The Preacher from Whiskey Ditch

The Preacher from Whiskey Ditch

C. H. Barnett, Jr.

iUniverse, Inc.
New York Lincoln Shanghai

The Preacher from Whiskey Ditch

iUniverse books may be ordered through booksellers or by contacting:

iUniverse
2021 Pine Lake Road, Suite 100
Lincoln, NE 68512
www.iuniverse.com
1-800-Authors (1-800-288-4677)

The views expressed herein are the sole responsibility of the author and do not necessarily reflect the views of iUniverse or its affiliates.

ISBN-13: 978-0-595-41189-4 (pbk)
ISBN-13: 978-0-595-67877-8 (cloth)
ISBN-13: 978-0-595-85545-2 (ebk)
ISBN-10: 0-595-41189-4 (pbk)
ISBN-10: 0-595-67877-7 (cloth)
ISBN-10: 0-595-85545-8 (ebk)

Printed in the United States of America

DEDICATED TO MY FIVE GRANDCHILDREN

Jill Elizabeth Schutz
Ronald Craig Stafford, Jr.
Amy Krista Corbett
Darla Jean McDonald
Michael David Barnett

Contents

Acknowledgements

I am deeply grateful to my daughter-in-law, Julie A. Barnett, who planted the idea that I write my autobiography for the benefit of my grandchildren who have always lived at a great distance from me. Along with the promised guidance and direction of my son, Dr. David K. Barnett, who skillfully managed all the work necessary to produce this book, I proceeded to search my memory with the excitement of a gardener in the springtime.

For the past eight months I have transplanted memories upon the pages of this book. Only God knows how grateful I am for my dear wife, Lois Jean Barnett, who offered many helpful suggestions throughout the process and typed and proofread most of the material. Together for more than sixty-two years, we have shared a lifetime of joyful service in ministry.

My grandson Michael D. Barnett has reviewed every chapter and offered encouragement for me to proceed. Dr. Stanley Joseph, a friend, has read the manuscript and critiqued the book.

I am grateful to God who by his grace inspired and strengthened me to write my story which I trust will encourage my grandchildren and others to keep the faith and discover the richness of His grace.

Introduction

Old photographs fascinate me. I can stare for hours at old pictures, looking past the smiling faces of people dressed in old-fashioned clothes, sneaking a peak into the world just over their shoulders; a world where old cars found now only in museums line the streets, where people traveled on trains and horses, where sprawling suburbs and vast shopping centers show up as plowed fields, where women hung laundry from clotheslines—a black and white world where people go to church and know their neighbor's names.

This book is the autobiography of one man and his family who makes up that background, people little noticed by the vast millions on their way to modernity. This is the story of my father, Clarence Barnett, Jr., who grew up in the Pennsylvania Dutch community of Whiskey Ditch and became a Methodist preacher for fifty years at the end of the 20th century. Spanning more than 80 years, his story is, I think, an archetype of his generation. Like millions of other children of the Depression, when duty called, he answered, going off to fight a war in Europe and in the Pacific. Unlike nearly half of the boys from his high school class, he returned home alive, but wiser, to face the challenges material prosperity would make on the soul of a nation.

As such, The Preacher from Whiskey Ditch is the story of a sea change in American life; a chronicle of the post-war transformation of a nation of farmers and shop-keepers tied to place and tradition into a mobile society defined no longer by religion as much as by television and consumerism. His story traces the sad demise of authentic Pennsylvania Dutch culture as the children of his generation, many of whom were the first to attend college, left the old ways behind in the upwardly mobile pursuit of the American dream.

Clarence Barnett, Jr. was never wealthy, never held political office, and was certainly never a celebrity. While he did not influence millions of people around the world, he did have a profound impact on hundreds of people in his family and thousands more in small towns and cities where he followed what he believed was God's call to serve; to befriend the lonely, to counsel the confused, to help heal the sick, and to preach Truth's case in a world increasingly colored with relativism.

In a world where families have been broken by the confused morality of the self-important, my father's love story witnesses to the power of self-sacrificing devotion to withstand separation, uncertainty, and deprivation. His family, like so many others those times, would feel the bitter pain of divorce and struggle to find healing and hope. But in the end, this is a story about the power of families to shape individual character and ultimately to change the world.

Sadly, this is also the story of the demise of Christendom in America, told not by cynical theologians in ivory towers but from the grassroots perspective of a country pastor who lived through the resurgence of the church during the post-war 40's and 50's, the struggles of the 60's, the existentialism of the 70's, the apathy of the 80's, and the revisionism of the 90's. Dad's story exudes a preoccupation with life, whether it was growing spectacular gardens, reshaping the Sunday school programs of an entire denomination, or doing what he loved most—encouraging the faith of his parishioners. He combines the rare quality of someone who could be both innovative and nurturing and his stories overflow with wisdom, humor, thanksgiving, and faithfulness to the One who transcends the fads and fickleness of human experience.

The Preacher from Whiskey Ditch is a witness to what endures in a world that is passing away.

David K. Barnett

1

Whiskey Ditch

I was born in Reading, Pennsylvania on May 9, 1924. Calvin Coolidge was President of the United States. Lenin had died and Stalin had come to power in the Soviet Union. First class postage stamps cost 2 cents. Milk cost 10 cents a quart at Peifer's Grocery, but we bought milk for six cents a quart from a farmer who lived about two miles away. My job as a youngster was to make the milk run every day. I'll tell you how long ago 1924 was—it was the first and last time the Washington Senators won the World Series.

I am the second son born to Eva Baer Barnett and Clarence Herbert Barnett, after whom I was named. My parents called me "Junior" for obvious reasons. But for reasons completely unknown to me, a friend of my older brother, Earl, nicknamed me Cork, and it stuck. My brothers and sisters always called me Cork and still do to this day. But most people called me Barney. Mr. Peifer would always welcome me into his grocery store by singing a song that was popular in the 1920s, "Barney Google, with the Goo-Goo-Googly Eyes."

I had three brothers and three sisters: Earl, who was five years older than me, Emily, Gertrude, Edwin, Donald, and Edna. The last five were born over the course of fifteen years at the end of a road in a village called Whiskey Ditch. The official name of the place was Gretna Lawn, but everyone called the six square blocks at the end of the bus line Whiskey Ditch. At one time it must have been a pleasant little valley between two green hills, but over time it became a working class neighborhood, a haven for drunks, and hence the unflattering name.

Our home was a very modest four room house at the end of Lincoln Avenue in the Ditch. It had two bedrooms upstairs, a living room and kitchen downstairs. We had no indoor bathroom. Privies were the norm in our community. When word got out that someone a few streets over had actually put a toilet inside the house, it was considered unsanitary. We did have a bathtub in the parents' bedroom. There was no wash stand, nowhere one could bathe or brush one's teeth except in the kitchen. So we had to develop a routine if everyone was to get ready in time.

Barnett's boyhood home in Whiskey Ditch

There were no clothes closets in the small rooms. I don't recall that we had a lot of clothes. So not having a closet was not really much of a problem. We hung our clothing on a hook fastened to the wall. Each of the children had his own hook. Our good clothes were hung in the attic on a wire stretched between some rafters. That's where the girls could hang up their best dresses and where Earl and I hung our suits.

In the children's room, three double beds were crammed so close together that one could hardly find room to walk. It took some coordination just for everyone to get into bed. All the children slept in one room except the baby who slept in the room with my parents.

If we were poor, we didn't know it. After all, we had wallpaper on the walls of our house. Many of our neighbors broke down cardboard boxes, opened them wide, and nailed them to the studding of the rooms of the house. Imagine decorating rooms with advertisements for Wheaties, Cornflakes, crackers, toilet paper, and every other kind of product.

Our family had a wonderful garden every year. It was ably managed by my father, who told my older brother and me when to start digging the soil for another year. Part of the area had to be dug early, because the potatoes had to be planted by St. Patrick's Day in March. I would dig and dig and dig until early May, when the entire garden was finally spaded, and we were ready to plant.

Planting the garden was a family affair. My mother and sisters and brothers and I would make a game of the work as we planted beans or corn or peas. And we had to do the job well. We had no sprays to keep our plants free from insects. Dad would strategically place tin cans half-full of gasoline alongside the garden. He showed us older children how to examine the plants every day, pick off the potato bugs and beetles from the bean plants and any other kind of critter that could destroy the leaves of our plants and toss them into the cans. At the end of the day when dad came home from work he would check our cans to see how many pests we had caught. Like a sergeant inspecting his soldiers, father would walk through the rows of vegetables and see how many bugs we had missed. We never quite measured up to his exacting standards, but when we did well, he was effusive in his praise. After emptying the gasoline tins filled with dead bugs, Dad would light a match and throw it onto the pile of carcasses. In one enormous whoosh of flame, the work that had taken us an entire day was burned up in a second or two.

Throughout my life, I planted a garden out back of every house in which I ever lived. Unlike those early days in Whiskey Ditch, I made sure that I had the world's best sprayer and all the latest pesticides. But around my garden you could still find a tin can or two with a tomato worm or a squash bug floating in a little gasoline.

2

My Earliest Memory

Psychologists say that your earliest memory can be a clue to how you see yourself. As I've thought about my earliest recollection it certainly gathers up some of the important themes of my life. My earliest memory is as a child at the age of five. Our family went to the Muddy Creek Church Festival held on the church grounds. These gatherings were times of fun and excitement that featured excellent food and good music by a band or country music group. On this particular night a band was playing stirring music. I remember my father and I were enjoying the music while my mom and other siblings were enjoying the chicken corn soup they served. I wanted to get nearer to the bandstand so I urged Dad to move closer. As we squeezed through the crowd, we got as close as possible. We were sure to get on the side of the bandstand where the baritone horn and tuba played. My Dad leaned over and told me that he used to play the baritone horn in the West Wyomissing Firehouse Band. He had only quit playing in the band when he no longer had the time to attend practice due to the demands of his growing family. I was dumbfounded to discover that my Dad had been a musician at one time and I had never known it. In a childish way I thought to myself, "Just think—my Dad could be up there playing that baritone horn."

As the music continued to play, I looked to my side and noticed that the man standing next to me was a total stranger. At some point I had lost contact with my Dad. Because I was smaller, I think I had gotten closer to the bandstand than my father was able to get. I realized that I was lost. I looked around but I couldn't see him anywhere. In my panic, I couldn't even hear the band playing, although I could see them going through all the motions of playing. I was lost. I was scared. Suddenly I was afraid. All the people standing around me, not one of them noticed the tears on my cheeks. I was lost and I knew it.

Muddy Creek Church Festival (author is boy in center looking at camera)

Five or ten minutes later, I caught sight of my Dad about 20 feet away. He was looking for me and I ran toward him. He looked 10 feet tall. I was thrilled to have been found. My Dad said nothing to me when he put his arm around my shoulder and patted me on the head. That was all I needed. What a joy to be found!

As I say, this memory captures so many of the themes of my life: my admiration for my father and my love of music. Some thirty-four years later, I told my father that our son, David, was playing a baritone horn in a concert given by the Sherwood High School Band. My father seldom drove out of Berks or Lancaster County, Pennsylvania. For him to make a 125 mile trip to Spencerville, Maryland, to attend that concert was something very special to him. He wanted the joy of listening to his grandson play the baritone horn. I can hear him say in a thick Pennsylvania Dutch inflection, "I lived out a dream just onct."

When I was about six years old, the joy of my life was to visit my Grandmother Baer, my mother's mom. She had a player piano with dozens of rolls of music stored in a cabinet. When our feet finally could reach the pumps at the floor, her son, my Uncle Melvin, and I would play and sing along with every roll. Most of the songs were written during the World War I era. In a couple of years we must have sung those songs dozens of times. It was always a joy and fascinating for me as a kid to watch all those keys on the piano play the most interesting beautiful music. The words to the songs were printed on the roll alongside the rows of holes that activated the piano keys. So we not only learned to sing but to read as well.

Melvin and I were always doing something with music. Both of us wanted to learn to play the guitar. He was fortunate enough to have parents who had enough money to buy him a beautiful Epiphone guitar, which he cared for like a jewel. He bought books that helped him to become an excellent musician by the time he was a teenager. He studied those books carefully and practiced for hours. He was able to join his brother Steve's dance band, so he was playing every Saturday night at State Hill. What a joy it was for me as a 15 year old kid to go with my Aunt and Uncle every Saturday night during the summer to hear the wonderful big band sounds. I enjoyed the great music that came out of the era of the 30s and very early 40s, some of the best music, I think, that has ever been written for singing and the most beautiful love songs that I have ever heard in my life.

There weren't many ways for a young fellow like me at that time to earn any money. My Dad would give me a dollar if I would work with him on Saturdays. When I was about ten or twelve, he challenged me to earn some cash by becoming the collection agent for his business. I guess he thought people couldn't resist a cute red-haired kid. Occasionally he would give me about twenty old unpaid bills owed him for work for which he had not been paid in full. The balance owed was seldom more than $15. Some of the invoices were several years old. He told me that I could keep all the money that I collected. I would jump on my bicycle, filled with hope, and peddle off to knock on the doors of past customers. After listening to a series of hard luck stories, my enthusiasm for collecting enough money to purchase a guitar just about vanished. But I pressed on to the next customer, and my perseverance would eventually be well rewarded by some honest old Dutchman who would give me a partial payment which was duly noted on the bill. At the end of the day when I had seen every prospect, I may have earned as much as four or five dollars which I tucked safely in my pocket. Back home I would go over the list with my father. Dad would smile and say, "You can try again in two or three weeks." Rarely did anyone pay the bill in full. If the payment was more than $10, I gave the money to Dad. I realized that he needed the money for better reasons than me. I was a bill collector for my father for several years. I finally managed to save five dollars and some change. This was enough, I thought, to begin my search for a guitar. The Depression was now in full swing and I knew the best deals would be in the local pawn shops in Reading.

I located a guitar in the second shop I visited. It was an inexpensive Kay instrument. All its strings and frets were in fairly good condition. I finally mustered enough courage to ask the shop owner for the price. He smiled, patted me on the head and said, "Three dollars for you". I tried to conceal my joy as I told him that I would take it. Before I handed over my hard-earned money, I checked the sound box and tuned it to make sure that the guitar would hold a tune. Only after I was finally convinced that it was worth the money, I purchased it.

I was one happy fellow as I walked up the street and into a music store where I purchased a set of new steel strings and a new guitar pick. After all that, I still had enough money for the bus fare to Whiskey Ditch.

I couldn't wait to show my guitar to Mom and play for her. Attending those festivals and carnivals, I noticed that most country and western songs could be played using only 3 or 4 chords. I studied Melvin's guitar books and learned how to strum and how to make the chords so I could play almost any popular song. As I learned new chords, I played that guitar for hours, coming up with new songs. My sisters and brothers would say, "Cork, give it a rest." But Mom often would sing along with me.

By the time I reached the ninth grade, I could play and sing nearly all the popular songs of the time. I loved to sing. It seems to me like I have been singing all my life. I have sung in glee clubs, church choirs, male quartets, duets, trios, mix quartets, but mostly solos. I have sung solos before or after or during virtually every sermon I have ever preached for the past sixty years.

Music is in my blood. I enjoy all kind of music with the exception of operas. My favorite music is that of a church organ playing hymns and spiritual songs of worship and praise. Especially in recent years the highlight of many worship services for me has been music well selected. My soul is often stirred to the depth of my being at the sound of music played in an exciting and different arrangement.

3

Vanishing Breed

To understand my family, you need to know something about the subculture that was our heritage. Actually, Pennsylvania Dutch was a counterculture. They didn't try to blend in. Although my ancestors immigrated to southeast Pennsylvania in the early 1700s, my father may have been the first to speak English. Today Pennsylvania Dutch culture has been taken over by marketers and tourist operators. You could say I am part of an endangered species, a vanishing breed. Today few Pennsylvania Dutch descendents carry on the ways of their grandparents or even understand who these Pennsylvania Germans were. Gone are the lilting cadences and odd expressions born of that ancient mix of German and English that filled my ears as a boy. It was the language and culture of a hard-working people, fiercely self-reliant, preoccupied with excellence.

All my mother's and father's ancestors were Pennsylvania Dutch. They weren't "Dutch" at all, if by Dutch you mean people from Holland, or what is known today as the Netherlands. They were first called Pennsylvania Germans, or Pennsylvania Deutsch, the German word for "German." The early English in America corrupted the term Deutsch to Dutch.

At the end of 18th century there was no unified country of Germany. The Germans were a loose collection of principalities, free cities, protectorates, and confederations. The country we know today as Germany didn't come into being until 1848 although the unification process started around 1800. Technically the Pennsylvania Dutch were immigrants to William Penn's American colony who came from everywhere the German language was spoken prior to 1800, places that are now part of Poland, the Czech Republic, Switzerland, Russia, France, and other areas as well as Germany.

We know a lot about our family history thanks to my sister, Edna, who spent 40 years researching my mother's ancestors, tracing the Baer family all the way back to its origins in Germany. She has written a book, *Our Pennsylvania German Families* (Edna Chelson, Mastof Press, 1998, ISBN 1-883294-78-9).

My ancestors came to Pennsylvania on ships named Pennsylvania Merchant, Snow Lowther, Phoenix, and Two Brothers. It often took as long as six months to reach the port of Philadelphia. The people on these ships were escaping religious wars between Catholics and Protestants that had destroyed villages and left the economy in ruins. One of the regions hardest hit by the Thirty Years War was the region known as the Palatinate, the area near the city of Zweibrucken where Germany, Switzerland, and the Alsace-Lorraine region of France come together. It is estimated that more than 100,000 German-speaking people from the Palatinate immigrated to Pennsylvania.

By 1800, 90% of the citizens of Reading and Berks County were German-speaking. During the American Revolutionary War, 9,000 Pennsylvania Dutch served in the Continental Army under General Washington's command. There were more soldiers from Reading and Berks County than from any other place of comparable area in size in all of the 13 colonies. George Washington spoke and understood Pennsylvania Dutch. One of Washington's officers was supposed to have remarked that the Pennsylvania Dutch were the best fighters in all of the Continental Army. "They know how to shoot straight," he said, "and the soldiers learned how to handle starvation well."

One of Washington's staff officers was Major David Gring, an ancestor on my mother's side. My great grandmother lived in Mohnton on the outskirts of Reading. Her name was Margaret Long Gring. (I remember that a trolley car ran behind the back porch and we had to cross the trolley tracks to get to her outhouse. So whenever a child would leave to go to the outhouse, my great grandmother would say "Watch out for the trolley.")

Another ancestor was the first Reformed minister in the state of Pennsylvania, the Reverend John Waldschmidt. He was responsible for bringing at least six other Reformed ministers to Pennsylvania and served as a minister of a German Reformed Church from 1757 to 1771 built on land donated by a man named George Hain. In 1766 it became Saint John's Reformed Church, but many people in Berks County continued to refer to it as Hain's Church.

From 1790 when one of John Waldschmidt's daughters married Major David Gring, my family's history has intertwined with Hain's Church for more than 200 years. Our ancestors are buried in its cemetery, including my father and mother. I was baptized in Hain's Church on August 24, 1924. I attended Sunday school and confirmation classes and was confirmed on May 11, 1940 by the Reverend Mr. Ralph Starr.

When my father was a boy, he lived on a small farm adjacent to Hain's Church. To this day at the boundary of the church's property, there's an old-fashioned water pump used to draw cool clear water from an ancient well. That pump once stood on the back porch of my grandfather's farmhouse. I visited Hain's Church in the early 1970s with David and his oldest daughter, Jill. My parents are buried in a plot not 100 yards from that farmhouse where Dad was born and grew up. I treasure a lovely photograph of Jill taken that day pumping water from the same siphon as did my dad at his boyhood home.

The Pennsylvania Dutch are characterized not only by their speech but by their cooking. They are renowned for pastries and pies, their love of sour flavors, and they eat much more pork than beef. Any green vegetable tastes better with a splash of vinegar on it. I no longer speak Pennsylvania Dutch and have lost the speech inflections, but when it comes to my favorite dishes, I am as Dutch as sauerkraut.

Author with granddaughter, Jill, at historic pump

Pennsylvania Dutch farmers were hard workers who helped each other. A farmer who owned a combine or a thrashing machine would do as many as a dozen jobs for his neighboring farmers. The Amish and Mennonites made it a community project to raise a new barn if someone lost a structure to fire. They never charged each other for work. Many of my Dad's family were farmers who also moonlighted at a second job. Uncle Paul Barnett not only worked on a farm, but he was also an outstanding automobile mechanic. He ran a garage and sold used cars. In spite of what most people thought about used car salesmen, Uncle Paul had a solid reputation for honesty. His children attended school where only Pennsylvania Dutch was spoken prior to World War II.

When my Aunt Mabel Harding wasn't helping her husband, Bill, on their farm near Fritztown, she made beautiful quilts and bedspreads.

The same was true with Mother's side of the family. Her dad, my Grandfather Baer, worked in a brickyard for $1.00 a day and would come home and craft furniture in his cabinet-making shop. He surely would have been "gabut" (tired) at night. My Aunt Bertha's husband, Ralph Crick, had a regular job but specialized in repairing electric trains, which were so popular at Christmas time when I was a boy. My uncle Steve Baer was by far the most outstanding of all my uncles. By day, he toiled in the mills. At night, he mesmerized audiences with his very own dance band. My Uncle Melvin was a welder at a local steel mill who became a virtuoso guitarist in my Uncle Steve's band.

Here are some Pennsylvania Dutch phrases I heard over and over again in my childhood.

- Don't "fress" (eat) like a "wutz" (pig).

- He was really "gabut" (tired) at the end of the day.

- Mom said to the children, "Be sure to wear your 'gum shoes' (overshoes). It is muddy outside."

- Don't be such a "dummkup" (dumb).

- My grandmother used to call for me, "Come here 'onct' (once)."

- Her dress had a "bissel" (little) tear in the sleeve.

- If I didn't use my head about something, Dad might call me a "glutz kupp" (dumb head).

- Quit your "grexing" (complaining) all the time.

- Sit down and be "ruich" (quiet or still).

- When my grandparents met Lois, they said that she was a "shae frau" (nice wife).

- My sister, Gertie, was fond of "schleck" (pastries), especially sticky buns.

- That girl simply "blabs" (talks) too much on the phone.

- I "dassant" (dare not) ask for another dollar.

- Someone might ask my dad for directions to a store. He would say "go up where the streetcar bends around."

I thank God that I was born a Pennsylvania Dutchman. Unlike most of my family, I became a wanderer after I left home for the Army. I never returned to live in Berks County as did virtually all of my cousins and my relatives that I knew as a child. They spent their entire lives in the same county. Nevertheless, we are Pennsylvania Dutch and proud of it.

Our son, David, found a Barnett coat of arms on an Internet site. I don't know how authentic it is, but something rings true about the motto: Nisi Faret Imperat, which is Latin for "Unless he obeys, he commands."

4

"Use Your Head"

Thinking about my life story, I've continually asked the question, "How did I grow up to be the person I am?" In so many ways I'm a duplication of my father. I not only have his name, I also have a lot of his characteristics. I look like my dad, though taller. He was only 5'5" tall. He was left-handed. I'm right-handed. But I cannot escape the fact that so much of what I am came directly to me through my father.

I accepted the work ethic he taught me. He had apprenticed with a man named Phillips for over a decade before he became a master plumber. He believed that any job worth doing was a job worth doing well. He always used the best equipment. His fleet of trucks ran on only high-test gasoline. He made it a point to clean up well after any job he did. Many of the rich German folks who lived in Wyomissing would have no one else come work in their homes except my father.

One day I went to the shop with my father and inside the door was a bag of brass fittings. He kicked the bag with his toe and noticed some strange writing on the burlap bag. I recognized immediately that the writing was Japanese. He called to my brother, "Earl, come here once." Earl came out of a nearby office.

"What's this pile of junk?" Dad asked. In those days anything made in Japan was considered of inferior quality. My brother explained he had ordered the fittings for a job they were working on.

"We won't use any of this junk. We only use material made in the United States," he said. And then he made this gesture that I must have seen hundreds of times. Dad would lift his left hand up to his ear and then drop it quickly to his knees. "Send it back," he said, punctuating the air. If equipment didn't have a familiar name he associated with quality, he would not install it in even the most modest home.

Another time a customer told my father that he had just bought all new bathroom fixtures and wanted my father to install them. My father said he wouldn't be able to do it.

"I'm in no hurry," the man said. "I just want you to do the job when you can."

My father told him a second time that he didn't think he would be able to help him. "Where did you buy this material?" my father asked.

"Montgomery Wards," the customer replied. Up went the left hand in that familiar gesture. Dad pointed at the man and said, "Then you go ask Montgomery Ward to install it. I'll have nothing to do with it."

My father confided in me later that the reason he refused to do the job was because whenever he tried to work with cheaply made materials, fittings would not fit and pieces would invariably break. He knew that it was not worth his time or effort to try to work with what he called "junk."

Dad did not suffer fools at all, even if it was his own children. One Saturday I was working with my father on a job. We were installing a new sewer line in Wyomissing, connecting a large three story home to the main line on Penn Avenue. Dad was working down in the trench. "Junior, go out to the truck and get me this tool from the toolbox." I had no idea what the tool was. But I wouldn't have dared to ask him what it looked like or how he was planning to use it. I was supposed to know what he wanted. Dad never seemed to catch on to the idea that others didn't know as much as he knew about plumbing and tools. When I got to the truck and opened the toolbox, I looked and looked, trying to imagine what tool he was talking about. I picked up a wrench, returned to the trench, and handed it down to him. A second later the wrench flew up from the ditch, heading straight at me. I ducked just in time. When Dad saw that it wasn't the tool he had asked for, he threw it at me.

"Use your head," he said.

I went to the truck a second time and brought another tool. Again he threw the tool at me and yelled, "Use your head."

A third time I returned to rummage in the tool box and it must have been a charm because I finally brought the tool Dad needed. After he finished making the connections and checking for leaks, Dad climbed out of the trench and told me to get busy filling in the ditch. Well, I understood that command. I worked most of the rest of the day back filling that ditch until I heard him call from the other side of the house, "Junior, come here once." I couldn't imagine what else he might want me to do.

Dad had a short temper. Whenever something didn't go right, he would curse or swear in Pennsylvania Dutch. He was very quick in expressing how foolish or dumb we children were when we couldn't do what he asked. Like many Pennsylvania Dutch men of my father's generation, he was a strict taskmaster. He had been raised to unquestioningly respect his elders, and I think he expected that same deference from his own children. But lest I give you the wrong impression of my Dad, he had a big heart. He visited his parents every day of his life until they died. He was generous to his family and with many of his friends.

Barnett family in 1950's(left to right front row, Edna, Eva (mother), C.H. Barnett Sr. (father), Gertie; Back row, Edwin, Earl, Emily, Clarence (author), Donald.

If my father was like a thunderstorm at the end of a hot August day, my mother was like the last few drops of a morning shower in the sunshine when every blade of grass lifts its face toward the skies and thanks God for the fresh drink of water. Mom did a wonderful job in raising her children without ever showing any hint of ostentation. She managed to keep her family happy, nourished, and clothed. Like my father, she had the highest respect for her elders. She worked hard, and she laughed often. She loved baseball and instilled in all of her children a love for the game.

Mother was the most compassionate person I ever knew. When I had to kill one of my pet rabbits when Dad was unsuccessful at hunting that day, she could not stand to watch us slaughter the rabbit and prepare it for supper. I confess that I also cried a lot on those days, and I never had much of an appetite at that supper. Mom took a lot of interest in my rabbits. I had six pens stacked one on top of the other in back of the outhouse in the backyard. She always reminded me to make sure they had food and water in their pens.

My mother was always busy working on an Afghan or a hooked rug made with scraps of socks and stockings. Some of the rugs were large enough to cover the floor of an entire room. I never recall her ever sitting idle in a chair any evening. She was always busy doing for others.

One day when I was about ten years old Mom was chopping down a small dead tree in our front yard. Apparently, I wandered too close to her as she swung the large axe. She struck me with the backswing of the axe, opening a large gaping wound above my left ear. I fell to the ground unconscious. Frantic, she ran into the house to get bandages and water and whatever else she needed to take care of me. In those days you couldn't call 911 in an emergency. You had to handle crises yourself. She managed to stop the bleeding and I regained consciousness. She asked a neighbor to take me to a doctor's office where I was stitched up with a large bandage that became my headgear for the next two weeks.

That evening at suppertime we all got a lecture from our father. "That was a close call and you should be grateful you're still here in one piece," Dad said. Then looking at all of us seated around the table he said, "You kids must learn to use your heads."

Dad's nature was to be strong and competitive. My mother was as meek and tender as anyone I've ever met. When I look at myself, I see my personality being much more like my Mom's than like my father's, although I look more like my father than any other of my siblings.

My brother Earl was not as interested in sports as the rest of us. His hobbies were crystal radio sets and building things. No one in our village could compete with the sleek, speedy four-man bobsled he built. I admired Earl. He was extremely smart because he had an imaginative, inquiring mind. He was always thinking of ways to be more efficient. As an adult he patented numerous inventions designed to save time or make work places safer in the plumbing business.

When we were boys, Earl had an idea for increasing the productivity of the ground adjacent to our garden. He thought there was an unusual amount of mica in the soil. He devised a plan to heat the soil and extract impurities. Since it was his idea, he told me to grab the shovel and start digging and he would supervise. So I started digging. When the hole was about three feet in diameter, I couldn't lift the dirt from the depth of the hole. Clever Earl solved the problem by building a winch over the opening of the hole using a heavy five gallon bucket attached to a lumber frame with some rope. With this contraption, I could be lowered into the hole and then extract the soil more easily by digging deeper for the rich mica. To keep our venture a secret, we piled the dirt behind some tall weeds nearby.

Earl encouraged me to keep digging saying the soil was looking better and better all the time. So I kept digging and digging until finally when I reached the depth of 12 feet, I struck water. This slowed our progress considerably, but we stayed with the project, convinced we were on to a great discovery.

One day Dad noticed the hole with the homemade winch suspended above it. "What are you doing?" Dad asked.

Earl tried to explain it all, but Dad just listened with an expression of mild horror as he looked from the hole to the bucket to the wench. As a plumber he knew how dangerous it was for me to be in that deep hole as Earl removed buckets of soil and water. He demanded that we stop digging immediately and that we start shoveling the dirt back into the hole as quickly as we could. I got into the bucket for the last time to go down into the hole to retrieve a shovel I had left there. I put the shovel in the bucket and as Earl hoisted it to the top, the handle of the shovel knocked the bucket off its hook. The bucket came crashing down and struck me on the top of the head. I can still hear Earl exclaim, "My gosh, my gosh." I fancy that I can still see the stars dancing in my head as I felt I was about to pass out from the blow.

"Hurry," Earl yelled at me. "Get back in the bucket and hold on as tight as you can. Your head is bleeding and covered with blood."

I got in the bucket and by the time I reached the top of the hole, I could feel the warm blood running down my neck and across my chest. Earl supported me as I stumbled the 100 yards or so across our backyard where I nearly passed out, but I remained conscious. All the way, Earl kept yelling, "Mom! Mom! Mom!"

She came out of the house and almost instantly knew what to do. "Get a basin of water," she barked. As Earl started to run, she said, "And bring some towels and get a clean baby diaper and come back as quick as you can." She stayed with me until Earl returned with the first aid supplies. She cleaned the skin and placed a large bandage on the wound to stop the bleeding. She told me to wear a baseball cap to keep pressure on the bandage that covered the top of my head. Because I never lost consciousness, I remember all that happened.

Later she determined that it would not be necessary for me to go to the doctor. At suppertime we all wondered what Dad would say. We weren't permitted to wear caps while at the table. Fortunately my position was at the far end of the table from where Dad sat. Eventually he saw that I had this cap stuck way down over my head. My brothers and sisters looked at Mom and waited for her to explain when Dad asked what happened. As she was about to speak, Earl spoke up and took full responsibility for the accident. When my father was convinced that I was okay, he told Earl that he was old enough and should have known better than to do such a stupid thing as to dig a hole and find mica in the dirt of our neighborhood.

Dad asked Earl and me, "When are you ever going to use your heads?" I knew better than to say anything, but the thought crossed my bandaged mind that I already had.

5

Role Models

Many people outside my immediate family had a strong influence on my life.

I learned some of the most important lessons in life from a man who never had the joy of being promoted to the fifth grade in school. I never realized that Ike Morris, our neighbor, was an alcoholic until I was about 12 years old. I don't recall if he ever worked a day in his life. He was free to take me fishing any time day or night. He taught me everything I know about fishing, including how to pack a fish in mud and throw it in the hot coals of a wood fire to cook. When you cracked away the dried mud, the fish was baked to perfection.

Sometimes Ike and I would stay out all night fishing in the Tulpehocken Creek under the Van Reed Bridge. Dad would stop by and bring us a can of beans, some fruit, bread and lunch meat and in exchange we would share some of the fish that we had caught.

Ike was good to me and I tried to return the favor. I never tasted his wine, although he offered it to me often. To this very day I'm proud to check "Never" on a medical form that asks if I've ever used alcohol. Although I learned many things from Mr. Morris, one lesson I never mastered was how to feel sympathy for a drunk. As a child, I had no difficulty spending hours and hours with an alcoholic, but as I matured and saw the devastation booze could have on individuals and their families, I lost much of that compassion for inebriated. Occasionally an intoxicated person wandered into a church service I was leading. I showed little patience with them and ordered them to leave. I somehow never transferred to my adult psyche the simple childhood capacity to care and to be concerned about alcoholics. I'm not proud of that.

Ike Morris (sitting) with author's father; the family privy is in the background

I had perfect attendance while attending West Wyomissing Elementary School. I have scant memories of my elementary school teachers, with the exception of my sixth grade teacher, Mr. Brossman. I was never very good at spelling and Mr. Brossman had a unique method for teaching the subject. He would line up students at the blackboard that covered three sides of the school room, the windows being on the fourth side. Standing in the middle of the room he called out a word to spell. God help you if Mr. Brossman caught you sneaking a peak at some other student's work.

If one of the kids was hesitating, he would walk behind the person and ask "Do you need a schtarter?" He had a thick Pennsylvania Dutch accent. If a student hadn't begun to write the word on the blackboard by his second trip around the room, he moved menacingly closer and asked again, this time a little louder, "Do you need a schtarter?" And suddenly he would slap the struggling speller on the rear end so hard it would slam you against the blackboard. Chalk dust flew as students rushed to print something, anything on that blackboard. I received a C in spelling in the sixth grade. Fortunately my report card never recorded how many schtarters I needed to earn that grade.

The teachers got better looking as I entered junior and senior high school. Interestingly enough, I became a much better student in all of my classes. I will never forget my athletic coach, Walt Risley. He was lean and muscular, 6'1" and weighed 185. He was a very demanding coach. I have him to thank for never taking up the habit of smoking. Mr. Risley would dismiss anybody from any team in any sport if he learned that the student had smoked a cigarette. He made a profound impression on my life. For years I aspired to be like Mr. Risley—physically fit, disciplined, and committed to excellence in everything I did.

I had few spiritual role models as a child. My parents were members of Hain's Church, as had been generations of Barnetts, but we attended services very infrequently. In my teens I spent nearly every weekend with my Uncle Melvin at my grandparent Baer's place. They were faithful worshippers at Hain's Church and I began to tag along. The Church was about to ruin our weekends by scheduling confirmation training on Saturday afternoons for nearly an entire year in 1939. Melvin and Charles Bergman (my cousin) were planning to attend that class and I decided to join. It was a large class of 36 young people led by Mr. Lamb, a funeral director in nearby Wernersville who also taught the teenager's Sunday School class. We were all confirmed in May, 1940.

I didn't think a lot about religion in those days. I equated spirituality with going to church which was just something that was expected in our community. Peifer's Grocery store was across the street from my elementary school. Carl Peifer and his son, Frank, were dedicated Christian men, although I didn't know it at the time. I only knew that there was something different about them. I couldn't ever put my finger on what it was that made them so caring and happy. They truly witnessed to their faith by living it. But I often think that if they had told me as a child or teenager about their personal relationship with Christ, I might have become a born again believer sooner than I eventually did.

6

Picking Up Speed

When I was a teenager I spent two summers working on the farm of my Aunt Edna and Uncle Vernon Stoudt in State Hill, Pennsylvania. Aunt Edna was my mother's youngest sister and was very much like my mother in her easygoing manner. We worked hard all day long in the garden or doing chores that had to be done on the farm and in the evening we sat on the front porch of their farmhouse and sang. My uncle was no singer, but my aunt and I enjoyed sharing a song.

One day when I was 14, Uncle Vernon asked me to load the hay wagon with corn cobs and deliver them to the State Hill Hotel. The hotel used corn cobs to kindle fires to warm up the rooms on winter mornings. State Hill was about two miles away and the road from the farm was winding and hilly. I hitched up two horses to the hay wagon for the trip. If I needed only one horse for a job such as raking hay, I harnessed the horse called George because he was easy to manage. The reason George was so gentle was that he was blind. The other horse was a mare named Topsy.

I loaded the wagon and made the uneventful trip to the hotel. After unloading the corn cobs, I stood in the front of the wagon and turned George and Topsy toward home. The empty wagon pitched and rattled back and forth across the stony country road, making so much noise frightened rabbits scurried from the underbrush along the road and even a couple of pheasants took flight from their grassy hiding place. Everything was going fine until I was about an eighth of a mile from the farm where the road descended into a little ravine. At the bottom of the slope the road took a sharp left turn. I held the reins as we started down the hill, trying to keep the horses walking. But as the wagon rumbled down the incline, its weight forced George and Topsy to pick up the pace. We continued to gain speed. The horses were moving at a fairly fast trot. The wagon vibrated so severely on the stone cobbles my cheeks flapped up and down and my eyes couldn't focus because of the intense shaking. Suddenly, when we were about 300 yards from the farm entrance, Topsy caught sight of the barn and she started to run. Poor blind George. It was all he could do to keep up.

In a split second the thought flashed into my mind that there was no way that old wagon would stay upright round the curve at the bottom of the grade, not at the speed we were traveling. I reacted instinctively to protect myself. Throwing myself backward into the bed of the wagon, I braced my feet against the front buckboard and pulled the reins as hard as I could. George and Topsy hurdled ahead into the curve, the wagon skidded and pitched, but by the grace of God, the horses kept the wagon on all four wheels.

As we headed for the barn, I was able to recover from the sheer terror of those few minutes on the run-away wagon. Back now on familiar turf, George and Topsy stopped in the barnyard. I unhitched them and led them to their stalls. I gave them two buckets of water because I knew they had to be thirsty after all that running.

I couldn't wait to tell my Aunt Edna how I had barely escaped what I was sure was certain death on the trip back. I told her what happened, and when I finished telling her how terrified I was, she simply smiled and said, "Ahah." She didn't say, "Oh child, how awful" or "What a brave lad you are." Merely "Ahah."

Sometime later my uncle arrived and I told him my harrowing experience. He listened as if with one ear and when I finished he smiled and said nonchalantly, "Things like that can happen." Here I had risked my life for his corn cobs and all he could say was, "Things like this can happen"?

I learned two very valuable lessons from this experience. First, an empty hay wagon makes a lot more noise on the rocky country road than a full hay wagon. I've used that illustration a lot in my sixty years as a preacher. And second, I learned that people aren't really interested in close calls. They are only absorbed by stories where there are crashes, things broken, wheels fly off, and the ambulance comes to take the dead and wounded to the hospital. Then people show interest in a story. Novels are more popular than autobiographies. It's the bad things that actually happen to others that arouse the fear that similar calamity could happen to us. I guess it's what makes news newsworthy.

The following summer I returned to the Stoudt farm and one job took the entire summer. Vernon and Edna had no running water in the house. They walked several hundred yards up a hill in their backyard to a spring house to fetch water. I was to dig a trench about 18 inches deep all the way from that spring to the back porch of the farmhouse. Day after day, week after week, I excavated that ditch. One day in mid-August my father arrived at the farm with a load of ¾-inch pipes. We had blocked off the spring at the top of the ditch. To test the flow of water we removed the boards and watched as water rushed down the slope with good pressure all the way to the back porch. Dad and I damned the spring while we finished laying the sections of pipe the length of the trench. Finally we connected the pipe to a faucet over a metal sink, removed the barrier at the spring, and for the first time my aunt and uncle had cold running water.

The following year I was working at an automobile dealership, doing odd jobs like washing and greasing cars to earn a little money. I was paid between 25 and 30 cents an hour; I don't think I made more than 40 cents per hour. When I turned 16 that spring and was able to work full time legally, the supervisor at the dealership transferred me to the body shop where the work was menial, hard, and undesirable. After fenders were straightened and bodies repaired, it was my job to sand the automobiles. Sanding the finish on a car could take me a day or two, sometimes longer. The surface had to be just right or the painter wouldn't accept the car.

Not long after I started sanding cars, a 1933 Chevrolet was wheeled into the body shop with two crumpled fenders. The rest of car was in good condition. The dealership had taken the car as a trade and immediately I became interested in purchasing it. I asked the salesman what he thought the price of the car would be. He told me I would need to speak with the sales manager. I did an extra fine job sanding that Chevy and when it was painted; it was beautiful indeed.

More interested than ever, I stopped on the way home from work on my bicycle that evening and noticed a sign on the windshield said $95. I told the sales manager I wanted to buy that car. I'll never forget how excited I was when I made the purchase. A couple days later I had license plates on front and back. I donated my 28 inch bicycle to my younger brother, Eddie. I had left childhood behind. I had come of age. What a wonderful feeling to own my own car!

Author in his 1933 Chevy

I drove around Whiskey Ditch showing off my new car. When I pulled up beside our house, Mom along with my younger brothers and sisters came running out to see the car. My older brother was serving in the Army in Iceland. Of course they all wanted to go for a ride. Mom jumped in the front and my smaller brothers and sisters clambered into the backseat. I drove them up and down the streets of our little community, hoping anybody or everybody would see us.

That September I was the one and only junior from Whiskey Ditch who didn't have to walk to school. My hard work when my classmates were goofing off all summer already was paying rich dividends.

But my favorite trip was the drive to the State Hill Hotel every Saturday night where from eight to midnight, Uncle Vernon, Aunt Edna and I tapped our toes and soaked up the harmonies of my Uncle Steve's big band orchestra. The Steve Baer Orchestra played in State Hill for many years. He was the brother of my mother and Aunt Edna. Two seats down from Steve my Uncle Melvin played an Epiphone guitar in the rhythm section. They played all the hits of the time, "It Had to Be You," "Sentimental Journey," and a lot of Tommy Dorsey songs.

The family was very proud of Steve. He played clarinet, soprano sax and bass saxophone. But when Steve picked up his violin about half way through the evening show, the crowd fell completely silent. One evening he played an arrangement of "Intermezzo" and segued into "Tenderly." The sound was ethereal. I remember when he finished the medley there was a second or two of stunned silence so beautiful was the music he had coaxed from the violin. I was so moved I went to a pawn shop and bought a violin. I thought since I played a guitar I could probably learn the smaller stringed instrument. I worked on "Intermezzo" and the more I practiced the more I came to admire the talent of Uncle Steve.

Uncle Steve had a big curly-headed Italian singer named Tony. As I listened to him crone those beautiful ballads, I fantasized that Uncle Steve would catch my eye, motion me up onto stage, lean down and say, "I want you to sing the next song." But it would remain a fantasy because Steve never asked me to sing. I figured it was because he didn't want to offend that big Italian.

That city of West Lawn sponsored an amateur talent competition each year. Many high school students vied for the prize as did some adults. They held the event in the firehouse hall. The place was packed. One by one the contestants came forward and did their song and dance. Some were musicians, some were dancers, but most were singers. When my name was called, I picked up my guitar and went to center stage. With a big smile I strummed on my guitar and sang one of my favorite love songs, "I Don't Want to Set the World on Fire."

> *I don't want to set the world on fire. I just want to start a flame in your heart.*
> *In my heart I have but one desire and that one is you, no other will do*
> *I lost all ambition for worldly acclaim; I just want to be the one you love.*
> *And with your admission that you feel the same*
> *I could build the world we are dreaming of, believe me.*
> *I don't want to set the world on fire. I just want to start a flame in your heart.*

I was pleased with the performance and it soon became obvious the audience also approved. Heavy applause filled the hall as I left the stage. After all the contestants had their turn, the announcer stepped to the microphone to announce the winners. Third place went to someone, and then second place to another. Since my name had not been called I thought I was out of running, but it had been a lot of fun anyway.

"Winner of first prize is Clarence Barnett."

I couldn't believe it. I was as happy as I could be. I walked proudly to the stage and stood beside the announcer who gave me first prize—a five dollar bill. I thanked the man, the audience applauded, and soon everyone began to file out of the hall. I celebrated by taking some friends to Smokey's where we feasted on large milkshakes and triple scoop ice cream cones.

Author and mother

As a high school senior I frequently played the guitar and sang in our high school assemblies. Regardless of the program, someone in charge would search me out and say, "Barney, sing a popular song." I made sure to always have my guitar out in the car.

In the 1942 edition of the Wilsonian, our high school yearbook, each senior is pictured along with a paragraph beside the picture by a yearbook staffer to identify something memorable about the individual. Beside my senior picture is written:

"Looking into an assembly, one would probably see Barney strumming on his gui-tar and singing some popular song. Even though shaving and literature held no attraction for him, a certain brunette does. His ambition is to become a successful husband. What a lucky girl his wife will be."

The same yearbook noted the glee club in which I sang put on an operetta that year called the Belle of Baghdad. I played the part of an aviator. I don't remember much about the musical except a certain beautiful brunette dancing in the chorus line.

7

Lois

In my senior year of high school I had a study period that met beneath the balcony of the school auditorium. Some girls were chatting and getting acquainted with a new girl in the junior class when a substitute teacher who was monitoring the study hall told the new girl to be quiet and stop disturbing the study hall. I thought it very unfair that she should be singled out to receive criticism. The substitute teacher had no way of knowing, of course, that she was a new student. When I stood up and explained to that teacher that we didn't treat new students the way she had treated this new girl, the study hall erupted in applause. The substitute teacher quickly apologized to the girl for what she had said. That new student was Lois Weinel, the girl who would eventually become my wife.

I came through the experience like a knight in shining armor. After defending her as I did, I thought I might have an entrance to this very attractive, well-dressed junior. I hoped she would become a friend and would not be embarrassed by my meddling in her affairs on her first day in Wilson High School.

I asked if I could walk her home from school. My car sat in the school parking lot, but I didn't have her parents' permission to drive her in my car. Our friendship grew during that school year.

But something strange was going on with my closest buddies, Uncle Melvin and my cousin, Charles Bergman. Charles was a year older than Melvin or me. He drove a Ford Roadster with a rumble seat. We rode around town with him every evening. Our favorite hangout was Smokey's ice cream stand. Lois would meet us at Smokey's and then we'd all set off in Charles' car with Lois riding in the rumble seat.

Clarence and Lois, 1942

I began to get this uncomfortable feeling that both Charles and Melvin were competing with me for Lois' attention and that was a problem. How could I keep peace with my relatives and at the same time not lose the friendship and attention I wanted from Lois? My strategy was that I would get better acquainted with Lois' parents.

Like most people in my family who took on a second job, I supplemented what I earned at the dealership by selling potatoes. One of my friends had an open trailer that could hold about 50 bushels of potatoes. I bought the potatoes for about 50 cents a bushel from a farmer who lived near Kutztown. I was able to sell them for 80 cents a bushel, making about $15 profit per trailer load. When I parked the trailer at the edge of Smokey's parking lot I could sell all 50 bushels of potatoes in a single evening. Smokey's was a hopping place.

One evening I went to Lois' house, which was less than a mile away from Smokey's. I knocked on the door and her mother answered. "Would you like to buy some potatoes?" I asked. Lois' father was seated across the room.

"Let me see what you're selling," he said in his gruff voice.

When I told him that I would have to go back to Smokey's and get the potatoes, he laughed at me for trying to sell potatoes with no potatoes to show. He was a sales manager for a large grocery chain and he knew salespeople had to be prepared.

Lois' mother was kinder and had more pity on me than her Dad. She ordered a half bushel of my potatoes, sight unseen. Lois asked if she could ride with me back to Smokey's to pick up the potatoes. I was delighted beyond words when her parents gave her permission to ride with me.

We returned a short while later to deliver the potatoes. I was so enthralled with Lois I didn't notice that as I made my way through the living and dining room, I left a trail of dust and dirt on the carpet. When I got to the cellar door in the kitchen and parked the beautiful heap of Kennybeck potatoes, I looked over my shoulder and to my embarrassment saw the trail of debris. I apologized and offered to clean it up, but Mrs. Weinel took it all in stride.

Lois' mom paid me more than I had asked for the potatoes. When she invited me to stay and enjoy a cold Pepsi Cola, I thought I had stumbled through the doorway to heaven. Mildred Weinel was a pretty lady who seemed to fully understand what was coursing through the veins of this tall, slender 17-year-old young man who was in love with her daughter.

Although I had gained a major victory over my competitors that night, the war for Lois' attention was not over with Melvin and Charles.

Lois was an excellent roller skater while clumsy would be a kind description of my roller skating ability. Lois's class was having a class party at the rink and she wanted to go. I had no desire to publicly humiliate myself, so I said I didn't want to go. A short, skinny guy asked Lois to go with him to the roller skating party and she agreed. Later she told me he was a nice fellow and they had an enjoyable time at the party, but I never liked that kid after that. That may have been my first real battle with jealousy. I hoped it would not happen often because it felt like someone kicked me in the stomach and it hurt. It was a battle I lost that night.

By December I had the confidence to ask Lois if she would go steady with me. We pledged our love and concern for each other and decided we would date no one else. We were now a couple. I didn't give her a ring because her family did not wear jewelry for religious reasons. But we made sure all our friends knew that we were going steady. I was greatly relieved.

Through the more than 60 years Lois and I have been together, Mom and Pop Weinel always expressed confidence and trust in me. We came a long way together from the day I sold them a basket of potatoes to the days when many,

many years later we laid both of them to rest in the arms of Jesus. They left imprints of spiritual virtues and values on our lives that have guided us faithfully through the years.

8

Spiritual Awakening

While the farmers in our family had second jobs, Grandmother Baer had both a church and a faith healer. Every Sunday morning she took Melvin and me to Hain's Church and every Sunday afternoon we went to a faith healer who lived off the main road up a long dirt path beyond Fleetwood. Grandmother had many aches and pains and she felt these visits were helpful.

Melvin and I would sit on the front porch in warm weather. In cold weather we would wait in the house. "Huck dich und sei ruhich," (sit down and be quiet) Grandmother told us before she disappeared into the room to have done whatever the faith healer did.

In many ways, this became a metaphor of my early spiritual understanding. I knew religion was important to my family, but I wasn't sure what practical difference it made.

Following high school graduation I went to work as a bench molder at the Berkshire Foundry. My job was to carry a large ladle that held about 100 pounds of molten iron that I had to pour into molds that I had made that day. Since I was the youngest worker, I was given a very easy pattern. Many of the men at the foundry had been bench molders for years and were extremely strong. I really felt like a boy among men, but I stayed with the job and learned quite readily. My work station was the furthest from the furnace. At the end of the day, I was wet with perspiration and so tired at times that I could hardly stand.

In late summer that year Lois's father was transferred to work in Allentown, Pennsylvania. He was a branch manager for Jewel Tea Company, a job necessitating that he move often from city to city. During Lois's four years of high school, she attended eight different schools: two as a freshman, three as a sophomore, only one when I met her as a junior, and two in her senior year.

Allentown was a pretty town with lots of parks. The Weinels rented an apartment there that I clocked on my Chevy's odometer as 38 miles from my house. The next county over was a world away for many of my friends and family, who said our romance wouldn't go the distance, but I was determined not to let that happen. So, almost every night after finishing at the foundry, though I was dead tired, I cleaned up and drove to Allentown. I would spend a couple of hours visiting Lois and her parents before it would be time to get back in the car, drive the hour or so back to my house, get into bed, and be ready to go to work again the next morning.

Lois's Mom often invited me to stay on Saturday night. If I did so, I felt somewhat obligated to attend church with them on Sunday.

They attended the Free Methodist Church in Allentown. Mrs. Weinel had grown up as a preacher's daughter in this small, conservative Methodist denomination that grew out of the abolitionist movement during the Civil War. While mainstream Methodism came more and more under the influence of modernism, Free Methodists were committed to maintaining the holiness tradition of John Wesley.

I had begun attending the Allentown church regularly. It was a tiny frame church with a handful of pews on each side of a center aisle. The building certainly wasn't impressive, but I was impressed that the people knew their Bible and they were beautiful singers.

The pastor was an elderly gentleman but one Sunday night in September, he invited a student from the Allentown Bible School to preach. There may have been 30 people present that evening as the young preacher made the point that whatever we aspired to be we would do better if we took Jesus and made him the Lord of our life.

All I knew was that I wanted to be a professional baseball player and get out of that foundry. Responding to an altar call at the end of the sermon, I left my pew at the back of the church and made my way to the kneeling rail. My motives were probably not what they should have been, but God accepts us at whatever point we're willing to start trusting Him.

I remember that as I began to pray I became deeply convicted about how I had treated my family, especially being such a lousy brother to my younger sister, Emily, who was the same age as Lois. I thought she was the laziest mortal who ever walked the face of the earth. It seemed to me that she never helped my mother as much as she should have with a lot of the work at home and I didn't mind telling her what I thought. All those hurtful things I said flooded my soul. I asked God for forgiveness and when I got up from prayer, I sensed that something had happened to me at a very deep personal level.

Back home the next morning the family was gathered around the breakfast table. I began with my sister, Emily. I laid my hand on her shoulder and I told her how sorry I was for all the mean things I had said to her. She looked at me, completely confused.

"What are you talking about, Cork?" she asked.

"Last night I responded to an invitation to become a born again Christian," I explained. "I've committed my life to Jesus Christ and made him the Lord of my life."

Emily stared dumbfounded along with the rest of the members of my family as I went from brother to sister, asking forgiveness. I tried to explain to them what conversion meant. While I talked, Mom and Dad listened carefully to this conversation that was so different from our normal table talk. I don't think a single member of my family understood what I was talking about. I can understand how strange it must have sounded. In spite of all my churchgoing and confirmation training, I never understood personal salvation through faith in the Lord Jesus Christ. I'm sure if the roles had been reversed and one of my siblings had told me they had been converted, I would have been as confused as my family was on that morning.

Mom was standing at the far end of the table next to Dad. As I apologized and asked forgiveness, she quietly muttered under her breath, "That's nice, that's nice." When I finished Dad simply said, "I hope it does you some good."

When my father told his minister of my conversion, Pastor Lutz said he was glad to hear such good news. Many years later, after I was ordained, Pastor Lutz extended an invitation to me through my father to preach in my home church. I wasn't able to honor that gracious invitation, but some years later I did attend a service with Dad and Mom. As I walked into that huge church with the balcony all around, seeing the big pipe organ up front, the high pulpit from which the pastor preached and the choir sitting on either side of the front of the church, all the memories of my childhood came flooding back. We sat in the same pew we did when I was a child. When the organ struck a chord and the choir sang "The Lord is in His holy Temple, Let all the earth be silent before Him," chills came over my body. I loved singing the hymns and going forward for communion. Everything that I learned came back to me naturally, but instead of not understanding, worship was filled full of meaning. I still have a deep appreciation for the liturgy that I learned as a boy. But how much more deeply grateful am I to the Lord Jesus Christ for making the benefits of salvation real to me and for giving me the courage to answer His call.

I continued to attend the Allentown Free Methodist Church every weekend over the next four months. I discovered that nearly every member of that congregation had been praying for my conversion and many told me they continued to pray for me as a young Christian.

I will never forget three very special people in that congregation. Mabel, Anna, and Helen were three old maid sisters who were the heart and soul of that congregation. I remember vividly how they dressed and their sweet voices. Anna was the youngest and a dynamic Christian, an able speaker, and a good Sunday school teacher. Mabel was tall. She was at her best whenever good meals were prepared and served to the members and friends of that church. Helen, the oldest of the three sisters, was a petite lady who must have worn a size 4 dress and was full of kindness and love. She had good penmanship. She wrote letters and mailed boxes of goodies to me while I was in the military.

Interestingly enough, following my conversion Mom and Dad got into the habit of attending church regularly. After returning from military service, my brother Earl was born again and became an outstanding Christian. My sister, Emily, had a profound spiritual awakening and is one of the godliest women I know. Brother Eddie served Christ faithfully as a devout Roman Catholic and Gertie became a pillar of their local United Methodist congregation. Edna is a strong churchwoman. In fact, every one of the people around the breakfast table that morning except Donald who never made a profession of faith became strong people of faith in their respective churches.

Nothing is wasted in the economy of God. I am so thankful for God's saving grace in Jesus Christ, which is as real in my heart today as so long ago on that September evening.

9

The Prexies

Baseball was the truly America's pastime in the world in which I grew up. Every town and village had softball or baseball teams. As I drive through the suburbs today I see fields of children playing soccer. But in the first half of the twentieth century, boys and girls filled ball diamonds.

My father was a left-hand pitcher for a local team. So, it's not surprising that I, too, would grow to love the game and became a pitcher for the Wilson High School Presidents, affectionately dubbed the Prexies. My best pitch was what today is called a sinking curve ball, but which we called a drop. I could throw a pitch that seemed aimed for the batter's head and by the time it crossed the plate, it was at his belt. Or if I threw it at his belt, would kick up dust in front of the catcher.

For three years I was a starting pitcher and a reliever. When I wasn't pitching, I played center field or third base. Our county was divided into four divisions. Called the Berks Scholastic League, Wilson High School was in the Central division and our biggest rivals were the Shillington Speedboys.

I still have the faded newspaper article of the divisional championship game proclaiming me the game's "number one hero." Our starting pitcher, Dick Doerrman, had given up four runs in the first inning. I came on in relief and pitched the rest of the game. The newspaper said:

> *Walt Risney's Prexies notched the first run in the fourth on a double by Barnett and a hit by Wayne Albright. They added a pair in the fifth when Barnett hit to the right field and scored Kochel and Zdraveski.*

We went on to beat Shillington 5-4. But the game I'll never forget was the 1942 League Championship when our Wilson Presidents met the Kutztown Cougars. The Reading Eagle called it "...one of the best-played championship games in the history of the Berks Scholastic League."

The teams met on a neutral field in West Leesport, a town north of Reading. In only the second time since the league was organized in 1927, a pitcher threw a nearly perfect shut out game, striking out eleven, giving up no hits and allowing only two walks. Unfortunately his name was Charlie Kutz, not Clarence Barnett.

I did pitch a pretty good game, however, giving up just five hits and only one run in the first inning. I walked Len Sayer who then stole second base. George Rhoads stood in at the plate and slapped an inside curve to the third base side of the infield. Our third baseman, Wayne Albright, couldn't get to the hard-hit shot in time. As the ball rolled into left field, Sayer rounded third and scored the Cougar's game winning run.

I saw Wayne Albright at our 50th High School Reunion. He said, "Barney, I'm sorry that I made that error at third base when they scored the run. They gave that guy a hit, but I should have made that play." After all those years, apparently he felt as badly as I did about losing that championship game.

It was not uncommon to see my father standing on the embankment above the athletic field while we were playing a game late in the afternoon after school. We did not have seating at our ball field. Dad was interested in seeing me play, especially if I was pitching.

I got word that baseball scouts from one of the major league teams in Philadelphia, the Athletics, were interested in signing me to a professional contract. The Athletics were the most winning franchise in Philadelphia history, clinching nine American League Championships and five World Series wins. Truly this was an answer to my every prayer. It was a dream come true.

But the United States Army took care of that dream.

10

Dear John

I toiled in the foundry until the middle of January, 1943, when I got my draft letter, or what we referred to as a "Dear John" letter from President Roosevelt, ordering me to report to Indiantown Gap for induction into the Army.

Every able-bodied male knew he was going to be drafted after high school graduation. As I look at my high school yearbook, I suspect 80% of the fellows with whom I graduated were inducted. Nearly half of them were killed during World War II.

Every weekend became more precious to me as I counted down the days I had left before reporting to the Army on the first day of February in 1943. Working in the foundry had made me strong. I was in great physical condition. Those weeks seemed to whiz by.

One Friday evening in November I was making the now familiar drive to see Lois and her family in Allentown. Suddenly I heard a rumble and felt my car lurch. I had fallen asleep and gone off the road, jumping the curb and had hit a building. There wasn't more than 6 inches between the curb to the corner of this large farmhouse. I awoke just in time to avoid a head-on collision, glancing off the corner of the house, and coming to a stop 25 or 30 feet on the front lawn.

I was paralyzed with fear for several moments but eventually gathered my wits, got out of the car, and walked around to inspect for any damage. Tires on the passenger side were flattened, a rear tire had a large gash in it, a front rim was severely bent, and I had dented my rear fender. The house was undamaged except for smudge of paint that had come from my fender. I waited for someone to come out of the house to investigate, but no one appeared. I didn't know what to do. I thought about knocking on the front door and apologizing, but I wasn't sure anyone was home. As I returned to re-examine my car, I noticed a car passing on the road slow and come to a stop.

"Can I give you a lift, buddy?" the driver called.

"You surely can," I said and jumped in his car. We were about two miles north of Kutztown and about halfway to Allentown. We drove down a long gradual hill that led downtown. The Chevy dealership was still open. I told the driver he could drop me off there and thanked him for his kindness.

Inside, several men were milling about the sales office, but I went directly to the garage. I found a mechanic and told him what had happened.

"Would it be possible to find two used tires and two inner tubes," I asked. "And I need a rim to replace my front wheel."

A few minutes later he returned carrying all the parts I needed. He went into the sales office, tallied up an invoice, came back and handed me a bill for about $30. I had plenty of money in my pocket so the price was no problem. Just as I was trying to figure out how I would get back to my crippled Chevy, a wonderful thing happened. The mechanic not only offered to drive me back to my car, but he installed the new equipment.

When I got back on the road, all I could think to do was to thank God for sparing my life and providing me with the help I needed.

Lois, her parents, and I had great fun on those weekends before I joined the Army. We played board games and sang. Lois's mother was a great sport and a good singer. I especially remember that first Christmas and New Year's season as a born again believer. It was the first time I had ever gone to a Christmas party and a New Year's celebration centered in the church.

But eventually the day arrived when I had to leave for the Army induction center at Indiantown Gap. Like my Mom I can scarcely get through saying goodbye to someone I love and respect without shedding a tear. I am a sentimental person, and often tears have dropped on the pages of this rough manuscript as I think and write about important events and people in my life.

When I watch reservists preparing for overseas duty say goodbye to their family, children, and especially their spouses, I flash back to my own farewells so many years ago. Often I cannot hide the emotions that flood my soul and bring tears to my eyes, and sometimes I don't wish to hide it. Getting used to Army life was much easier for me than saying goodbye to my love ones at home.

It was especially difficult to say goodbye to Lois not knowing what would happen to me in the Army. I purposed that this beautiful brunette would one day become my wife, God willing, if I was spared the death and the destruction of war.

11

You're in the Army Now

The train ride from Reading to Indiantown Gap took about an hour. The coach was filled with noisy young men going off to war.

We had settled down in the barracks that first night when a sergeant came and asked, "Is there anyone in here who knows how to drive a truck. I mean a big truck."

Several guys volunteered.

"Good," said the sergeant. "Follow me."

The men climbed out of their bunks and dutifully followed the NCO outside.

"Over there," the sergeant said pointing, "you see a large pile of soft coal that must be delivered to all of the barracks you see down this road."

The volunteers nodded and began looking for the big trucks they would drive.

"Over by the pile you'll find wheelbarrows," the sergeant continued. "You will fill those wheelbarrows and deliver a load of that soft coal to every one of these barracks."

That night I learned Lesson Number One: Never volunteer for anything in the Army.

The first days at the induction center were hectic and a little embarrassing. First we had to pass a physical exam. We lined up, stripped naked, and then one by one passed down a line of doctors like a car being poked and jabbed on the assembly line. Each doctor looked for specific physical ailments. One listened to the heart, another checked the lungs, one examined feet, and still another checked the spine by having us raise our arms as high as we could and twist this way and that. We read eye charts and went through all kinds of motion tests to qualify our physical dexterity. The most embarrassing moment was the hernia examination. That doctor stuck his fingers up in your crotch, instructed you to turn your head and cough, and then repeated the process on the other side.

If you made it that far along the medical gauntlet, you received several shots before finally arriving at a dentist who examined teeth. If a recruit had a problem that needed attention right away, the doctors scheduled him to report the following day to such and such a place and have the problem corrected.

The second day I went through another line. This time we were given a large duffel bag and walked along counter after counter of shoes, shirts, and every imaginable part of our uniform. We put every article of clothing we would wear for the next three or four years into the duffel bag. From behind the counter a man would eye each recruit as he passed by and ask what size shoe he wore. If the soldier didn't know his shoe size, the man leaned a little way over the counter to see the GI's feet, and within moments, slammed a pair of boots down on the counter.

On down the line I went. Shirts, socks, underwear, even a heavy winter overcoat—I stuffed it all into the duffel bag.

Next we came to a room with several barber chairs and some anxious barbers who seemed to be getting paid by how fast they could sit you down, grab their shears, and strip every hair off your head. When I saw my bald head in the mirror of that barbershop I knew I was really in the Army.

Finally, we completed numerous aptitude tests to match our skills and interests to the job of which we were most capable.

Within a week or so we were split into smaller groups and assigned to different basic training camps throughout the country. I was to go to Camp McCain near Jackson, Mississippi. I thought to myself, "Mississippi? I've hardly ever been outside Berks or Lancaster County and they're going to send me to Mississippi."

I really didn't care where they sent me as long as it was away from Indiantown Gap. The train ride to Mississippi took three days. Somebody said we're about an hour from our destination. I looked out the train window and saw nothing but swamps. I wondered where there could be an Army camp in this bog, but it wasn't long until the train pulled into the Camp McCain station.

The first item of business was getting our Ml rifle and a bayonet. We spent a great deal of time the first day getting our rifles ready to fire by cleaning away the grease and waxy substance the manufacturer put on the metal parts to prevent rusting.

I enjoyed the days at the rifle range where we practiced shooting the M1. The shooting instructors had a funny way of humiliating someone who shot and completely missed the target. The person operating the target pit would raise a long pole with ladies' underwear on it and waved it back and forth. Everybody along the firing line would shout, "Maggie's drawers, Maggie's drawers," and we all would have a big laugh.

The first two weeks of basic training we hiked and did a lot of calisthenics. We built our strength and endurance with what seemed like endless repetitions of push-ups, chin-ups, sit-ups, and jumping jacks.

The most difficult and frightening exercise of basic training was crawling through the live fire range. This was a muddy area larger than a baseball infield that was covered with barbed wire perhaps twenty inches off the ground. We had to crawl across this swamp with our rifles cradled in our arms while live ammunition was fired from a machine gun just above the barbed wire. They told us, "If you stand up, you will be killed." With bullets whizzing over my rear end I had no trouble staying on my belly and keeping my rifle low enough so that I would not be hit.

We drilled in bayonet fighting by practicing six or eight jabbing and slashing movements before sticking the bayonet into a burlap bag packed tight with straw. We paired off with another soldier who came at us using the same movements. The routine ended by sticking the bayonet into the bag of straw as far as you could, symbolizing how we would prevail in hand-to-hand combat with an enemy.

Basic training was not difficult for me; in fact I enjoyed a good part of it. I got to like the food, especially the lamb stew. But the water at Camp McCain was horrible. It had a strong sulfur smell, like rotten eggs. The only time I didn't mind the water was when I got to take a shower after getting myself filthy crawling on all fours through the live fire range or when I had worked especially hard. The shower felt so good I didn't even notice the stench.

Everyone in basic training pulled KP duty. KP stands for Kitchen Police which meant we cleaned floors or washed dishes, but mostly KP meant peeling several bushels of potatoes. One day as I was peeling potatoes with a couple of fellows I remembered some folks back home saying potatoes could cure warts. I had developed a serious wart on the joint of my forefinger. This seemed like the perfect time to test the folk medicine remedy. I cut a potato in half and rubbed it on the wart. I rubbed and rubbed some more until I got tired of rubbing over that wart. Then I would slice off a piece of the potato and throw it in the pot. I took what was left of the potato to the barracks and every evening, or whenever I had time, I sliced the potato and rubbed it on the wart. Within a week the wart was completely healed. So, the old Pennsylvania Dutch remedy worked even in Mississippi.

The only work worse than KP was latrine duty. This entailed cleaning all the urinals, toilets, showers, and mopping everything down with disinfectant. It was a terrible job, and one I was always glad to finish.

I decided one day that I would ask for a pass to go into town. A group of us GI's couldn't wait to jump on the bus and head into Jackson. Most of the guys went straight for the barrooms in town. I wasn't a bit interested in drinking or carousing, so I walked up and down the streets looking in shop windows. I didn't see much that interested me until I found a little ice cream store. I went in and ordered a triple scoop ice cream cone. As I sat there eating ice cream, I was transported in my mind back to Smokey's. I really enjoyed that simple moment as I reconnected with home and my life outside the Army.

The best part of the entire day at basic camp was mail call. The CQ (charge of quarters) stood on the weapons carrier with a fist full of letters and parcels at his feet. Each man waited anxiously as the CQ called out soldier's names who had received mail. When he called a name, the soldier said, "Over here," and the CQ would toss the letter in that direction. Standing at the back of the group meant your letter or package passed through three of four sets of hands before reaching its recipient. If the CQ called out "Barnett" and the return address was from Allentown, my closest buddies would know that the old maids had sent me another box of cookies or candies and something interesting to read. They always included several religious tracts, and I would make sure to hand out those tracts to everyone who shared the sweets from my three old maids in Allentown.

Basic training lasted almost three months. During that time our platoon developed a strong sense of camaraderie. We learned to respect each other, work, laugh, and yes, we even cried together at times. I was the only soldier in our barracks that attended church or went to chapel services on Sunday. I studied the Bible whenever I had the opportunity. The base chaplain did not always give me much to think about as a Christian. I would read an entire book of the Bible at one time to gain a deeper understanding of its meaning. I was a new Christian in a very spiritually challenging environment and I needed a lot of divine help.

The big day of basic training came when we completed all the requirements, passed all the physical exams, proven marksmanship, demonstrated that we could obey orders, and survived the live fire range. At last we had finished basic training. Not everyone made it through on the first try. Some men waited anxiously to learn if they would have to repeat another period at Camp McCain. I wasn't concerned because I had scored well in just about everything. Nevertheless, I had to wait several more weeks for my first assignment.

We passed the time marching and doing more calisthenics. Gradually orders started coming in and men would celebrate their reprieve from Camp McCain to get on with their next assignment, usually a training school in whatever job they had been assigned. It wasn't until about half the men had left that I finally received my orders to report to Camp Butner, North Carolina.

12

Extracted

While I was in basic training, Lois's family had moved again, this time from Allentown to Washington, DC. I greeted this as great good news because I could take the train into Washington on a weekend pass from Camp Butner. I was trained to be an MP, military policeman.

It was several weeks before I got my first pass. When I arrived at the train station in Henderson, North Carolina, I discovered I wasn't the only one with a ticket on the northbound train. A large crowd of GIs stood around smoking and chatting on the platform. As the train chugged into the station, I could see in the windows that every coach was filled with people. Almost no one got off. Those weekend trains headed for Washington were so crowded that many times I had to stand in the aisle holding my suitcase over my head until someone moved just enough that I could claim a little floor space in the passageway where two cars joined. I would upend my suitcase and sit on it from Richmond to Washington. It was a rough ride, but I was thrilled to be on my way to Washington.

Lois had written me with step-by-step directions from Union Station to her house in southeast Washington. When I got off the bus at Greenway Apartments, I was one long block from her house. I walked as fast as I could until I finally arrived in front of her house. I had to stop for a moment and catch my breath. I was very excited as I climbed the steps on to her front porch. I took a deep breath and rang the doorbell. When the door opened, I dropped my suitcase at my feet and embraced Lois with the warmest and most tender embrace I could manage. As we kissed, I was overwhelmed with love and the joy of seeing her once again after so long a time.

Mr. and Mrs. Weinel welcomed me warmly and seemed glad to see me. Lois's younger brother, Jack, who was about 8 years old, wrapped his arms around my legs. He was fascinated with the buttons and belt on my uniform and wanted to wear my cap. I obliged him in every way that I could.

Lois' mother, Mildred, and father, C.D. Weinel

That evening was filled with love and conversation as we spoke openly about our hopes and plans that Lois and I could be married at the earliest possible time. When I asked Lois's dad for permission to marry his daughter, he answered with a typical dour look on his face.

"What is she worth to you?" he asked.

I was dumbfounded and didn't know how to answer. My face turned red and after catching my breath, I said, "She's worth everything I have and ever hope to have. I promise you, with God's help, I will love her and take care of her all the days of my life."

He turned away smiling and I took his answer to be yes. Those days were some of the happiest moments in all my life. The three days I spent with Lois and her folks seemed to fly by. All too soon it was time to go back to the Army base. I packed my suitcase and prepared myself for the horrible ordeal of saying good-bye. I minimized some of the pain of leaving by convincing myself that I could get another pass in a month or two. But I knew that I was in God's hands and took great comfort that Lois and her family were praying for me every day.

Back at Union Station, I was fortunate enough to get a seat in a coach. As the train rolled southbound through the night, I sat back in my seat, cherishing and reliving all of the precious moments that we shared, and I thanked God for permitting me to be with people that I loved.

I was surprised when I returned to camp and learned that our company of military police was scheduled to ship out in a couple of weeks. We went to Camp Patrick Henry near Newport News and Norfolk, Virginia. While there we got another physical exam, more shots, and another dental examination. When the dentist looked into my mouth, he told me I had three wisdom teeth that should be extracted.

"Three!" I exclaimed. "Three? At one time?"

The dentist insisted the wisdom teeth had to come out, that it was better to do it now than to get overseas and have tooth problems. I reluctantly agreed and the next day I climbed into his antique dentist's chair for the procedure. Within a few moments of receiving something to numb the pain, he pulled and yanked those teeth out of my jaw. As each tooth was extracted, the nurse pushed a cotton wad into my mouth and told me to bite down. When it was finally all over, my mouth was filled with more cotton than a Mississippi plantation.

"Keep pressure on those cotton wads," the nurse said.

As I left, the dentist handed me a bag of cotton wads and said, "Good luck, private."

By the time I walked back to my barracks, I looked like a casualty of war. My face was swollen and I had to spit out blood-soaked cotton wads every 20 to 30 minutes at first and then every hour or two. That night, I slept very little. The dentist told me to rinse my mouth with salt water for pain. I was up and down most of the night.

At four o'clock that morning we were awakened and told to pack all of our belongings in our duffel bags. We were leaving in 30 minutes to board ship for a trans-Atlantic passage to Europe.

Next to me was a large Jewish man named Abrams. He and I had gotten somewhat close since the Army did everything alphabetically and my name came after his on our company roster. He reached over, touched my arm, and said softly, "Barnett."

"Yes," I whispered.

"I'm leaving soon, so don't look for me."

A moment later I saw him sit up in bed and slip on his shoes and uniform. What happened next was indeed strange. He fastened his bayonet on the end of his rifle and standing near the head of his bunk, Abrams rammed the bayonet through the composition board of the barracks wall. Leaving the bayonet in the wall, he laid the butt of his rifle on his bunk and hid his duffel bag under his cot. I watched as he opened the screen door and quietly made his escape. No one noticed that Abrams wasn't present until we boarded ship. He was supposed to sit next to me on transport truck, but when he didn't show, the sergeant thought maybe he had gotten into the wrong truck. Nobody was too concerned until they checked all the areas and discovered Abrams was gone. He told me some time before that there was no way he was going overseas in any field of combat.

I never saw Abrams again. I don't know if he got away, if he was able to elude the guards and sentries stationed all around the camp. I imagined Abrams fleeing through the alligator-infested swamps that surrounded much of Camp Patrick Henry.

When we arrived at dock side, we boarded a large Canadian luxury liner called the Empress of Scotland. The ship had originally been named the Empress of Japan, but Churchill declared no Allied ship should carry the name of the enemy. Since 1940, the ship had been converted into a troop transport that could accommodate about 12,000 GIs. Bunks were arranged six deep in every possible compartment of the vessel. With only two feet of space between bunks, we were stacked like a can of sardines. There was no room to store our belongings, so we slept somehow with our duffel bags at our feet.

I was assigned as an MP to accompany the ship and see to it that soldiers didn't get into trouble. I knew that we were going to pick up German and Italian prisoners of war and bring them back to the United States.

The most dangerous part of the trip was getting out of port because German submarines had been spotted at the mouth of the Chesapeake Bay. Our course lay directly across that very hot spot. Troop transports did not travel in a convoy, but relied on speed to outrun and outmaneuver any German submarines that might be in the area.

During the first few days aboard ship my mouth was still very sore. I persuaded a crew member who worked in the ship's dining hall to give me some salt, so I continued the dentist's instructions. Finally the bleeding stopped on the fourth day at sea, but as a precaution I continued salt water rinses during the entire trip.

Onboard we were continually drilled on what to do in case we were attacked. When the alarm sounded call to quarters, the decks cleared in a blaze of activity. Men who had been shooting craps on the open deck outside my compartment could grab their dice and money and be gone in a matter of seconds. Anti-aircraft guns had been mounted topside. They made an awful racket when fired during those practices.

In the spring of that year President Roosevelt had announced that 18 year-old men were being drafted but would not see overseas service. I looked around at the men crowded on that vessel, and I saw a lot of guys who looked younger than I was. I had just turned 19 the month before.

It took us about five days to reach our destination in Casablanca. As we sailed into the harbor, three P38 fighter planes came roaring toward our ship. Those hotdog pilots flew upside-down directly over the ship. The men waved and shouted from the decks, but whether they cheered the fancy flying or were just thankful to be off that cramped ship, I couldn't tell. It was quite a scene that welcomed us to Casablanca.

13

Prisoners

As an MP my job was to supervise the orderly unloading of GIs in Casablanca. When our troops finished disembarking, we began the slow process of getting German and Italian prisoners of war on board the Empress of Scotland. It took three or four days to load an estimated 8,000 prisoners. The ship's capacity was limited somewhat by the fact that wounded prisoners couldn't be crammed as tightly into quarters as healthy men had been. The wounded lay on litters and were carried aboard first. I made rounds with the doctors and helped to translate based on the little German I had learned from my Pennsylvania Dutch relatives.

I don't know what I was expecting when I first laid eyes on these Germans. Posters and newspaper cartoons pictured them as evil ogres. But I was struck by how much they looked like me and my family. They had the same complexion and hair color, even their accent was familiar. Many of them were tank men who had fought in Rommel's Africa Corps.

We were careful when loading the ship not to have Germans and Italians in the same compartment. They hated each other. Many Germans told me that the Italians were lousy soldiers. In some campaigns in North Africa the Germans used Italian divisions as a buffer between Allied forces and themselves. The Italians did not want to be caught in the middle and so they simply surrendered to U.S. forces. Some Germans told me on board the ship the Italians were only interested in eating bread and loving women. We military police were able to keep things under control on our way back to the United States.

When we announced that we had landed in Boston, many Germans refused to believe us.

"Boston! Nein, nein," they said. Their propaganda reported that the German Navy had shelled Boston and New York and destroyed them. As we carefully unloaded the wounded, thousands of prisoners came out on the deck to see the great American city. It wasn't until they saw signs that the Germans were finally persuaded they really were in Boston.

Our Military Police company returned to Camp Butner in North Carolina. Several weeks later we received orders to start the cycle again, returning to Camp Patrick Henry to board another ship crossing the Atlantic. This luxury liner was the USS West Point. Built in the United States, the ship was by far superior to the Empress of Scotland, which we had taken to Casablanca on our first trip for prisoners.

In many ways the second trip was quite pleasant. The food was better, or maybe it was that I could chew again without pain as my mouth was now completely healed. We did not encounter any submarines or threats as our huge vessel zigzagged across the ocean. Arriving again in Casablanca, we disgorged thousands of GIs who would in a few weeks fight and die in the invasion of Sicily.

Back we sailed to the United States. Once again our Military Police company returned to North Carolina. Camp Butner was our home base for about nine months in that year of 1943. We had been back from the second trip about a week when we were rewarded with five-day passes. The fellows with relatives in the eastern part of the United States were anxious to visit their homes and families. I signed up for a pass to Washington, DC.

The train left from the town of Henderson. As I waited to get on the train, the platform was packed with soldiers. My spirits fell as the arriving train was already so crowded with soldiers most of us were not able to board. I decided to walk to the edge of town along the main street going north which happened to be US Route One. At the edge of town I started thumbing to get a ride. I thought if I could reach Richmond I could hop a train there sometime later. It didn't take long until a man in a pickup truck stopped to offer me a ride. He told me he was going as far as Petersburg which is about 25 miles south of Richmond. I climbed in and off we went.

We had gone just a few miles when I became aware that the man was too intoxicated to be driving anywhere, especially on such a busy road as Route One. Thankfully it was early evening and by this time the highway was relatively free of traffic. I offered to drive.

"Don't worry, soldier," he said, "I'll get you to Petersburg." I didn't know what to do. I wanted to get off the truck, and I wanted to keep going. I prayed all the way, and it was an interesting, wild ride.

Arriving in Petersburg, I thanked the man for the ride but I thanked God even more for keeping me safe. I vowed that never again would I hitch a ride anywhere with anyone.

At the train station I discovered that I had missed the last train, so I had to wait all night for the early morning train. But it worked out as I had planned. I was able to get a seat and finish my trip to Washington.

When I reached Lois's house I rang the doorbell. I remember how happy I was when she opened the door. I was just as excited to see her this second time as I was the first. We had a wonderful four days together.

My days with Lois ended too soon. Back at Camp Butner, we seemed to be marking time. We picked up trash around the grounds and occasionally did formation drills, but we had no mission. It was like the Army didn't know where to put us.

After a couple of weeks in limbo we got new orders. We were going to a tent camp outside the small town of Windsor, North Carolina to guard about 500 German prisoners of war. A prison camp was a tent city surrounded by guard towers. The tents were arranged in orderly rows. The MPs lived in the same kind of tents, too. Our tents were located adjacent to the barbed wire that confined the prisoners. Each tent accommodated four men and was equipped with small coal burning stoves because it did get cold in North Carolina. We shared outdoor showers, protected from the cold air by only a tent flap.

Prisoners worked at various sites in towns as far as 35 miles away. We supervised the work teams. Some felled trees and cut the logs into lengths for delivery to pulp mills. Some teams unloaded railroad cars of lumber onto large conveyors that carried the wood up into the pulp mills. I supervised prisoners working in a local lumber yard. The owner of that lumber yard told me one day in his thick southern drawl, "You know, I'm really happy to have these prisoners working. I used to have about 15 head of niga', but these Germans are much better workers. I am happy that you and your prisoners are here and doin' such a good job for me."

Race relations were very poor in those days in the South. If a white woman was walking on the sidewalk in town and a black man came from the opposite direction, it was common practice for the black man to step off of the sidewalk and stand in the street until the woman had passed. Only then would he get back on the sidewalk and continue where he was going.

We had no trouble with the prisoners of war. They were good workers. The Army became concerned about warning the citizens in town to be on the lookout in case any of the prisoners attempted to escape. We passed out leaflets instructing townspeople to call the camp if they saw any German POWs wandering around unsupervised.

We decided to test the effectiveness of our brochures. We asked a trusted German prisoner to go into town, walk around, order a meal in a restaurant, and then come back to camp. The prisoners were easy to spot because they wore their German uniforms. We never received a single call. The Germans were model citizens. They were respectful and never complained. They were delighted to be in the United States. Most volunteered for work programs, preferring to be active than to sit idly in the camp.

Two guards drove a 2-1/2 ton truck that carried 12 to 14 prisoners to a work site. These prisoners were happy to get out of camp and see the countryside. In most cases there was good rapport with the prisoners and the soldiers guarding them. The prisoners had their own cooks and did all their own house work, or perhaps I should say, tent work. The POW camp functioned almost entirely without incident.

About the middle of October I went to our captain's quarters located in an abandoned railroad freight station at the edge of town and not far from our camp. I walked into the office and saluted sharply. Captain White saluted back. Captain White was about 50 years old who had a reputation for fairness but he could be rough at times.

"What can I do you for you, Barnett?" he asked.

I said, "Sir, I'd like to ask for a three-day pass to go to DC and make some final arrangements for our wedding."

Captain White smiled and asked, "Why do you wanna buy a cow when milk is so cheap?"

The statement surprised me. I recovered my composure and said, "Sir, I would like to make final plans because we intend to be married sometime as early as February. I hope at that time I could be granted a seven-day pass to go to Washington in order to marry a very special girl that I love with all my heart."

He sat there for a moment and finally he said that the pass could be arranged if there were no unforeseen problems in the camp. A week later I received a week-end pass. I rode a bus from Windsor to Richmond where I got on a train to Washington.

We spent the weekend making wedding plans. We selected the date of February 6, 1944 and began to make all the necessary contacts for the wedding. Members of our wedding party were all in the armed services, and we hoped they could all get passes to participate in our special day.

When I returned from that visit to Washington, I was one very happy camper because all our plans were made. On the return trip I boarded a train in Washington and went as far as Richmond where later I was able to board a bus that was scheduled to get me to Windsor by 7:00 a.m. in the morning.

I went into a diner where several others were seated at the far end of the counter. When I sat down, a young waitress asked if she could take my order. I said that I would like some scrambled eggs and fried potatoes.

"Don't you want some grits?" she asked.

I told her I didn't know what grits were.

"You may as well take it as it comes with the order."

So that morning I tasted grits for the first time and I've been eating them ever since. As I ate my breakfast, I noticed the waitress kept looking at me. I suspected that she wanted to know if I enjoyed the grits. She approached where I was sitting, leaned her elbows on the counter, put her face in her hands, and stared at me.

"Are you really a Yankee?" she asked.

"I'm from Reading, Pennsylvania," I said. "Does that make me a Yankee?"

"I don't know where Reading is, but I sure have heard about Pennsylvania. If you come from way up thar', you must be a Yankee."

I finished my breakfast and left a small tip. As I walked out the door she said, "Y'all come back, ya' hear?"

In December, 1943 our camp was hit by a terrible snowstorm with nearly a foot of heavy, wet snow. Our poor tents were doubled over, sagging beneath the weight of the snow, and some nearly hit the ground. Tent poles snapped under the weight of the snow and our tent came down on 4 cots. The temperature dropped to about 15° and we had only one blanket. We lay on our cots with the tent hanging down in our faces buried under our heavy overcoats to keep warm. One GI fired up his coal stove until it was white-hot. When some fool stoked the fire, sparks flew up the stove pipe and set a neighboring tent ablaze.

The prisoners suffered equally. The guards in the towers left their posts as the blizzard worsened. Pipes froze in the kitchen tents and many people thought we needed to make sure that the shower didn't freeze up through the night. So before retiring, we were ordered to open the faucet so that there was a slight water drip coming out of the shower. Next morning we went to check on the situation and found a cone of ice about three feet in diameter at the base that lead right up to the shower head. It was several days before anyone had any idea of taking a shower. Fortunately most of the snow melted in a few days and we were once again able to take showers, although we did so quickly as the air was still rather chilly.

Within a week we repaired the damaged tents and replaced the one that had been burned. We were able to settle back into a regular routine. I do not recall ever going to church in town during the six months I was stationed at Windsor. I cannot explain the reason for that neglect. We had no Army chapel, but I faithfully read and studied my Bible. My tent buddies started calling me Preacher Barnett. I was determined to keep the commitments that I made to God the night of my conversion, and I surely would not do anything to break the trust placed in me by Lois, her family, and my dear friends in the Allentown Church.

As Christmas approached, there were few if any holiday decorations in the tent at camp. Most soldiers received extra packages filled with gifts at mail call during the Christmas season. Not many were given passes during the holiday. Since I had been promised a pass for our wedding, I wasn't going to make another request. Since married soldiers were permitted to spend nights with their wives when they had no guard duty, I began to look forward to the time I could have a life with Lois outside the tent city.

14

That Moment Divine

In January I began to look for a place for Lois and I to stay after we were married. I found a large house on a tree-lined street in the best section of town with a sign on the front lawn saying "Rooms for Rent." I inquired about the rooms and an elderly lady showed me a well-furnished room on the second floor. A long outside stairway ran along the side of the house, connecting to a second-story covered balcony that ran around three sides of the large house. I told the landlady that I was going to be married on February 6 and that I would pay rent for the month of February, 1944 in advance. The lady was very kind to me.

There were many such places in southern towns in those days. They were referred to as tourist homes. They rented rooms for sleeping only. I felt fortunate to find such a nice place, but there was one drawback that had me a little concerned. The room was heated with a wood stove, and I wondered whether Lois would be able to keep a fire going if I was on duty all day and then had night duty as well. Lois wasn't keen on the idea of tending the stove. I told her that I would teach her how to stoke a fire and get it started again the next day. But I could tell from her letters she was not looking forward to that part of our new life together.

I wrote letters to everyone in my family and to ladies in Allentown, telling everybody about our wedding plans. At first we were concerned about relatives who had to drive great distances because gasoline was rationed. But guests coming from great distances persuaded family members and friends to share extra gas stamps to make the trip. Lois's grandfather, the Reverend F.T. Diddle, made the long drive from Pittsburgh to Washington, DC to officiate at our wedding service. Members of our wedding party were all in the armed services. In the providence of God the best men, Gerald Diddle, and the maid of honor, Gladys Stein, were able to come on that day to Washington.

Most family members arrived at the Weinels' home on Friday or Saturday. The wedding service followed a Sunday morning service held in the East Washington Free Methodist Church on Minnesota Avenue where Lois's grandfather was the visiting preacher that morning. Before the benediction, the congregation was invited to attend the wedding service.

In 1939 Oscar Hammerstein II and Jerome Kern wrote a beautiful love song titled "All the Things You Are." It was one of my favorite love songs when I was a senior in high school dating Lois. I must have sung it dozens of times. On our wedding day that song kept running through my thoughts. Its lyrics so perfectly expressed my feelings on that wonderful occasion:

> You are the angel glow that lights a star.
> The dearest things I know are what you are.
> One day my happy arms will hold you
> And someday I'll know that moment divine
> When all the things you are, are mine.

Members of the wedding party joined Lois and me before the altar of that small church. As her grandfather started to speak, I could hear my heart pounding in my chest.

"Dearly beloved, we are gathered here in the presence of God in this house of worship to join together Barney and Lois in holy matrimony, which is an honorable estate by God in the time of man's innocence. In the scriptures marriage is often used as a symbol to indicate the close relationship between Christ and the church. Marriage is therefore not to be entered into unadvisedly, but with reverence and love."

By the time he finished that first paragraph of the wedding liturgy my heart had slowed down somewhat. The wedding party managed to get through the entire ceremony with no one passing out from nervousness (which has happened quite frequently at weddings I have conducted throughout the years). It was a beautiful experience for me and Lois and our friends.

Instead of a formal wedding reception, Lois's family hosted a great dinner. Since no members of my family were able to attend the wedding, we decided we would make our "honeymoon" a two day visit with my family. After we finished eating, we left the Weinel home about 3:30 in the afternoon. Someone took us to Union Station where we got on the train to Philadelphia where we transferred to the Reading line that took us back home.

We arrived in Reading about 6:00 and boarded the local bus that ran to Whiskey Ditch. My family gave us such a warm welcome. It was the first time my mother and father had ever met Lois. My sisters, Emily and Gertie, remembered Lois from her days in high school. Emily was in the same grade as Lois. The only one who seemed to have difficulty with this beautiful young lady now leaning on me or standing close to me was my youngest sister, Edna, who was about ten years old. I think she saw Lois taking a lot of my attention that would have gone to her, but she soon enough came around. My family was really impressed with Lois, and told me they thought I had made an excellent selection. The big thing was that we were all so very happy to be together as a complete family with a new beautiful wife who was pleased to be called Lois Barnett.

We spent two days in Pennsylvania visiting my immediate family and my grandparents. My mother's parents spoke English. My grandparents congratulated us several times before we left, both of them kept saying, "It's so good to see you, Junior. You have a very beautiful wife." I learned that Uncle Melvin had been drafted during the summer of 1943.

Next we drove about five miles to my dad's parents in West Lawn. There conversation was more difficult because they spoke only German, although they understood a little English. Lois could only sit and smile pleasantly and listen as I kept up the conversation. Whenever they said something about Lois or asked a question about her, my grandparents would smile at Lois while they spoke to me. They told me that she was very pretty and more than once they said that they were so pleased that we had come by to visit them. Their youngest daughter, Edna, and her husband lived with my grandparents and helped take care of them. Edna helped to interpret their Pennsylvania Dutch.

My grandmother made the best apricot pies that I have ever tasted and she had remembered that apricot pie was my favorite as a child. Before we left, Aunt

Edna said we should go to the kitchen for some pie and milk. Sitting there eating apricot pie brought back memories of the many times my grandmother called to me as I crossed the playground of an elementary school located across the street from her house. She stood on the porch and waved to get my attention, calling "Junior, come here onct" and I remembered thinking that was exactly the same way my father called me when I worked with him as a boy. I'm not sure which was better that day—the apricot pie or the golden memories.

Lois and I returned to my parent's home on Lincoln Avenue. All the family was there except Earl, who was serving in the Army in Iceland. As I looked around my boyhood village I couldn't find anybody that I knew. All the young fellows my age who had never been out of the county were now in the Armed Forces scattered throughout the world.

15

Surprises

Back in North Carolina, Lois and I would soon discover a shocking surprise. But we were oblivious to anything but starting out new life together as we walked from the bus station in Windsor to the house where we would live. We laughed that this would be the first night that we would actually sleep alone in our own place. It was freezing cold so I started a wood fire in the stove. Soon everything was just as cozy and comfortable as could be.

Early the next morning I woke, stoked the fire, and tried to explain to Lois how to keep the fire burning until my expected return later that afternoon. I kissed her goodbye and walked to the camp hoping to get there early enough for breakfast.

When I rounded the turn in the road where I should have seen the guard towers surrounding the camp, there was nothing. Everything was gone. There wasn't a sign anywhere to indicate that a week earlier a military installation with 500 German prisoners and 125 military police had occupied the space. Confused, I ran back into town. On the way, I met a local man and asked him if he knew what had happened to the camp. He thought for a moment and then said he thought they had left the site about a week ago, but he didn't know where they had gone. When I got back to our room and told Lois that the camp had disappeared, I'm sure she must have wondered about the strange unpredictability of Army life.

I asked our landlady if she had any idea where the Army had gotten off to. She told me she thought the camp had relocated to the neighboring town of Williamston, about 13 miles down the road. At the Windsor Post Office I was able to verify that my landlady was correct. I don't recall how we settled up the rest of the rent I had paid in advance, but I will never forget that the people of North Carolina were as kind and friendly toward GIs as any place I have ever been.

Later that day Lois and I hopped the bus to Williamston. There on the north side of town just as the road crosses the river I saw the familiar guard towers watching over the coming and going of trucks, materials, and other equipment. It looked just like our old camp at Windsor, only it was much larger.

The next day when I reported to camp I learned that several hundred Italian prisoners had been added to our responsibility. Needing more room, the site was moved to the more spacious site at Williamston. I made arrangements for Lois and I to stay in a small hotel located in the center of town. It wasn't much of a hotel and the room we were assigned left much to be desired. It was a second-floor room overlooking the only stoplight in town, not 12 feet from the street. Huge trucks loaded with wood headed for the pulp mills screeched and chugged to a stop outside our window. The entire room vibrated as the truckers shifted gears pulling away from the red light. But worse than the traffic noise was the fact that the room came furnished with two simple cots. This represented cruel and unusual punishment for newlyweds.

Thankfully, our stay at the hotel was only temporary. I didn't have to report for duty at camp for several days. This gave us time to search for a more appropriate place to live. We found a lovely tourist home about a block from a small restaurant that served good food. We saw the sign in the window, "Rooms to Rent." The home was in good repair. The lawn and shrubbery were immaculately kept. Lois and I decided we would inquire. We walked up the stairs onto the porch, knocked on the door, and an elderly lady opened the door. Mrs. Rogers was a sophisticated southern lady who greeted us warmly and invited us inside. I told her that I was a soldier that had just come to the camp on the edge of town and that we needed a place to live. Her home was truly exquisite. She showed us a room off the right side of a grand hall. It was large and well-appointed with a nice carpet and comfortable furniture. A private bath with every imaginable fixture adjoined the room. When Lois saw a modern oil heater that required no attention throughout the winter, we said we'd take it.

She asked if we would have supper with her and her daughter, Mary. Mrs. Rogers told us she had been married to the president of the largest bank in town who had died several years earlier. She wanted to minimize the loneliness by making rooms available for tourists. We spent many enjoyable hours with these kind and gracious people. They treated us like family. Practically every evening Mrs. Rogers invited us into the parlor for conversation or to play some board games followed by a wonderful dessert before retiring for the night. Lois and I felt we were so blessed to have found what we thought was the perfect arrangement.

Many years later when we made trips to Florida, we were sure to go by way of Williamston. When our children were 9 and 12 years old, we stopped by to say hello to Mrs. Rogers and her daughter, Mary, to thank them again for the six months of kindness they showed us. Thank God for warmhearted people who know how to welcome strangers and make them dear friends.

Our six month assignment in Williamston was relatively easy duty. Our schedules for guard duty in the towers were posted well in advance and we had virtually no trouble with German or Italian prisoners as long as they were segregated into their own camps. Each had its own kitchen and dining hall. They did not go out together on work assignments.

The most undesirable work site was a large fertilizer plant located close to the camp on the Roanoke River. Workers there had to wear a mask and by the end of the day, we were all covered with a fine, white dust. It wasn't a very healthy place to work, but MPs and prisoners worked there every day.

Some places we worked were quite a distance away. We took work groups as far as Elizabeth City, Plymouth, Edenton, Ahoskie, and many other places on the eastern edge of North Carolina near Albemarle Sound. Most assignments involved cutting trees for pulp mills or lumber yards in the area. It was easy duty for the military police. Our most important responsibility was to be certain that we returned to camp at night with the same number of prisoners as when we left that morning. Prisoners never attempted to escape.

Lois and I attended a Presbyterian Church every Sunday I was off duty. It happened to be the home church of our landlady. Occasionally members of the church invited us to join them for lunch at a very fine restaurant.

Then, one day like an unexpected clap of thunder suddenly startled and surprised, our Military Police Company received orders that we were being transferred to Fort Lewis, near the city of Tacoma in the state of Washington. The news came as a complete surprise. We usually picked up information around camp when something important was about to happen, but not this time. Rumors flew around the camp. Some said we were just being re-assigned to guard duty at Fort Lewis. Others were concerned that we would be attached to an infantry division headed to the Pacific theater of operations.

We were given about a week to prepare to leave until we were yanked out of that lovely southern town and sent so far away. Married soldiers like myself who had enjoyed having our wives with us while stationed in the tent city at Williamston were probably the most distraught as we tried to plan for this unexpected reassignment. We were a sad bunch of GIs as we loaded our duffel bags into our trucks and headed back to Camp Butner for further preparations. Within a week we were driven to Henderson, North Carolina where we waited to be attached to a troop train headed for the Pacific Northwest.

Lois left Williamston and took the train to Pittsburgh to join her parents. Her father had been transferred again while we were living in North Carolina. She got a job working in an ice cream store to earn enough money for train fare to Tacoma.

It was very hot at that time. We were assigned to Pullman railroad cars that were on side tracks as we waited for the arrival of the troop train. We waited and waited in the sweltering heat. One enterprising farmer saw an opportunity. He had a load of watermelons in his pickup truck. He pulled up beside our coach and started selling his watermelons for 25 cents apiece. When the GIs in other cars saw what was going on, they swarmed that truck like flies at a picnic. The farmer couldn't keep control of the sales. He did the best he could, but after awhile, the soldiers reached into the truck for melons, threw money into the bed of the truck, and returned to the railroad cars to enjoy their treat. We cut the melons with our bayonets and made a sticky mess of our compartments.

The troop train finally arrived and the Pullman cars in which we were finishing up our watermelon were hooked to the end of the train with a jolt and a lurch. As the engineer blew the whistle signifying our departure from the station, two soldiers still attempting to buy watermelons almost missed the train.

We rode west on that train for days. We had many layovers all the way to the west as we waited for civilian trains to pass. After leaving Pittsburgh on our way to Chicago, our layovers were often in smaller cities. At almost every stop we were met by volunteers from the Red Cross and other service organizations. They lined up alongside the cars on the train, handing out sandwiches, coffee, cocoa, and many other goodies to the GIs free of charge. People were enthusiastic about supporting members of the armed services in those days.

From Chicago we were attached to a sophisticated civilian train that ran from Chicago to Seattle, Washington. We crossed the Mississippi and saw the night skyline of Minneapolis and St. Paul. Skirting the Missouri River we followed the trail of explorers Lewis and Clarke across the plains of North Dakota, through the big sky country of Montana, and finally arriving in Tacoma.

My first concern was to arrange a place for Lois and I to live near Fort Lewis. The first Sunday I didn't have duty I sought out the Tacoma Free Methodist Church. I introduced myself to the congregation telling them that I had just arrived in town and I hoped to find living quarters for my wife in Pittsburgh who hoped to join me as soon as possible. At the close of the service a lady introduced herself to me as Mrs. Tremain. She offered Lois and me one of her first floor bedrooms. Her husband was sick and seldom left the house. I wrote to Lois the good news that I had located living quarters.

When Lois earned enough money for train fare, she made arrangements to come to Tacoma. That trip would take five days and required her transferring trains in Chicago. That took a lot of courage for someone who had never traveled on her own before.

One morning on the train ride to Tacoma Lois woke early to discover that her feet were nearly frozen. The baseboard water heater that ran along the floor had sprung a leak while the train was passing through the Rocky Mountains. It was cold enough that the water that had leaked on to the floor had frozen and her shoes were frozen to the floor of the coach. She finally arrived on schedule, but I didn't know there were two train stations in Tacoma. I was waiting and waiting but no train arrived according to the schedule Lois had mailed me. I asked the station master if her train had already arrived, thinking I had missed it. He suggested to me that she had probably come in on the other line. I hurried to the other station located about three blocks away from where I had been waiting.

I found Lois sitting on a bench anxiously waiting for me. I ran and embraced her. Lois told me she had gone to the other station to find me. A lady on the train told her that there were two stations in town and perhaps I would be found at the other station. While I was going back and forth looking for her, she was doing the same thing. We must have walked on opposite sides of the street so that we never caught sight of each other. Once again we were together in a new place with new challenges.

16

Catheters and Roller Skates

Mr. and Mrs. Tremain were happy to have Lois join me as a tenant in their bungalow-style house. We always enjoyed our evening meals together. My duty schedule was light. I was free many weekdays and every weekend we went to church with Mrs. Tremain on Sundays.

Soon after we were settled, Lois went looking for a job at the shipyards. She was given two choices: one was an office job that paid $25 a week; the other job was as a ship's tank cleaner for $65 a week. Lois decided on the higher paying tank cleaning job. She cleaned calcium deposits from the large water tanks and scoured sludge from the oil tanks in the bowels of ships. It would take her a whole day to clean the inside walls of these storage tanks, some of which were so large she worked from a ladder to reach the entire surface. Many women went to work for the first time to support the war effort. In many cases women had to do jobs that had been previously reserved for men. That was why it seemed so out of character when I saw Lois who was usually impeccably attired go to work dressed in coveralls under a big cap and wearing hard-toed work boots.

The Army often did irrational things. Basic training taught us to unquestioningly obey orders because it could save our lives in combat. But it had as much to do with learning to adjust to the Army way of life. Case in point. After only a month in Tacoma, orders came in for some of our group to ship out. My name was not on that list, but within a few weeks, I was ordered to report to Fitzsimmons General Army Hospital in Denver, Colorado, on September l, 1944. So the Army had dispatched me from North Carolina to Denver by way of Tacoma, Washington. Ours was not to reason why, as the old saying goes.

I rode from Tacoma to Denver on a beautiful train with dining cars. As we sped through the stunning vistas of the Rocky Mountains, I ate my meals at a table covered with a white tablecloth. The silverware was sterling silver. Smiling stewards brought delicious food and served us like royalty.

The picture changed dramatically when I arrived in Denver. An Army bus met us at the train station and drove us to Fitzsimmons General Army Hospital located on the outskirts of the city. It was then I learned I was going to be trained as a combat medic.

Duty as an MP was easy compared to medic training in Denver. We lived in barracks and for the first several weeks we did vigorous calisthenics exercises to get us in peak physical condition. When classes began, many were conducted outdoors where we learned how to bandage flesh wounds in battlefield conditions. In the classroom, we learned physiology. In time we paired off to practice our new skills on each other, such as inserting catheters or stomach feeding tubes through the mouth or nose, administering shots, and many other medical duties. Practicing on each other meant you had to take special care to get it right. I learned what it felt like to insert a stomach tube and what to tell the patient to do to feel as little pain as possible. I was careful when I did the work because I knew soon the roles would be reversed and tubes would be inserted in my body. So it was important to do as good a job as possible because I certainly didn't want to have the other guy pay me back for a botched exercise when it was his turn to do the work.

We were appointed to various stations in the hospital during our three-month training. One month I served on a medical ward with long term patients. Many were older GIs afflicted with heart problems or leukemia. During rounds with the doctors, female nurses showed us what was expected in caring for very ill patients. I was assigned for two months to a psychiatric ward where I had some of the most interesting experiences in my life.

After I got my first weekend pass, I made my way to the Free Methodist Church in Denver for a worship service. Once again I told that congregation essentially what I told the congregation in Tacoma that I was a new Christian having been recently converted in a Free Methodist Church in Allentown, Pennsylvania. I told them I was looking for an efficiency apartment so that my wife could join me and that she was currently in Tacoma, Washington. Once again the response of this Christian community was overwhelming. Following the worship service, a grandmother told me that I should write to Lois and have her come as soon as possible. Her name was Mrs. Hughes and, like Mrs. Rogers in North Carolina, she shared her house with a young lady, her teenage granddaughter.

How fortunate we were in those early days of our marriage to have such wonderful people care for us and love us as if we were members of their own families. Mrs. Hughes explained that there were only two bedrooms in her house, but if we were willing we could sleep in her living room which had a sofa that opened into a bed. She promised she would be on the lookout for an efficiency apartment near the trolley lines that went to Aurora and eventually to the hospital. Mrs. Hughes even said she would meet Lois at the train station. I didn't get many passes on week days during medical training, so her offers to help were a true God-send.

Mrs. Hughes made good on all of her promises. She helped locate an apartment near the trolley line. How blessed we were when Lois finally arrived in Denver. I felt that we were privileged people when we were in her home. At church, Mrs. Hughes introduced us to four or five military couples in that congregation. Soon we became very close friends. The guys were good singers. We formed a male quartet and often sang in the church services all the time I was stationed at Fitzsimmons General Hospital.

Our efficiency apartment in Denver left much to be desired but it was a place to get away from the Army and spend the night. The most undesirable thing about this apartment was that we shared a bathroom with another tenant who lived down the hall, but we never met each other, coming or going.

That apartment was our home for five months. During that time, Lois found a job with Montgomery Wards. In addition to a large retail store, Wards also operated an enormous catalog warehouse were orders were filled and shipped all over the world. Lois worked nine hours a day pulling orders from the warehouse, mostly for wallpaper and paint, as she remembers. The management had discovered that people could carry much more and process more orders if instead of walking, they wore roller skates. Lois enjoyed the job because she loved to roller-skate.

At Christmas time she was transferred to the toy department. The pay was modest but it was a good experience.

Since I did not get many days off during the week, the weekends were precious. On Sundays we went to church and in the afternoon we visited with our friends who often took us sight seeing in the city as well as up in the mountains. They tried to teach me to ice skate without much success. We all laughed when I told them I thought I would do better wearing snowshoes.

17

Cuckoo's Nest

During my training at the hospital in Denver, I had the most horrible experience in the entire time I was in the Army. Late one night, probably around two a.m., I was awakened by man trying to get into my bunk. It took me a couple of seconds to get awaken before I realized this weirdo was a homosexual. All the genes I had ever received from my father mobilized instantly. I gave the guy a shove with my right shoulder and my hip and he landed flat on the floor beside my bed.

"Get away from me, you jerk", I said. "Don't touch me, you pervert."

"Aw, come on," he said. He wanted me to play his fun and games, and I wanted no part of it.

"I'm going to report you to the sergeant first thing in the morning" I whispered loudly.

"Aw, come on, "he kept repeating as he walked away from my bunk. I was so angry that it took more than an hour for the impulse to follow the creep and beat him to a pulp finally subsided. I know that is not very Christian, but it is exactly how I felt that night. To this day my anger is aroused every time I remember that horrible experience.

One day about noon time one of my coronary patients suffered a very serious heart attack. Doctors arrived by his bedside in a matter of moments and injected a large dose of digitalis directly into his heart. A nurse turned up the oxygen supply as the practitioners started pumping on this man's chest. In those days mouth-to-mouth resuscitation was not practiced. I stood at the foot of the bed and watched as the doctors and nurses did everything they could for the man, but in spite of all their efforts, the patient died. During the chaos of trying to save the man's life, someone had delivered a tray of food and placed it on the bedside table.

The doctor who was in charge turned to me and said, "Barnett, take care of him". I knew exactly what he meant for me to do. My job was to remove the tubes and close all body openings. If the patient had false teeth, I was to remove them. I attached a death card with his name and serial number to his big toe. Finally, the body was to be covered and rolled on a gurney to the morgue in the basement. Well I did everything I was instructed to do except one minor detail.

After I had prepared the body, I washed my hands carefully, and looked at that tray of food and thought it a shame if all of that was to go to waste. So I pulled up a chair to the dead man's table and enjoyed a delicious lunch he never had the chance to eat. Hospital food was far superior to anything we got in the mess hall, so I enjoyed it before wheeling the body to the morgue.

When I told this story to my granddaughter, Darla, she was mortified that I would do such a terrible thing. Her reaction surprised me because at the time it seemed quite natural. I'm quite certain that I was not the first person to have done that nor would I be the last.

But in spite of eating a dead man's lunch, as a medic I was strongly influenced by the example of my mother's kindness to others. I often experienced deep compassion for many of the young, severely injured soldiers that had been returned to Fitzsimmons General Hospital from the theaters of war. Many had been injured fighting in France and Germany. In that month of duty in the medical ward, I learned a lot about how to care for very ill people.

During my last two months at the hospital I worked in the psychological ward of the hospital. It was large and populated with men who had severe mental disorders. Many of them were diagnosed with "shell shock," a term developed in the First World War to describe those suffering from traumatic stress. Traumatized by what they experienced in the killing fields of Europe, they were haunted by the horrors day and night.

Others who were psychotic and schizophrenic were much more difficult to handle than those suffering from the daze and confusion of shell shock. We had several dozen men who became so violent at times that they were put into solitary confinement. The walls of the rooms were padded and contained only a mattress on the floor. This solitary was not for punishment, but for the protection of others and to protect the insane from injuring or even killing themselves.

We noticed that these violent patients seemed to have episodes almost on schedule. So at certain times or if we saw behavior starting to escalate, we wrapped them in cold sheets. Bed sheets were soaked in ice water and while two of us would hold a man down, the other would wrap the icy sheet around his body. The patient was then laid on a gurney and restrained with cloth straps to make certain they would not injure themselves or others when they exploded in a raging tirade.

I remember my arm around the head of man who was thrashing back and forth and with the other hand I tried to pry open his jaw so another medic could try to force nourishment or medicine into the patient. Sometimes all we could do was hang on until the episode passed and the individual's energy was spent and he was completely exhausted. Then we would let them lie there for a while and when we saw that they had some sense of control, we would return them to their room where they spent the rest of the day sleeping.

Some of the men in the psych ward were bucking for Section 8 discharges. Anyone who has seen the character Klinger in the TV show M*A*S*H, will recognize the behavior. These guys were faking their mental illness in hopes of getting out of the Army. We developed some interesting tests for spotting psychological malingerers. One that worked very well was to have some attractive female nurses engage the suspected faker in a conversation. We would observe how these men who had been away from women for a year or more reacted. If the soldier remained passive and disinterested, we knew he was probably seriously disturbed. But many times the men perked right up with this female attention and were soon engaged in normal, jovial conversation. This became one of the most productive ways of distinguishing who legitimately belonged in the psychiatric section of the hospital and the cowards who just wanted a way out.

A critical part of our care for these patients involved medications, both pills and injections. Another test we developed to be sure a man was not faking a mental illness was to use placebos. By keeping careful records we could often separate fact from fiction in treating the mentally wounded.

Once I was on night duty and I had to give injections to all of the men on this large psych ward, perhaps as many as 50 men. I proceeded to make the rounds, carefully checking medical records with the names written on the hypodermics I was to administer. All the needles were arranged on a tray according to where the men were in that ward. I had completed giving shots to about half the men. I laid the tray on the table next to the man who I was preparing to inject next. I swabbed his upper arm with alcohol just like I had routinely done to all the others. As I lifted the needle, suddenly this man sat up and struck me a hard blow on my chest. I'm sure he was swinging for my chin, but he missed and struck me under my neck. Stunned for a moment, I tripped over the table with the needle tray. Like pickup sticks, they flew everywhere and I landed on the cot next to the patient.

Another medic at the far end of the room saw what was happening and came running. Together we managed to get control of the belligerent man by wrapping our arms around him and persuading him to sit down. We talked with him for about 10 minutes. Finally he was persuaded to sit down on the bed and ultimately to lie down. We then persuaded him to get the shot. I told him if he absolutely refused to let me give the shot, I would have to report it to the doctors. At last he gave in and I gave him his injection.

There was never a dull moment at Fitzsimmons General Hospital. Those men in the psyche ward were very unpredictable. The most difficult people for me to attend were the young men in very deep depression. They lay in bed staring at the ceiling for hours and would barely move their eyes. If you managed to get in their line of sight, they looked right through you to something far away. If they were sitting up, their gaze stayed fixed on the floor. They sat without moving a muscle for minutes on end without giving any expression of life. I sometimes had the strange feeling that they had become a lifeless thing rather than a human being. I felt such pity for these fellows, but I could not express it in any tangible way.

About 50 years later, long after I had been ordained as a pastor and was in the final year before my retirement, my mind would flashback to those men as I visited elderly members of my congregation suffering from deep depression. I saw again the faces of those despairing solders. The training I received in the Army made me a better pastor. But I thought so often that here we were, fifty years later, with patients given the most up-to-date medication, treated with the finest care, the best doctors available, and I still couldn't tell the difference between depression today and what I witnessed in those young men who returned from war to Fitzsimmons General Hospital.

Denver was a beautiful city in a majestic setting. We made dear life-long friends there and enjoyed the vitality and hospitality of the church. But of all the places I had been to that point in my life, I think Denver stands out as the place where I became aware of my compassion to serve people.

18

Paris in the Rain

After six months I was yanked out of Fitzsimmons General Hospital expecting to be assigned to another Army hospital somewhere in the States. When my orders arrived, I was surprised to learn that I was to report to Camp Maxey near Paris, Texas, an infantry training camp. The Army did it again. In a year I had switched jobs three times: MP, medic, and now infantry.

At my first opportunity to go into town, I searched for a place where Lois and I could live. I quickly became discouraged when I saw a sign "Soldiers and dogs stay off the grass" posted in the front yard of house near downtown. But further down the street I spotted a "Room to Rent" sign in front of an old dilapidated house near downtown. I inquired about the room and learned that three or four other soldiers' wives rented some rooms in the big, ugly building. Having no other prospects, I committed to renting a room for a week while I continued searching for a more suitable place for Lois to stay when I was in camp.

Heading in a different direction from downtown, I found myself in what appeared to be a better section of the city. About two blocks down that particular street, a large, brown brick house caught my attention. I walked slowly past the well-groomed lawn. There was no "Room to Rent" sign, but I did see displayed in a front window a small banner on which was printed a gold star. The gold star meant that someone from that family had been killed in action during the war. I also spied a small building currently under construction in the backyard. It was obviously living quarters of some kind. I turned around and went back to the house. As I walked up the steps, I thought that, at least, I should find at this house someone who might be sympathetic to a soldier's need.

The door opened. I introduced myself and learned that the Gold Star Mother was Mrs. McWherter, an attractive lady with sandy-colored hair. I told her that I was looking for a place to bring my lovely wife who was presently in Denver where I had last served at Fitzsimmons General Hospital.

"I couldn't help but notice your back building," I said, "I wondered if you might rent it to me."

"I'm buildin' it as my maid's quawtahs," she said in a Texas drawl. "But I haven't told her when to move in. I'd be happy if you and your wife would live there while you're stationed heah."

Almost immediately I recognized this lady was cut from the same pattern as Mrs. Rogers, Mrs. Tremain, and Mrs. Hughes. She told me the sad story that her son had been killed in action recently. He was a pilot operating out of England and his plane had been shot down over Germany.

Mrs. McWherter informed me that the little house would soon be ready. I wrote to Lois and told her to come to Texas. She arrived about a week later. This was the middle of February, 1945, during the rainy season. It seemed to rain every day. When Lois arrived, I went to meet her at the train station. We rode a banged-up old bus back to the center square of town, and then walked the rest of the way in the rain to the old rooming house I had rented for the week.

The landlady showed us our room. It was dingy and had one naked 25 watt light bulb that hung from the middle of the ceiling. It was dark and depressing. I was determined to get out of that place as soon as I could. We stayed there two or three nights.

A few days later I stopped by again to see Mrs. McWherter. She told me that while the landscaping had not been completed because of the rain, the building was suitable enough to move in.

"Mr. Barnett," she said holding a key chain, "you can move in whenever you're ready and stay as long as you and your wife are in town."

I unlocked the door and stepped into an ample-sized room with a nice bed, several pieces of furniture, and a full bathroom. Compared to the rooming house, it felt like a castle. We moved in that very day.

My days at Camp Maxey were filled with target practice at the rifle range and rain, lots of rain. In addition to gaining proficiency with our M1 rifles, we also learned to handle the Browning automatic rifle and 50 caliber machine guns. It rained every time we went to the firing range. When we moved from one firing range to another, the long line of GIs wearing rain ponchos and helmets looked like a parade of penguins. The rain turned the clay soil into what the locals called "gumbo," a thick mud that clumped to the bottom of our boots sometimes two inches thick until we could hardly walk. Back at the barracks, it took hours to clean our boots at the end of the day. It was said that Paris, Texas was the only place in the world where you could stand in mud over your ankles and have the wind blow sand in your face at the same time.

Fortunately I was able to get home just about every night. Lois and I enjoyed a little restaurant on the corner of the downtown square. It was the only place I ever remember that the special of the house was fried fish eggs.

Mrs. McWherter would sometimes make the most delicious bread and invite Lois to the main house to share a snack with her during the afternoon. One day Mrs. McWhirter served a particularly tasty meat sandwich. Lois couldn't identify the taste and asked what the mystery meat might be.

"Tongue," said Mrs. McWherter. Lois told me later she liked the sandwich better before she knew what it was.

Mrs. McWherter became like a second mother to Lois and me. I think I became a temporary surrogate son to fill the vacuum in this grieving mother's heart. I suspect that in some ways she may have needed us as much as we needed her. I had very little contact with Mr. McWherter. He owned several grain elevators out on the edge of town. He was a tall man who always wore a ten gallon hat and fancy Texan boots. Twice he may have referred to me as Mr. Barnett. I remember he would smile and say "Howdy" when we greeted one another.

While we were in Paris, Lois' father was transferred back to the Baltimore office of the Jewel Tea Company. It was fortunate her parents lived in Baltimore when I got my orders to go overseas. Of all the goodbyes I had said to Lois, this farewell was the most difficult. I knew that in a few days I would be on a large troop train headed for Camp Stoneman, near San Francisco, and then ultimately to the far side of the world where an unknown future awaited.

The train trip across the country was long and lonely. Fortunately we were able to stretch out and sleep in Pullman cars and the black porters made us feel very special. During those lonely days I read a lot of scripture. I was studying the book of Joshua and the words God spoke to Joshua became God's word to me on that west-bound train.

> *As I was with Moses, so I will be with you; I will never leave you or forsake you. Be strong and courageous…Do not be terrified; do not be discouraged, for the Lord your God will be with you wherever you go. (Joshua 1:5-6, 9)*

I read how Joshua faced many conflicts, nevertheless, he prevailed and God fulfilled his promise to Joshua. As we arrived at Camp Stoneman in California my faith was strengthened that God would be with me wherever I went. I was confident that I would survive combat and one day return to my wife and family.

19

The Call

Something very important happened to me in Camp Stoneman. I cannot fully explain what happened on that day, but the experience forever changed my life and continues to have a profound impact on me to this very day. But in 1944 I had a very difficult time dealing with something I could not entirely explain.

Our days at Camp Stoneman were spent attending classes and watching Army training films designed to acquaint us with Japanese war tactics and to help us identify various enemy aircraft. I was in the theater one afternoon watching one of these films when I heard or felt (I'm not sure quite how to describe it) a voice say to me, "Hey there, Barnett." It was so real but no one sitting around me appeared to have heard it. I'm not sure if my eyes were opened or closed, but I knew it was the voice of God. Somewhat startled, I responded, "Yes, Sir" (remember I was in the Army).

"What do you hope to do when you get out of the Army?" the voice asked.

Without a moment's hesitation I said, "I would like to play on a major league baseball team, preferably with the Philadelphia Athletics."

Not sure this was the proper thing to say to God, I added, "Or, I suppose I could work with my Dad."

"Would you be interested in something with a far greater challenge than you would have in the major league or working with your father as a plumber?"

"Of course," I responded.

"Listen carefully," I heard God say. "Would you consider being one of my disciples?" I suddenly remembered reading in the Gospels that Jesus once said that to be a disciple one would have to deny himself, take up a cross, and follow Him. I didn't know all that this meant, but after a moment's hesitation, I responded, "Yes."

When God spoke again He said, "Will you give yourself fully in my service as a minister in my church?"

I thought again for a moment and finally said in my spirit, "Lord God, if you guide me and protect me so that I will one day return to my wife and family I will do anything you want me to do and I'll be all you want me to be."

The voice said, "Well then good."

With those words I saw again the flickering image on the large theater screen. I looked around to see if others were watching me, but all the GIs close by seemed to be perfectly normal. I didn't know if I had been dreaming or had God in some way really called me to be a minister. I thought about that for a long time. I didn't tell Lois about it until I got home after the war. The reason I chose not to tell her was because she had often stated that she did not want to be a minister's wife because she was tired of moving every year or so, and ministers in the Methodist tradition were often re-assigned every other year. She not only wanted more stability in her life, but she had witnessed many ministers' wives being unjustly criticized and often burdened with duties in the church such as teaching Sunday school, leading the women's groups, or even cleaning the church. All the time I was overseas in the Pacific I hoped and prayed that God would somehow help me to break the news to Lois, because each day I became more and more convinced that the call was genuine. I began to think of myself as a minister in training.

I kept renewing my commitments to God. Often I would read God's promises to Joshua for example and substitute my name instead of his in all verses God promised to be with him and to protect him and to guide where ever he went. I read those words again and again to be God's words a promise to me.

20

Etchings

Camp Stoneman was the primary jumping off point for troops going into combat in the Pacific. The place hummed with activity as lines of men carrying duffel bags on their shoulders marched up gangplanks and into the many troop ships that would steam them across the ocean. Leaving camp we walked under a portal that read "Through these portals pass the best damn soldiers in all the world." As I walked under the archway, I wondered what the sign might read on the other side when we returned. I hoped I would have the opportunity to read it one day.

I will never forget the feeling of awe mixed with uncertainty as our ship passed beneath the Golden Gate Bridge. It wasn't long before that magnificent structure faded from view and the coastline of California disappeared beneath the eastern horizon. We were on our way to some place in the Pacific where Americans were fighting and dying.

Many GIs passed the lonely days and weeks on board ship playing cards and shooting craps. I spent a lot of time walking around the outer deck of the ship for exercise. I also did a lot of reading. Leaning on the ship's railing watching the water slip past far below, I thought long and often about what the future might hold for Lois and me. My reverie would sometime be interrupted by a seasick soldier struggling to make it to the rail in time to throw up over the side. In all my time on the high seas, both in the Atlantic going several times to Casablanca and returning, and crossing the Pacific to only God knew where, I was never seasick. But I did miss Lois terribly. Each evening I wrote a small note to her in a diary that I kept all the time I was away. I also wrote several letters to her during the trip, but I could not mail them until we finally reached Manila in the Philippines.

The Philippine capitol had sustained considerable damage when the Japanese attacked and over-ran the city some months earlier. Debris littered the streets. Some soldiers said the Filipinos were probably waiting for the United States to do all the dirty work necessary to clear the streets and restore the city to its former grandeur.

We were loaded on trucks and convoyed a few miles beyond the city to Clark Field where we received our assignments. Most of us ended up in various companies of the 33rd Infantry Division. I was assigned to Company B, 108th Medical Battalion attached to the 33rd Infantry Division. Yes, I was once again a medic, now attached to an infantry division on the island of Luzon in the Philippines.

Our group was loaded on a narrow gauge railroad train made up mostly of flat cars that had been modified with wooden walls built up about two feet around the edge of the car. Once we found a place to sit on these open air cars we rode through villages and into the jungles an hour or so north of Manila. When the train stopped, we scattered in different directions on trucks waiting to take us to our specific duty assignments.

I did not know exactly where we were located; all I knew was that we were engaged in what was called "mopping up action." We were tasked with going through the area recently taken by US forces and clearing any remaining enemy troops that might be left. Company B had a fleet of ambulances with drivers, a squad of litter bearers, several Jeeps, a weapons carrier, and numerous other trucks. We had a first-aid tent loaded with supplies.

The first time I recall coming under enemy fire was near a town called Aringay in North Cotabato Province near the San Fernando River. We came under mortar attack. We were quite sure the mortars were being fired at us from across the river on the hillside that dipped sharply down to the river's edge. Enemy soldiers were hiding out in caves which had been bypassed when the infantry and artillery units advanced before us. The river was over 200 yards wide.

From a distance, the mortar makes a sound like "flup" when fired. It's frightening to know that within seconds the ground somewhere around you is suddenly going to explode with fire and shrapnel. Our leaders called for air support to bomb those Japanese bunkers across the river. Within minutes P47 Thunderbolt fighter planes roared down the river valley about 50 feet above the water. The noise was deafening as the planes buzzed by overhead with machine guns rattling and at the last possible second bank away from us and let loose their bombs. The explosions echoed through the valley. Those planes repeated their sorties on those positions until the mortars were silenced. Our Company sustained no fatalities in that attack.

The 33rd Infantry Division advanced north on the island of Luzon and captured the city of Baguio, called the summer capital of Luzon. Some US troops may have gone beyond that, but that was as far north as any of our medical battalions progressed. Our ambulance drivers transported the sick and wounded to larger medical facilities south of our position. We patched up our GIs as well as any wounded Japanese soldier who chose to surrender to our forces.

With the enemy mortars wiped out, our campsite received many improvements, not the least of which was our latrine and shower facilities. It was amazing the work that the local Filipinos were able to do with a large bolo knife and a pile of bamboo. Squatting with their knees sticking almost above their heads, the Filipinos wove together bamboo poles cut in half to create as fine a fence as you could imagine. Everything was held together with long green strips of bamboo which, when they dried, created joints as strong as if they were held together with steel bolts. Almost all of the houses in that part of the country were all made exclusively with bamboo.

In Aringay I met the first avowed Christian in my two years in the Army. I first noticed Ed Romig back at Clark Field, but I never had the occasion to talk with him there. I knew he had to be much like myself, because he refused free beer or cigarettes when passed out to the men. I learned he came from Doylestown, Pennsylvania which wasn't far from Philadelphia. When I told him my hometown was Reading, he said, "I thought you were a Pennsylvania Dutchman. Your speech betrayed you."

As soon as he said this, I realized he must be a student of the Bible because that phrase came directly from the lips of a little girl who thousands of years earlier accused Peter of being a follower of Christ. "Your speech betrays you," she said.

Without any risk of personal embarrassment I said, "You must be a born-again Christian."

"Yes," he said, smiling broadly. "And you, too?"

From that moment on Ed Romig and I were bosom friends. Ed was much more mature in matters of faith and biblical knowledge than I was. He was a member of a Plymouth Brethren Church. I told him I had never heard of that church. When I told him I was a Free Methodist, he said, "I never heard of Free Methodist." He was a great Christian and helped me so much as we would study the Word of God together.

While in the Philippines, I became interested in making artistic engravings on aluminum. I had always been pretty good at free hand drawing. I discovered that with a little pressure the knife from a GI mess kit could score a clean line in aluminum. I would first make a pencil sketch on the metal and then scratch in the details. I created etchings of a Filipino man in that familiar squatting position and a GI taking a picture of a small child, pictures of everyday life I saw around me.

The locals told us that a Japanese Zero fighter had been shot down in a field about a mile distant from the camp and that the plane was not severely damaged. So Ed and I decided to take a Jeep out to see this legendary aircraft. I was also interested in getting a piece of the aluminum flap from the trailing edge of the wing on which I could do some engraving.

We found the downed aircraft drove the Jeep alongside. As we explored the crash site, I was impressed with how good the plane looked. As we moved around to the other side of the aircraft, suddenly rifle shots pierced the silence of the open field. We heard the bullets whiz over our heads. We scampered back to the other side of the plane and hunkered down on the ground for a long time. We could see a stand of trees about 400 yards away at the edge of the field. We suspected we were being pinned down by a Japanese soldier with a sniper rifle hiding in those trees. Fortunately he was a poor shot. We had our carbine rifles with us but we made no attempt to return fire because we couldn't see movement anywhere along the tree line. After 15 minutes of silence, we decided to make a run for the Jeep. We sped away as fast as we could. Several weeks later we returned to the plane with no trouble, and I was able to get all of the aluminum I needed for my art work.

One night I was on guard duty at our company motor pool. All of a sudden the silence was broken by the sound of footsteps in the wooded area just beyond the perimeter of our camp. I stopped walking and focused my attention in the direction of the approaching sound, but I saw nothing. I readied my carbine and waited as the sound became louder. It seemed to move through the underbrush with a steady rhythmic cadence. I remembered all too well the surprise of being shot at by the sniper in that open field and I imagined this might be the same Japanese soldier who was determined to get me this time. My heart froze as I heard heavy breathing and saw movement at the edge of the clearing.

"Halt" I said, lifting my rifle.

Whatever it was ignored my warning. Adrenaline surged through my body. I was just about to pull the trigger when out of clearing emerged a friendly old caribou, the common beast of burden in the Philippines. I lowered my rifle, exhaled a deep sigh of relief, and felt like giving the large animal a hug.

I learned to admire how well rural Filipinos adapted to their limited crude surroundings. I watched mothers with babies strapped to their backs wade along a river bank, thrash in the shore grass and catch enough shrimp in cloth netting for the family's evening meal. Little children were curious about all we did at camp. If they had any kind of skin wound, we would dress the wound with sulfadiazine ointment and bandage them up. One day a little boy kept looking at me with a puzzled look. Finally, he came over and touched my arm. It finally occurred to me that I was probably the first person he had ever seen with a light complexion with freckles. At any rate the touch satisfied his curiosity.

21

On the Ropes

I would soon learn the limits of my physical strength and endurance in the summer of 1945. We were scheduled for amphibious landing training out in the Lingayen Gulf. We were ferried by landing craft out to troop transport vessels anchored a mile or two offshore. We took all our gear with us because we would spend a week on that ship. Each day we were supposed to make at least two practice landings on shore where we would find men lying all over the beach with notes tied to them stating the nature of their injury or whether they were dead. We were to treat the "wounded" and bring them back to the ships.

What made this training so difficult and dangerous were the rope ladders or rope netting that hung from the side of the ship and down which we were to climb into landing craft. These rope ladders were 10 or 12 foot wide and twenty or thirty feet long and reached just to the top of the landing craft that had pulled alongside the ship.

If you were fortunate enough to get assigned to the stern or middle of the ship, getting into those landing craft wasn't too bad. But if you happened to catch a position near the bow, that could be a real challenge because the rope swayed further away from the side of the ship. You were literally dangling in space.

Three of us crawled down the rope ladder at one time. The landing craft bobbed up and down far below us in the ocean swell. One minute the craft would lunge at you almost knocking you off the ladder and the next it would drop away four feet or more below the bottom rung of the rope netting. It was almost impossible to time the jump from ladder to landing craft. It wasn't unusual to fall three or four feet into the bottom of the landing craft.

When the craft was loaded with medics, we made our way to the shore. The way it's supposed to work is that when the front end of the landing craft is dropped and everybody scrambles forward, you should only be six or eight feet from the shoreline, allowing you to wade ashore with water below your knees. But sometimes the landing craft operators misjudged and dropped the front too far away from the shore. Then you had to contend with water up to your waist or shoulders.

We scampered up the beach and ran for the men we saw lying there. We would read the note describing their wounds; for example, "broken femur" or "serious chest wound." We dressed the wound and if necessary we had litter bearers carry the wounded soldier to the water's edge.

When the next landing craft hit the shore with another load of medics, we loaded our "wounded" onto the landing craft and headed back out to the transport ship. Then came the hard part.

The landing craft pulled alongside the rope ladders. This time three of us medics had to climb up the netting simultaneously with a "wounded" man suspended on a litter. When we finally reach the ship's railing, somebody could lean over and help us get the patient aboard ship. We did that twice a day and at the end of the day we were totally exhausted. This training went on for five days.

One day we heard the news over the loudspeaker that our B29s dropped an atomic bomb over Hiroshima. Reports said it would be a hundred years before anything would grow in the area and that hundreds of thousands of people were destroyed. On board that ship, we were dumbfounded trying to comprehend how a single bomb could wreak such destruction. The good thing about it was that the following day we were told that there would be no further amphibious landings in the Lingayen Gulf. A day later we made our way back to shore and to camp.

We learned later that my Company was scheduled to have been in the sixth wave of an amphibious assault on the Japanese home islands. Expectations were that our forces would suffer 60% casualties. The Japanese had vowed never to surrender and to fight to the last person. Some estimate that it would have cost over a million US casualties and prolonged the war at least a year or more. When people began to criticize the President for ordering dropping two atomic bombs, thousands of US soldiers like me knew if not for that fateful decision by President Truman, we would have likely never gotten home. The atomic bomb probably saved my life.

22

Japan

Within two weeks we broke down our equipment and loaded all of our vehicles aboard ships and left Luzon for Japan. We had the roughest seas I have ever experienced in all my travels. Nearly everyone was seasick. I managed to avoid the sickness by rarely going inside to my compartment. Waves were 15 to 20 feet high. The ship lurched up and down so violently that in the forward compartments it was like trying to stand on a roller coaster ride. In less than a day the bathroom facility in the front of the ship couldn't keep up with the number of seasick men and the violent shaking. Urinals and toilets were full and overflowed everywhere. The stench was terrible. It was impossible for anyone to clean out the facilities. Men lined up at the toilets that still worked. The seas stayed angry all the way to Japan.

We finally landed near the town of Wakayama on September 5, 1945, less than a month after VJ Day ended World War 2. Ours was one of the first battalions of GIs to set foot in Japan. A few Air Force units had arrived a day or two earlier in other cities.

It's impossible to describe the difficulties we had getting our equipment off the ships and on to shore. Landing craft were loaded first with trucks, ambulances, and weapons carriers and then, if there was room left over, a few GIs scampered down the rope ladders and jumped into the landing craft. Usually the landing craft stopped after hitting bottom eight to ten feet from shore, which meant we could wade ashore in water up to our thighs with little trouble. But sometimes a landing craft would drop its door at the same spot where earlier an LST had gotten stuck and created a large hole on the sandy bottom with its propellers. Our weapons carrier was loaded on the front of a landing craft. Reaching shore, the driver got into the heavy vehicle, drove down the ramp and disappeared clear out of sight, falling into one of these holes. At first we were stunned but then the soldiers laughed and ballyhooed when a moment later we saw the driver bob to the surface.

The rest of us on the landing craft jumped out the front gate and immediately sunk in water over our heads. We had to tread water until we were finally able to touch bottom and could wade the rest of the way. We moved up the shoreline about 50 yards and watched as other landing craft had the same problems we experienced. A large wench attached to a two and a half ton truck pulled out the vehicles stuck under water. The driver of the vehicle swam with the winch cable to the site of the sunken vehicle and wrapped the cable around the front bumper. Slowly the winch would pull the dripping vehicles out of the surf like a fisherman reels in a catch. The vehicles would not run after being submerged and so nearly half of our trucks and weapons carriers had to be towed from the beach through little villages until we reached the city of Wakayama.

I thought of what might have happened if this had been the invasion and Japanese machine gunners and artillery had been waiting for us to hit that beach. In Luzon they estimated 60% of us would be killed or wounded if we had to attack Japan. Watching the chaos unfold on the beach, I knew that estimate would have been highly optimistic.

From the beach we walked two miles or so up narrow roads that led through several small villages untouched by the war. Japanese policemen stood at every turn in the road directing us to our destination. They stood at attention until our entire battalion passed. As we walked two abreast alongside the tiny houses close to the road, we might see a pair of eyes looking out between some bamboo blinds. Those Japanese villagers were frightened to death. During the war, their government propaganda said Americans would rape and kill their women and children.

Reaching Wakayama, we found the train station where we would catch a train to the city of Kobe. Our Lieutenant informed us that we would need to bivouac at the station until morning. So we spent our first night in Japan sleeping on the wooden platforms of that train station. By that time our clothing was dry, but everything in our rucksack was still soaking wet. Fortunately it wasn't cold that night as we stretched out on the wooden boards to sleep.

Next morning we boarded the train. It wasn't long until we saw what remained of a once great city with a large harbor. Kobe had been virtually leveled. Only a few buildings stood higher than the rubble. Block after block where once had stood commercial buildings and homes, all that remained were bare foundations, and in some cases the foundations had been cleared to make room to grow turnips which were starting to sprout. The nearby harbor was littered with sunken vessels and reminded me of the harbor in Casablanca, North Africa.

We made our battalion headquarters in what had once been an office building. We hadn't been there long until two barbers appeared and wanted to show their hospitality by offering to cut our hair. Some of the men joked about letting any Japanese near their throat with a blade, but we agreed. I sat down in the chair. The Japanese barber shook his cloth and snapped it smartly before pinning it behind my neck. How ironic, I thought, two months ago a Japanese soldier was trying to kill me, and here I was getting a shave and a haircut from a Japanese barber in Kobe. That was the first time I ever had anyone shave me with a straight edge razor. The barber warmed my face with large warm towels and then lathered my face well. When I saw him raise that straight edge to shave my cheek and around my chin down my throat, I knew the world had changed for the better and how I thanked God for it.

Being in the infantry meant we were always on the move. From Wakayama our company was trucked about 35 miles to the town of Himeji. Our campsite in Himeji was an old cavalry camp. We were in a large stable. We set up our kitchen and dining facilities on the first floor and our whole company slept under the rafters in the loft. To a soldier, these accommodations were quite comfortable.

We were warmly received in Himeji and in a month or so we learned that some of our guys had been received a little too warmly. I was getting requests for penicillin to treat the first signs of gonorrhea.

The most interesting thing that happened all the time I was in Himeji was befriending a Japanese family. Mr. Ouchi was about forty years old. He operated a photography studio where he sold and developed film. When I took my first roll of film for development, I noticed his lovely wife and two darling little girls, probably ages three and four. One of the little girls suffered a dermatitis problem. Her head was covered with sores. Mr. Ouchi spoke a little English so I asked how they were treating the condition. The mother said she was soaking a towel in salt water and applying it to the girl's scalp, but she showed no signs of improvement. When I returned to pick up my developed pictures, I brought along sulfadiazine ointment. I dressed her head and covered it with loose gauze bandages. The girl beamed to be given such special attention. In a few days she had greatly improved. We cleaned her head with water and applied another application of the ointment. In a week she was completely healed. After that, whenever I went to the Ouchi home, this little girl would run to me and wrap her arms around my legs. Her parents treated me as if I were a god.

The Ouchis couldn't do enough for me and my friend, Ed Romig. I was a regular customer at Mr. Ouchi's photography store and it wasn't long before they invited Romig and me to have supper with them. It was my first introduction to

Japanese customs. We took off our shoes before entering the house. We were ushered to the dinner table which was only about 14 inches high. Instead of sitting on chairs, we sat on a pillow on the floor, crossing our legs under the table. Dinner that evening was squid and rice. The food was placed in the center of the table and we were served one dish at a time. I embarrassed myself trying to eat with chopsticks. The little girls used their chopsticks so efficiently and tried to help Ed and me. We all laughed.

One day we decided we would reconnoiter a hillside where there was a lot of timber. As we drove higher, the mountain road became a dirt trail. We heard the whine of high speed saws cutting wood. At the top of the hill was a village of about a dozen houses. As soon as we appeared, the children who had been playing in the road scampered inside their houses. The men working at the sawmill fled, scared to death that we meant them harm. As we proceeded slowly past the houses and up to the sawmill we turned and saw some children peaking around the corners watching us with a great deal of curiosity. We tossed chocolate candy bars back in the direction of the children. When the men from the village saw that we weren't going to hurt them or destroy their village, they gladly showed us their sawmill.

23

Black Market

Company B didn't have much to do at Himeji. We had regular shifts of guard duty and KP, but as an invasion force our primary task was to keep the peace. We had considerable time on our hands. We played basketball a lot. Sometimes Romig and I would hop in a Jeep and go explore the countryside. On one excursion we found an airfield with dozens of planes lined up like they were ready to take off at a moment's notice. Bombers and fighter planes were fully loaded with ammunition. There was only one problem—they had no gasoline. Our troops first unloaded the weapons and then large bulldozers mashed the planes into one large pile before being doused with gasoline and set on fire. Before long our planes were using the airstrip.

One evening I was going into town to see Mr. Ouchi when a weapons carrier pulled up beside me on the road. It was driven by one of our sergeants from our mortar pool. He offered to give me a ride and I agreed. He pulled off the side of the road and I jumped in the back. As we bounced our way along, I noticed something wasn't quite right about this situation. I wasn't quite sure what it was until I noticed two 50 gallon drums of gasoline in the back of the vehicle. I was aware that some GIs were getting involved in the black market, but I couldn't believe anyone in our company would do such a thing.

When we reached town, the sergeant pulled the weapons carrier into a narrow back street. I watched as two Japanese men ran from the shadows and helped him unload the two giant containers. When the deed was done, I saw the sergeant take a big roll of money from one of the men. He said goodbye and as he passed me in the back of the weapons carrier he said, "Barnett, you didn't see anything."

I was really disappointed that we had a scoundrel in our camp dealing in black market. I wondered if I should report him, so I sought the council of Ed Romig on the situation. We discussed the situation at length and decided that the risk was too great if I turned him in. If he was unscrupulous enough to deal in the black market, he might think nothing of arranging an accident in which I was involved or something worse. After considerable discussion, he suggested that I not report it and I didn't.

I suppose my compromise with the black marketer steeled my resolve about taking bribes when I was in charge of the first-aid station. Those guys with venereal disease were always offering me money if I would issue them pills and not enter the diagnosis in their medical records. I told them that I was accountable for all the medications that were dispensed from our station and that I could not in good conscience honor their request.

I earned a little extra money by making watchbands from the aluminum I had salvaged from the Japanese fighter plane in Luzon. I charged four dollars for each watchband. I probably made 10 or 12 as the different fellows would request one. I didn't intend to sell them originally. I would simply make one when a soldier requested it. I inscribed the bands with anything the men requested. I made about $50 for my hobby as I waited out my last six months in Himeji.

On the horizon not far from our camp was a large castle built in the center of an ancient fort. Built in the early 17th century, Himeji Castle, as we referred to it, was the oldest surviving structure from medieval Japan. With it's six-story stone walls and tile roofs, the locals called it the "Giant White Heron" Castle. It dominated the entire landscape in Himeji. One day Ed Romig and I drove a Jeep up to the castle. To my surprise we were the only people on site. We walked up many flights of stairs to the top floor where we discovered a large gong with a telephone pole-sized log fastened to a sling that was used to strike the metal gong. It must have made a tremendous noise when struck. As we stood there looking out over the city of Himeji, I wondered how the world would change now that the war was over. Looking at the enormous gong used to summon people to this great castle, I thought about going home and how I would explain to Lois that I believed God was summoning me to the ministry.

Men who had been in the service longest began to be discharged. Every day we checked to see who had earned enough points to leave. A soldier received a point for each month in the service and two points for each month served overseas. A steady stream of older men in leadership positions were the first to leave, creating vacancies into which the rest of us were promoted. In four months I was upgraded steadily to the rank of Staff Sergeant in charge of that first-aid station.

The highlight of any day was still mail call. Since we were staying put in one location longer packages arrived more regularly. During Christmas and New Year of 1945 turning into 1946 we received many parcels from home. I expected packages from my friends in Allentown, my family, and Lois's family, but when I got a package from my brother Earl I was surprised. He had entered the Army two years earlier than I did so I shouldn't have been surprised to know he was home. When I opened Earl's package and found several pairs of socks and some fresh fruit, I knew he remembered what we got too little of in the Army.

24

USA!

All the time I was away I kept diary mostly of love notes I addressed to Lois at the end of each day. I would also note anything of significance that had occurred that day, such as, "Had supper with the Ouchis tonight." My last diary entry was dated January 11, 1946, the day I received notice to prepare for my move back to the United States. I packed my diaries along with everything else that belonged to me in my large duffel bag.

We were convoyed by truck to Kobe where we boarded the same kind of ship on which we had sailed from Luzon. Fortunately, the seas were not as rough going home as they had been on the trip to Japan. I was so happy to be going home after being gone for such a long time.

Our trip across the Pacific was not without incident, however. The first few days we sighted four mines floating in the ocean. The Navy was obligated to destroy any mines for the safety of ships traveling the high seas. When a mine was spotted, the Captain ordered the vessel stopped and batteries of gunners would make it a contest to see who could hit the mine bobbing in the ocean. The mine may have been a half a mile or more away from the ship and you could only see it when it rode the crest of a wave and then it would disappear into the trough a second later. The largest gun, a six-inch gun on the fantail, started the shooting followed by all the gunners on one side of the vessel blasting away. A gang of soldiers gathered on the open decks to watch this spectacle hopeful that one of the batteries would eventually blow up that mine so we could get going. No one ever exploded the mine on the first try, so the captain would order gunners on the other side of the vessel to shoot at the floating bomb. Eventually, a rifleman from an Army infantry company would begin making fun of the navy gunners.

"You get me an M1 and I'll take care of that mine for you," said the soldier.

After two days at sea, we sighted no more mines.

It took about a month to cross the ocean. When we finally caught sight of the Golden Gate Bridge and the city of San Francisco, we were a happy gang of GIs.

When we were still about a mile or mile and a half from passing directly beneath the bridge, one of the officers got on the intercom and said, "All right men, it's time to police your quarters." In spite of that order, no one standing out on the open decks moved. We were not going to miss the spectacle and excitement of passing beneath that great bridge, a symbol of the country for which we had fought so long and hard. As we stood in silence slipping through the water beneath that magnificent structure, it was a moment that sent chills up and down my spine.

When we got through into the harbor it really felt like we were back home. We disembarked the ship and we walked up that same roadway and under that portal through which we passed all those months ago.

"Welcome home—thanks for a job well done," I think it said. I was ecstatic to be back in the USA.

We re-traced our way by train across the country. I arrived in Baltimore five or six days later. We spent a few days at Fort Meade and then a group of us returned to Indiantown Gap near Harrisburg, Pennsylvania. While at Indiantown Gap I was given a brief medical exam and a dentist offered to fill a cavity in one tooth. I was urged to continue the $10,000 serviceman's life insurance policy. I could choose to take the full $10,000, but I thought the premium for that amount of coverage was more than I could pay. So, I kept $2000 of that policy. I paid the premiums for a couple of years until the interest earned was enough to pay for the policy. Anything extra went into the cash value of the plan. At the present time that $2000 policy is worth more than $10,000.

I had told Lois to meet me at the train station in Harrisburg. When I got off the bus and saw her at the station, she was more beautiful than I had ever remembered. I thought she was the most attractive lady I had ever seen in my life and I loved her more than ever. That moment we embraced and the night we spent together in Harrisburg were pure bliss. Being home with my wife was more wonderful than I had ever imagined.

The following morning we took the train to Baltimore and soon arrived at Lois's parent's home who were then living in Dundalk, a suburb of Baltimore. Lois continued to work in her father's office where he was still a manager for Jewel Tea Company. Lois told me she would often go into the ladies lounge at work and pray regularly for my protection while I was overseas. She came to believe that God was testing her because as she prayed, her statement that she didn't want to be married to a preacher kept coming back to her mind and it bothered her. She said she finally came to the place where she promised God that if I returned safely and if God wanted her to be a minister's wife she would accept whatever God might ask of her. I had told her nothing about my call to the ministry a year earlier in the theater at Camp Stoneman. As she told me this, I was overwhelmed by the power and goodness of God who had prepared Lois even as he had prepared me. When she learned of my call, she made good on her pledge.

One of the great benefits of having served in the military in those difficult years was the GI Bill. This was legislation that guaranteed veterans could attend college. I made application to take advantage of the program which would not only pay for college education, but also give a married couple $90 a month to help with living expenses.

I began to make preparations to enroll in the closest Free Methodist college, Roberts Junior College, about 10 miles west of Rochester, New York. The college was building new apartments on campus for the GIs who were expected to arrive on campus in September. Apartment 3A was reserved for us.

We looked forward to going away to college, but classes wouldn't begin for six months. I needed a job in the meantime. While Lois continued working with her father, I got a job as a civilian medic at Camp Holabird which was about half way between Dundalk and Baltimore. My job with an ambulance crew was much like the work I had done in Luzon and Japan. We transported soldiers who were too ill to be cared for in our camp facilities to one well-known hospital in the city of Baltimore.

The only real emergency that I had in those six months came when the day we got a call from the base laundry. A man who worked in the laundry had gotten his hand and arm stuck in a pair of gears driving a huge piece of equipment. The gears continued to draw his arm deeper and deeper into those crunching teeth-like cogs, finally jamming mechanism. His arm was stuck nearly up to his shoulder and he was bleeding profusely. No one in the laundry seemed to know how to work the machinery. Finally, someone figured out how to reverse the gears and the man's mangled hand and arm were liberated from the machine. We rushed him to the nearest emergency room. I don't know if the doctors were able to save his arm, but if we had not acted quickly, he might have certainly bled to death.

I was very active in the Dundalk Free Methodist Church. I was invited to preach two or three times that summer. My first sermon text was from Luke's Gospel, chapter 5 verse four in which Jesus advised the discouraged disciples who had been fishing all night and had caught nothing "to launch out into the deep". The sermon wasn't very long and consequently the members of the congregation thought it was good. At the same time I had the opportunity to teach and work with the church's youth group. Members of the congregation recommended that

I be given exhorter's license which was the first step on the road to become an ordained minister.

I was busy those six months. I spent time with Lois's younger brother Jack who was about 11 years old. Back Creek flowed behind the Weinel's house and a small rowboat was tied to the fence at the end of their backyard. Jack wanted to go out in that rowboat in the worst way. He wasn't permitted to take the boat out by himself so whenever I had time we went together in the boat. He always wanted to do the rowing. It made him very happy when I was willing to become his friend. A few years later there was nothing that he wouldn't do for his sister and me. When Jack started to work at the age of 14, he bought overcoats for his sister and looked after us.

Finally summer came to an end and it was time to leave Baltimore and drive north on Route 15 to the little town of North Chili, New York, where I was going to study and learn how to become a preacher.

25

College

Roberts Junior College was approximately 400 miles from our home in Maryland. We moved a living room set, two bedroom sets, a sofa, a few end tables, along with some odds and ends. Eight hours later we arrived in North Chili and learned that our apartment was not ready for us to occupy. Plans were made for us to go to the home of the president of the college, Dr. Merlin Smith, where we were given a large first-floor bedroom. We went to the college dining hall for our meals. Our furniture was stored in the larger of the two bedrooms in our apartment.

The Smiths were warm and cordial toward us. Mrs. Smith was a beautiful singer and an excellent pianist. If she happened to be playing the piano when I came in the house from classes, she would ask me to come over and sing with her. She sang familiar hymns and gospel songs, such as "What if it Were Today" and "Glad Day."

Apartment 3A in the GI housing area was finally ready about a month later. Lois and several other ladies from this college were able to get jobs at Eastman Kodak Company where they were processing color film, which was beginning to become more popular at that time.

I was employed as a glass blower at Taylor Instrument Company. My work shift was from four in the afternoon until eight o' clock in the evening. I started by making thermometers. That was easy—just blow a ball of liquid glass at the end of a tube. I was soon promoted to the more difficult job of making a circular mercury unit used in hotel room fire alarms. This required much more skill as we had to not only blow the glass, but bend the stem without twisting it. If the stem wasn't exactly right, it could give an erroneous reading.

My German supervisor thought I was a very good glass blower. He permitted me to make a number of units over that which was required per day. I found time to study by working ahead and storing these extra units. If I had an exam, my supervisor would say, "You don't need to come tonight. I'll take care of filling your card and seeing you get credit for having been here and completing your work."

Taylor had this contract for about seven months, but when the contract ended, a lot of us were out of work. The supervisor promised me that he would get in touch with me when the company got another contract. Before I left he said to me, "If the preacher business doesn't work out well for you come back and see me. I promise you I will have a job for you."

Like my ancestors and my father before me, I approached every job as a perfectionist and always gave my best. Unlike my progenitors, I was the first Barnett to attend college.

There is not much to say about my college class work. I had several outstanding professors who were dynamic Christians and I shall always be indebted to them for they not only knew their subjects, but they knew the Lord personally as well, people such as Mr. and Mrs. Updike, Professor Anderson and Dr. Stanley McGill, who once told me, "I'd rather burn out for the Lord than rust out for the devil."

I didn't have time to get involved in sports while in college. But I did participate in a gospel team made up of ministerial students. We had various singing groups that visited churches in the area and assist by providing music for their worship services as well as preach in Sunday evening services. Around Christmas time of my freshman year four or five of us were invited to assist in the morning services at a place called the "pony barn." Several people from the Rochester church were hoping to establish a new church in a suburb named Greece. I worked with that group for about a year and a half until I completed my sophomore year.

Lois and I were fortunate to secure jobs in the General Motors plant in Rochester. I was a drill press operator and Lois made locks for glove compartments and automobile trunks. We worked from 4:00 p.m. to 8:00 p.m. The plant operated a cafeteria where we had a good meal before going home.

While we were away at college, Lois's dad retired from his job as manager in the Jewel Tea Company office in Baltimore and took a job as pastor at the Rockville, Maryland Free Methodist Church. The salary of a minister was peanuts compared to the wages he had made with the company. Pop Weinel would not let us talk about the pay cut that was involved in the move from manager to preacher. Somehow Mom Weinel was able to make the adjustment. Pop Weinel had been a local preacher for a number of years, and since there was a shortage of ministers due to the war it was difficult to get anyone to take responsibility for leading a small church. I was always proud of him in the work that he did as a pastor and then later as a conference superintendent. His skills as a manager served him well in his church work.

Lois terminated her work there about September 1, 1947, while I continued working there beyond Thanksgiving. Lois was pregnant with a due date sometime the third week in October. We decided that she would stay with her parents who were now living in Rockville, Maryland. We wanted Lois and the baby to have the best prenatal care. For the month before the baby was born I drove from North Chili to Rockville and back every weekend.

Our first child was a big, strong, healthy baby boy with long black hair. David was born in Suburban Hospital in Bethesda, Maryland on October 20, 1947. The nurses adorned him with large blue ribbons. Lois's Ob-Gyn was Dr. Linthicum. He had delivered David and given Lois the best of care. When I asked him how much the charge would be, Dr. Linthicum spoke in his southern aristocratic drawl, "Mr. Barnett, would $40 be all right with you?"

Dr. Linthicum knew I was a ministerial student in college and he seemed reluctant to charge me anything at all. Looking him in the eye while I shook his hand, I expressed my deep thanks for all his kindness to Lois. Seldom could anyone today find a person that was half as considerate as Dr. Linthicum.

I continued to do well in my studies at the college. A lady named Vida Belardi wrote our class play entitled "God through History." In this play she re-enacted Christian history from the time of Jesus to our own day. She asked me to play the part of Martin Luther. I enjoyed being the German Reformer for a month or more in our rehearsal sessions and as we presented the play in two different venues.

After I was laid off at General Motors Company, I was able to secure a full-time job as a custodian at the Railway Signal Company, a large office complex with dozens of dozens of cubicles and offices for white collar workers who managed the railroads. I cleaned the restrooms, emptied waste paper baskets, and cleaned the wooden floors with a dust mop. Sometimes I got so sleepy by the end of the shift that I couldn't remember if I had cleaned offices earlier in the evening. I'm sure there were some nights that I did my work in my sleep. I worked from four until midnight and got home at about 12:30 or 12:45 p.m. The next day I had to be in class at 8:00 a.m. and stay in school until three in the afternoon at which time I needed to drive back to work again. By the end of the week I was so exhausted that I could hardly stand. I carried 15 hours of college credits and worked full-time. This was my routine for six months until I was ready to graduate from Junior College.

Clarence, Lois and friend, Wanda Stein, at Robert College, 1946

The winters were brutal in upstate New York. There were times when snow would drift up to the roof of our apartment house and to get out we had to dig tunnels from our porch to the street. Temperatures sank to below zero and the wind blew violently off Lake Erie. I decided I would finish my college degree at the University of Virginia in Charlottesville while I worked as pastor of a struggling little church in the town of Waynesboro, about 35 miles over the mountain from the university. The church had been without a pastor for about twelve years, and I would soon know why.

26

Baptisms and Other Beginnings

David was eight months old when we left North Chili for my first full-time preaching assignment in the hills of Virginia. My first church appointment was to the Free Methodist Church in Waynesboro. When we pulled into town the moving van had already arrived ahead of us. I pulled up behind the moving van and the driver of the truck climbed down from his rig and came to the side of the car.

"Reverend, are you sure this is the right address?" he asked.

"Yes," I answered. "I'm quite certain this is the right address."

"I don't believe you're going to put your furniture in that building," he said jerking his thumb in the direction of the house. "You won't believe what you'll find when you walk around that first floor of that house."

I saw that the door was open. "Let's go have a look," I said. So the moving van driver and I walked inside. He was right—I couldn't believe what I saw.

In the dining room two uninstalled windows leaned against the wall. The kitchen floor was not tiled and there were no plumbing fixtures in either the kitchen or bathroom. The house had no refrigerator. It looked like plasterers had moved out the day before and forgot to clean the splattered mess.

I was afraid to go to the car and tell Lois what shape the place was in. We had decided to come on the strong sales pitch of the conference superintendent who told us that Waynesboro church had "one of the nicest parsonages in the entire conference." Talk about buyer's remorse! If this was one of the best, I hated to see how the other minister's were living. As I looked around at the unfinished house, I thought until finally deciding upon a plan.

The back bedroom on the first floor was the most suitable place to store the furnishings, so the movers unloaded and stacked the furniture and boxes there. I returned to the car and told Lois that the house was not livable in its current state and I would take her and David back to Rockville to stay with her parents while I got the house ready.

Although she was upset, Lois took the news matter-of-factly. I think all we had been through together during the war years made us more flexible and less likely to complain as to approach the situation as a problem to be solved.

I estimated I could finish the work that needed doing on the house in two weeks after which I would bring Lois and David back and we could get on with our life as a family. In my many moves as a pastor over 50 years, it's normal that someone from the congregation would plan to meet you when you arrived in a new town. But no one from the Waynesboro church was there to meet us or help us move in that day. I'm not sure I would volunteer to meet a new preacher so I'm not sure I'm in any position to complain.

Some time after the moving van left, I saw a lady approaching the house. Mrs. Angel (and the irony of the name is certainly not lost on me) was sometimes referred to as the "queen bee" of that small congregation of believers. She handed me the keys to the house and apologized for the mess. Mrs. Angel explained that the church had been without a pastor for twelve years and the superintendent had taken it upon himself to build the house. There had been a lot of miscommunication between him and the plumbers and carpenters who were supposed to have finished the work before we arrived. She blamed the superintendent for not following through on his promises.

In two weeks I was able to get a lot of work done. I engaged plumbers and carpenters to install the windows and fixtures. While I had no restroom facilities, the lady next door was kind enough to let me use hers. Finally, the details were completed and I returned to Rockville to get Lois and David.

The church in Waynesboro was only a basement. Those who had originally built the place had either run out of money or interest or both and never bothered to finish the rest of the church. Driving by on the street, you saw some concrete blocks sticking up about two feet from the ground. It looked like a bunker.

But within a few weeks the church began to grow and prosper. I think a lot of people came to church out of curiosity and wondered what kind of preacher would take on an assignment like this. But we had a great response from those people who had been without a pastor for so long that they soon became willing to do just about anything I would suggest. Most of our members were poor people who worked in the large apple orchards that surrounded the town of Waynesboro. Some of the men worked in a small sawmill up in the hills behind Stuarts Draft. They loved me and I sincerely loved them.

The church board had concocted an interesting compensation program for me. They knew I received $90 a month from the GI Bill so they felt no compulsion about providing me with a regular salary. For the first month or six weeks that I was pastor I received whatever was left from the offerings after all the bills were paid. Sometimes I got as much as five to seven dollars.

The church had no budget so I decided it was time to get things organized and running on a more solid footing. I established a budget and arranged to be paid a regular weekly salary of ten dollars.

The church attracted new people and we were making new converts among both young and old. Mrs. Fields was 73 years old when she professed faith for the first time. The normal practice of Free Methodists was to baptize by sprinkling, but that just wouldn't do for these rural Virginians who wanted a real baptism service down by the river. They may have been converted in the Free Methodist Church, but their ideas of baptism were strictly Baptist.

Some members said they knew a spot that would be the perfect place for an outdoor country baptism. They made arrangements with the farmer who owned the land. Our congregation would meet there Sunday at two o'clock in the afternoon. We walked through a large meadow in the full bloom of early summer until we reached a lovely spot where the stream was 45 or 50 feet wide. The members of the congregation gathered on the bank and twelve candidates for baptism lined up in front of me on the shore of the stream. Everyone brought song books from church and when it was time for the service to begin, I welcomed them and began the baptismal service.

"Dearly beloved," I read from the liturgy, "for as much as all men have sinned and fallen short of the glory of God and our Savior, Jesus Christ said unless one is born of the water and the spirit he cannot enter the kingdom of God, I beseech you therefore to call upon God our Father through our Lord Jesus Christ that He would grant us His boundless goodness on all of these persons about to receive the baptism for the forgiveness of their sins, be baptized with water and the Holy Spirit and be received into Christ's Holy Church."

Then I asked the candidates the following questions.

"Do you truly and earnestly repent of your sins and accept Jesus Christ as your savior?"

Together they responded, "I do."

"Do you believe in God the Father Almighty, maker of heaven and earth and in Jesus Christ his only Son our Lord and the Holy Spirit the Lord the giver of life?"

They answered, "I do."

"Do you desire to be baptized in this faith?"

Again, they all said, "I do."

"Will you then obediently keep God's holy commandments and walk in the same all the days of your life?"

As one they answered, "I will."

"Will you then obediently keep God's holy commandments?"

"I will by God's help," they responded.

After offering a prayer, I turned and waded into the water. I was about half way out into the stream where the water was waist deep. From there I called each candidate by name. He or she stepped forward, came down the bank into the water and walked out to face me. I gave some brief instructions, reminding each person to keep their feet on the ground as I put them under the water.

I called the first young person by name. He moved quickly into the water beside me like you would expect any eager teenager to do. I explained to him what was about to happen. He smiled and said "Let's go."

I secured him in my arm and, putting him under the water, I said, "I baptize you in the name of the Father and of the Son and of the Holy Spirit. Amen."

I brought him up from the water and he returned to the shore. He stood beside the other candidates proud and happy that he had gone first and that everything had gone as expected. Then I called the others one by one to join me and I repeated the same procedure.

The last person to be baptized was Mrs. Fields, the 73 year old convert. She had snow white hair and a very, very large body. I explained the procedure carefully to her.

"Remember to bend your knees, but keep your feet on the ground," I said.

She nodded. I tried as best I could to put my arms around her. I said, "I baptize you in the name of the Father and of the Son and of the Holy Spirit. Amen."

She must have wanted to experience her baptism with all her heart and soul. When I put her beneath the water, her feet came flying up to the surface and I could see her gray hair disappearing beneath the water. The current was strong enough and she was so buoyant that I was afraid she might float downstream. I grabbed her and as she got her feet under her again, she shot out of the water, raised her right hand and let out a whoop, "Thank you, Jesus." She wrapped me in an exuberant bear hug and nearly took us both under again. Meanwhile up on shore the congregation was singing "Shall we gather at the river." I had survived my first baptismal service without major incident although it was a scene I shall never forget.

27

Under the Gun

In July, 1948 I attended my first annual conference and camp in Spencerville, Maryland, about 105 miles from Waynesboro. Most churches in the Maryland-Virginia Conference clustered around Baltimore and Washington, DC and in the countryside in between. My church in Waynesboro was located furthest away from all the other churches, a forgotten outpost. Few people in the Waynesboro church went to annual conference, but I attended with a great deal of joy and pride because we had seen considerable growth in the few weeks since coming as pastor. That year the superintendent who had told me about that wonderful parsonage retired and a new man was elected to take his place.

The Reverend Dewey Yale was very attentive to our needs and took an exceptional interest in that church way down in Waynesboro. Here's just one example of his attentiveness. Conference and camp meeting took place over two Sundays during the first week in July. When I returned home from the camp and conference, I wondered what my pay might be for those two Sundays that I was away from the church. Nothing was said for several weeks. Finally the treasurer finally came to me and said, "We haven't offered to pay you anything because you were not here those two weeks."

I don't know who got Superintendent Yale involved, but he told the board members of the church that it was standard procedure for the minister to be paid when they attended conference. It wasn't a vacation and I should be paid because I was representing the congregation as their minister.

We had been using only half of the basement auditorium and the other half of the bunker was completely unused. To accommodate our growing congregation, we needed some additional seating. Superintendent Yale told me there were two abandoned churches in the villages of Keene and Alberene on Walton's Mountain (yes, there really is such a place but we never suspected it would become a popular TV show) near Charlottesville. These defunct churches had some pews that could be put to good use in Waynesboro. The superintendent asked me to go to the courthouse in Charlottesville and check if the county had anyone identified as trustees from the churches. At the courthouse, I was met by old, thin man who wore a green visor. I explained my mission to him and asked if he had records of two vacant churches that I knew as Keene and Alberene Free Methodist churches.

"Let's go check," he said.

I knew if there were any living trustees from those churches, I would need permission to remove anything from the buildings. But if there were no registered trustees, then I had written authority from the superintendent to take any furnishings that might be put to good use in our Waynesboro church. We spent about five hours digging through musty books, researching the information. He worked diligently and seemed to know just where to go to give me the answers I needed. But no records of trustees were found. He told me one church was near an old slate quarry on a hard surface road. He told me how to reach that place. I had all the information I needed.

Back in Waynesboro, I contacted a church member who was a lumberman and had access to a large stake body truck. The following day a young person from the church and I got in the truck and I drove to Keene and Alberene. We located the church at Keene with no trouble. When we opened the door of the old church building, we found that the electric company was using the building to store equipment. The church was filled with transformers, large roles of electric wire, a lot of insulators, and all kinds of electrical equipment, but no pews or anything our church could use.

The man in green visor told me that not far from the church I would find a dirt road leading up into the foothills of the mountains. That road would take us to Alberene. We didn't travel far until sure enough we spotted a dirt road and turned off. We bounced along that rutted dirt path as it climbed higher in the hill and became little more than a path. There wase nothing on this dirt path, no road signs, no signs of human life. Trees had grown over the roadside. Branches slapped the cab and pulled at the stakes of the flatbed, making a terrible racket.

Up ahead we spotted what looked like a building, and as we got closer, it was easy to tell it had once been a small country church. I stopped the truck and we got out to explore. I noticed a cabin about 200 yards away, but it looked abandoned. The teenager and I entered the church. It looked exactly like the day they had held the last service there. Everything was in place. A large lantern hung from the ceiling. A wood stove stood in the corner and a pulpit slightly off center in the front. But we were most excited to see a dozen pews made with three-inch wide slats of lumber.

"We can sure use those pews," I said. "Let's get our tools and load these on the truck."

I had left the hammers and crowbars in the truck. As we walked toward the truck, we saw a woman about 60 years old standing beside the truck. She had long, straggly hair that hung to her shoulders and she was missing several front teeth. In her left arm she cradled a shot gun.

"Hello," I said trying to be friendly.

"What you 'uns think you're doin' here?" she asked menacingly.

I told her who I was and that I had permission from the Free Methodist superintendent to check out these abandoned churches for any furnishings we might use in our church building in Waynesboro.

She continued to glare at us, her expression unchanged. There was something about her face that looked familiar to me; she reminded me of someone. Then the name came to me of someone who could have been her twin sister, but who was younger than this guardian hag. The woman I knew attended the Free Methodist Church in Washington, DC, where Lois and I had been married. It occurred to me that her last name was Barber.

"Your last name wouldn't happen to be Barber, would it?" I asked.

"Now why would you ask me that?" she said surprised, but I noticed her eyes brightened.

"Well, I know someone who looks a lot like you who lives in Washington. She goes to a church where Alma Frederick is the pastor."

Alma Frederick had been the last pastor to serve these little churches twelve or fifteen years before. I heard stories about her from people in my congregation. Some of the mountain people used to say she would preach like a chicken picking up corn.

The lady's face brightened because she knew the Reverend Alma Frederick and the lady who lived with her as her companion, Lillian Kelly.

"That lady preached like a chicken picking up corn," she laughed, lowering the shotgun and propping it against a tree.

"My daddy donated the land for this church," she said nostalgically. "He was the last living trustee, but he died some time ago."

"Let me tell you all about this church," she said. "You certainly can take whatever you might find useful to your church in Waynesboro."

As we lifted those pews with our crowbars and hammers, she told every detail about the church, who built it, how many people attended, and the good times they once had enjoyed. My helper and I were careful to drive out all the nails that would still be left in the pews as we prepared to load them on the truck. We secured the benches to the stakes along the bed of the truck with large ropes. As we pulled away, I thanked her again for her kindness and generosity.

We made our way slowly back to the little trail and onto the dirt road and finally to a hard surface road that connected Charlottesville and Waynesboro. I couldn't help but thank God for the grace and presence of mind to transform that angry woman with a shotgun into an ally.

Unloading the pews back at the church, we discovered the benches were too long to negotiate a sharp turn at the bottom of the stairs into the basement auditorium. But when we knocked off one end of the pew we were able to make it by bending those three-inch boards one by one just enough to slip around the corner. Once all the pews were inside, we reattached the ends and set them carefully in place.

Those crude benches were enough to accommodate the growing numbers of people attending our services. I often thought as I sat on those rough hard benches, whoever had to sit here for Sunday services would certainly learn what the Bible meant by "suffering for righteousness' sake."

28

First Funeral

In September I started attending the University of Virginia in Charlottesville. About a semester's worth of credits from Roberts College were not accepted at the University, most of which were Bible classes. I was not surprised to learn I would be classified as a sophomore, but to this date I receive letters from the University in which I'm referred to as a 1952 graduate even though I attended the University only one year.

I was impressed with most of the professors at that school. One of my classes was in medieval history. There were easily 150 students who met in a large auditorium. I liked the discipline and respect that was shown to the professors. The students arrived in the class prior to the starting time and at the exact hour the class was to begin, the professor would stand in the doorway and the class rose to their feet. The professor walked across the front of the room to his desk. He looked from one side to the other of the large classroom before finally saying, "Be seated." He would then proceed to lecture for fifty minutes without interruption. The time sped by because he made the medieval world come alive. Few students wanted to skip his classes and they were always filled to the brim.

Another professor was so good I took four classes from him. One was entitled, A History of Naval Sea Power and another was Classical Greek Architecture.

I enrolled in one class in which I soon discovered I was in way over my head. I thought it would be beneficial to study Greek. Of the eight students in my Greek class, I was the only undergraduate, and the others were all specializing in foreign languages. About halfway through the semester I realized there was no way I was going to keep up with these linguistic whiz kids, so rather than flunk the course, I dropped out to receive a grade of incomplete. It was difficult to keep up my full-time work at the church as well to carry fifteen credit hours at the University.

I was so busy with school and work that I began to notice that I wasn't giving enough time to my wife and son David who was now approaching one year old. I began to ask the Lord in prayer to help me with this problem. In late summer a new family began attending our church. Harry Baldwin was a chemist who had been transferred from a Dupont plant in New Jersey to the facility in Waynesboro. He and his wife, Frances, were experienced church people who became a great help to me in all matters pertaining to the operation of the church. Harry was committed to continuing the growth we had seen in that first summer. Frances was elected our delegate to annual conference. They were an answer to my prayer. I was able to spend more quality time with my family.

The tranquility of that late summer was broken by a traumatic event for which nothing in my training or experience had prepared me.

We had a fine group of young people at our church. Jack Clark was 18 or 19 years old and active in our youth group. Jack was a timid person from a family in which several children had learning disabilities. He was such a loving person and he expressed his feelings in very simple and genuine ways. It was not unusual for Jack to stop by the parsonage almost any evening. He knocked on the door and I would answer.

"Preacher, I have a gift for you and your wife." Then he would hand me a Hershey's Almond Chocolate candy bar. If I asked him to come in for a visit, he became a little uncomfortable and told us he had to be getting back home. He climbed into his pickup truck and drove away. He did this any number of times. He brought us a small bag of apples and he always would say, "Preacher, I have something to give to you and to your wife." He was a simple, but entirely genuine person.

Then one day the phone rang.

"Hello," I said, expecting another routine call.

"Reverend Barnett, I'm a friend of Jack's and I'm calling you from the hospital. Somethin' real bad's happened to Jack, Reverend."

There was a long pause and I thought the young man might have been crying. "Jack shot his self," he managed to say. "I drove real fast and tried to get him to the hospital, but by the time I got there he was dead."

I told him I would come right away. I hung up the phone, jumped in the car, and sped to the hospital as quickly as I could. Some nurses told me where to find the boy. We sat down and he explained to me the sad story.

He and Jack had been out fox hunting when they came across a hole beside a large rock. "We thought it may well be a foxhole. So we decided to build a fire right inside the opening of that hole. When it got burning good we put on some damp leaves to make it smoke. We fanned the smoke back into the hole and hoped if a fox was in there, he'd come out and then we'd shoot it."

He paused a moment to collect his thoughts and then continued.

"We thought we heard somethin' stirrin' inside that hole. Jack had left his shotgun in the bed of his pickup with the barrel hangin' over the tailgate. He was so excited, he ran to the pickup and grabbed the gun by the barrel. As he pulled it to himself across the bed of the truck, the butt of the gun hit the tailgate and the gun fired with that muzzle no more than six inches from Jack's chest."

"I put him in the truck and I drove with Jack sitting up beside me. He was talkin' until we got about halfway to Waynesboro and…" Here his voice trailed off. And he wiped away a tear.

"By the time I got him here to the hospital he had collapsed. That's when they told me Jack was dead."

I had patched up a lot of chest wounds in my training as a medic and I could only image the horrible scene that would be indelibly etched in this young man's memory forever. I spent a great deal of that afternoon with Jack's friend assuring him that he should not blame himself for this tragic accident and that Jack was safe in God's care.

The sun had just gone down and it was just turning dark when I drove out to Jack's parent's home near Stuarts Draft. As I got out of my car I heard moans and crying such as I had never heard before. It sounded like the voices coming from behind the house. When I knocked on the door, Jack's mother answered. I could see other family members crumpled up with grief in their small living room. As I stepped inside, Jack's mother laid her head on my chest and I put my arms across her shoulders. All I could think to say was, "I'm very, very sorry, I'm so sorry."

We stood there together for some time, everybody in the room was crying. As she regained her composure, she told me she wanted me to be in charge of the funeral in Waynesboro. I told her that I would do everything I could to help them through these rough hours of grief and pain. I had prayer with them before going outside. I walked around the house and back to a pig pen where I tried to comfort Jack's father who was moaning and groaning. As I approached him he said, "I'm very sorry, preacher, I just can't talk with you right now."

"Okay," I said. "I understand."

I left him and got into my car and drove back to the parsonage wondering all the way what I could say and do to help and comfort this family in this terrible hour of their grief and pain. I truly shared their sense of loss for I loved that young man for the many kindnesses he had shown to me and Lois.

All of the funeral arrangements were made and in a few days I met Jack's family at the funeral home for the service. I'm not sure any class I had taken in preacher's school could have prepared me for my very first funeral. A large crowd of family members and friends filed past the open casket before the service began.

Many of them cried and called out his name, most touched his body, and many family members kissed him on his cold cheek. Sounds of grief were beyond anything I had ever seen before or since that event. I had no idea how they might respond to my service and sermon. I had never witnessed such freedom in expression of grief as I did during that funeral service.

We got through the service and everything went well and then came the hard part. Jack was to be buried in the family cemetery in the mountains above Buena Vista, Virginia. A family member had taken the funeral director to the remote site the day before so he would know the way. It must have been more than 50 miles from Waynesboro to the family cemetery in a little clearing at the top of the mountain. Many who had attended the funeral made the drive to Buena Vista. I rode in the hearse with the funeral director. On the way he told me we were in for a rough ride on that mountain road, so rough he was afraid that the body, tossed around in the coffin like a drumstick in shake and bake would not be fit for viewing.

As we pulled into the clearing, we saw a large group of really strange looking people waiting for us to arrive. Most of the men wore coveralls and about half of them had a rifle or shotgun by their side. Racial intermarriage which was strictly taboo in the south in those days was obviously being practiced here as I saw about half the young people had pasty white skin covered with brown spots. Many others were seriously deformed from incest I suspected. Still others were covered with growths on their faces. Their appearance was gruesome. I told the funeral director that if these folks were anything like the family I had witnessed back in Waynesboro, they were going to insist that the casket be opened. My prediction turned out to be true because those mountain people made it known in no uncertain terms that they wanted to see the body.

When the casket was positioned over the grave, the mourners drew closer to the graveside. Those who had driven from Waynesboro stood to one side. Just then a man shouted, "We want to see Jack." The funeral director looked at me anxiously. I wasn't sure what he would do. Then the whole crowd took up the chant, "Yeah, we want to see Jack."

I cupped my hand over my mouth so that my voice didn't carry out to the crowd, and I said, "If you want to get down off this mountain alive you better open that casket." He nodded and slowly moved to the front of the bier and lifted the lid. I saw him adjust the body to make it more presentable. I took my place at the head of the casket and the funeral director stood at the foot of the body.

The mourners filed past the open coffin. Their blank stares and halting pace reminded me of a line of zombies from a movie. One by one they approached the casket. Some wept wildly. Others simply stood and stared at Jack. "Why'd you do it, Jack?" one sighed.

A mother with small children stopped in front of the grave. She lifted the two little boys so they could see inside the casket. "Now, this here is your cousin Jack," she said. "You ain't never seen him but this is your cousin Jack. Say hello to Jack."

The children, who were probably eight or nine, politely and shyly said "Hello."

"We have to be leaving now, Jack," the mother said. "Boys, say goodbye to Jack." And the children responded sadly, "Goodbye, Jack."

As people slowly filed past I would nod my head to them since none of them offered to shake hands. It took quite awhile as many stood there talking to Jack's body and finally saying goodbye. After the last mourner said farewell, the funeral director moved quickly to close the casket. He gave the signal to some of the men standing nearby who began lowering the casket with ropes into the grave. Almost immediately men from the family laid down their guns and picked up shovels lying about the dirt piled behind the casket. Groaning and crying, they shoveled dirt into that grave. When they had nearly filled the grave and as soon as we could get around the crowd, the funeral director and I made our way back to the hearse.

Many of the cars that had followed us had already started back to Waynes-boro. I heard later from some of our church people who had been at the intern-ment service that they were scared to death. The funeral director turned the hearse around and we re-traced our way back down the rough mountain trail, the chassis reverberating every so often as we scraped the bottom of the vehicle on another large rock in the road.

On the ride back to Waynesboro the funeral director and I said hardly a word to one another. There just wasn't much left to be said after the unforgettable funeral of Jack Clark.

29

Visitation

One afternoon a woman came to the parsonage because she had a problem and she said she needed to talk with me.

She was a prominent lay leader during the twelve years the congregation had been without a minister. When I first arrived in Waynesboro she was very helpful. She chauffeured me to meet most of the church members at their homes. But as time went on she seemed to distance herself from me. She became less supportive of my leadership. So, I wasn't entirely surprised when she dropped by the house that day.

We sat down in the living room and she began to enumerate a number of changes I had made that did not meet with her approval. She was calm as the conversation began. I listened and responded that I understood how she felt, that she was upset because I wasn't consulting with her about how the church would be run. I told her it was natural for her to feel left out now that members of the congregation were coming to me with their questions and problems instead of coming to her as they always had. She became more excited as she continued telling me all the things she disliked about my leadership. Soon she was screaming at me, her face shot red like an erupting volcano, her words spewing in such a torrent that she quickly became completely incoherent.

Immediately my mind flashed back to the psychiatric ward at Fitzsimmons General Hospital where I had seen this behavior many times and learned how to handle men who were out of control. I quickly moved across the room taking a position above and beside her. I put my hand on her shoulder to prevent her from getting up from her chair. Foam sprayed from her lips and ran down her chin as she continued screaming at me. Hearing the racket, Lois came into the room. I asked her to bring a cold washcloth. A few moments later Lois returned and placed the cool compress on the woman's face and wiped away the foam that had gathered around her mouth. We gave her a glass of cold water. I told her to sip the water slowly knowing that at least while she was drinking she would not try to speak.

Finally the lady grew calmer. When I was convinced that she wouldn't try to get up and start running through the house, I lifted my hand from her shoulder and returned to sit on the sofa across the room. My visitor was physically spent. She sat in the chair for several minutes without saying a word, breathing deeply and obviously recovering from exhaustion, not to mention embarrassment.

"Is there anything I can do for you?" I asked.

"No, thank you," she said with a note of exasperation. She picked up her purse and without saying a word opened the door, walked to her car and drove away. She returned to church the following Sunday and every week after that. We never had a moment of trouble with her ever again.

If this encounter had taken place in the first century church, her strange behavior might have been recorded in the Bible as a case of demon possession. I was so grateful for the training I had received in the Army that enabled me to react so quickly to keep this lady from hurting herself or others. But my family background also had a profound impact on shaping my pastoral temperament in dealing with the woman and the many other people like her I encountered during 50 years of ministry. I could empathize with people as my mother did without compromising what I believed to be right as my father had deeply instilled in me.

David learned to talk before he walked. He was a very inquisitive little fellow, forever asking "Who is that?" or "What is that?" During church services, he liked to stand on the pew beside Lois and push the side of her face to turn her head to see the person seated behind them. "Who is that?" he asked loudly.

I take responsibility for David's inquisitiveness. Whenever I was outdoors with him I pointed out every bird or squirrel. I would ask, "What is that?" and he would proudly answer "robin" or "squirrel." I made sure he saw an airplane overhead and before long when a plane could be heard but not seen, David would look up into the sky and say, "Airplane."

In warm weather I enjoyed putting David in a stroller and walking to a small grocery store located several blocks from our parsonage. The grocer always stacked soft drinks on the floor just inside the door. When David saw the bottles of Pepsi he pointed his finger to the stack and said, "Daddy, buy some." For the longest time Pepsi was known in our house as "buy-some."

Lois seldom went with me when I made pastoral visits. But that changed on a particular day when Lois and David accepted the invitation of one of our church members for all of us to come to her house. This lady was a faithful member and she was always dressed impeccably. Her shoes were highly polished and she wore fashionable but not gaudy dresses. We had no reason to expect what we saw as we pulled up in front of her house.

Chickens over-ran the house, some were on the front porch, and as she ushered us inside, chickens were roosting in her house as well. There were no screens on the doors or windows so the house was filled with flies. She welcomed us cordially, totally ignoring the flies and chickens scurrying under foot. David was completely fascinated with the chickens, but never left his mother's lap.

"What is that?" David asked with wide-eyed fascination.

"Chickens," Lois said without moving her lips under a polite but not altogether sincere smile.

When David became restless our host suggested that Lois let him sit on the floor. He was dressed in a white suit and there was no way Lois was going to put him on that floor. We continued our conversation while brushing flies away from our faces. Lois had about as much of this as she could handle when she said we needed to go home because it was time for David to eat.

"Oh, that's not necessary," said our host. "I've got a cow out back and I can get plenty of good, fresh milk for the boy."

"That's not necessary," Lois replied, with a slightly sick expression.

"Say, why don't y'all just plan to take supper here with me and my boys?"

Lois looked at me with desperation in her eyes. Once again we talked our way out of staying for supper, insisting that we needed to return home. We did our best not to offend the lady and apparently succeeded because she kept coming to church faithfully.

Church attendance continued to improve throughout that year. Most new members were coming from the country, but I wanted to attract townspeople from the surrounding community. I went door to door, introducing myself to folks who lived near the church. The residents were cordial but never attended. I became convinced that our basement bunker didn't measure up to what most Virginians would want to identify as their church. I suggested to the congregation that we should make plans to complete the building. The majority of the congregation agreed that local residents would be more likely to come to worship in a more traditional looking church building.

I talked privately with several of the most influential members of the church about a plan I had devised and they gave me their blessing.

"It's either going to be the most courageous or the most foolhardy thing any preacher here ever did," said one.

I ordered a load of sand, several bags of mortar cement, and some cinder blocks. Next morning, I mixed the ingredients into "mud" and started laying blocks on the rear corner of the building. Lois was my helper, carrying blocks and "mud." Being a pastor's wife meant you had to be flexible.

I laid a corner, three or four courses high. I did not intend to do any more than that. I simply wanted people in the community to see that changes were underway to transform the ugly bunker on the corner of 12th Street.

I was determined to move that congregation off dead center and get a building program underway that I decided after classes broke for the summer I would discontinue my school work to devote all my energy to building that church. Our annual conference was only two months away and I planned at that time to notify my superintendent and bishop of my plans to discontinue school.

30

East Washington

Each year the thirteen churches that made up the Maryland-Virginia Conference held its conference in conjunction with a weeklong family camp meeting that featured good preaching, Bible study, and afternoons for fun and play. We packed several suitcases for our ten-day stay at the Spencerville campground. Bishop Leslie Marston presided over the 1949 annual conference. The annual conference was the occasion for churches to do their collective business. Committees and congregations gave reports about attendance, offerings, and special concerns. When I gave my report to the conference, in addition to the statistical information, I stated my intention to discontinue my schooling so that I could give all my attention to constructing the church building in Waynesboro. Shortly thereafter I was notified that the bishop wanted me to attend the meeting of the stationing committee later that evening. The stationing committee makes recommendations to the Bishop about relocating pastors.

At the committee meeting the bishop made it very clear that he would not permit me to stop my schooling. He told me other arrangements could be made so that I could continue my degree work at a church closer to a university. Without telling me the name of the church, he asked if I would be interested in such an appointment. I told him I was.

At that time, ministers were appointed to churches with little foreknowledge or previous consultation. Lois and I waited anxiously until the final session of the conference when the Bishop read the appointments.

"Clarence Barnett," Bishop Marston said, reading from the appointment list, "East Washington Park Free Methodist Church."

This church was in southeast Washington, DC, located on Minnesota Avenue and F Street. Ironically, it was the church where Lois and I were married in February, 1944.

I was sad to leave the congregation in Waynesboro, but I was also glad to be moving to Washington where I planned to continue my studies at the American University located on the other side of town.

The next day was Sunday. Lois and I put on our best clothes and drove to Washington to scope out my new congregation. We parked our car on F Street and walked up the steps toward the front door of the little stone church where we were greeted by a stone-faced woman. I introduced myself, Lois, and David. She looked us over carefully and then said to me, "Is this the best the conference could do for us?"

Lois and I stood there awkwardly, the smiles slowly melting from our faces. I couldn't image someone being so rude and inconsiderate. I thought to myself, here's another "queen bee," another Mrs. Angel.

Thankfully, we met other people that morning who turned out to be more gracious. We didn't stay long before returning to the campground with very little enthusiasm about our new responsibilities. We stayed throughout the remainder of the weeklong camp meeting before returning to Waynesboro.

We had lot of work facing us. We had to pack up the house and then I made arrangements for a moving van. I preached my farewell sermon the following Sunday morning. I never do well saying goodbye, but I managed to get through it. The people at Waynesboro were gracious and wished us well in our new work in Washington.

The East Washington church was better-organized and slightly larger in membership than the Waynesboro congregation. The parsonage was a comfortable two-bedroom bungalow with a full basement, finished attic, and a detached garage. A small lawn surrounded the house in a clean residential neighborhood.

The church was a stone structure in an excellent location. One of the first things I did was to put up an outdoor bulletin board facing the high traffic corridor of Minnesota Avenue. I made good use of that bulletin board during my four years as pastor.

Washington was a very different city in those days. Even though it was the nation's capitol, it had little of the hurly-burly hustle and bustle of today's city. There wasn't even a Beltway. Washington was a predominantly white, southern city.

Pictures of our life in East Washington come to mind and still bring a smile to my face. Across the street was a nosy neighbor who peeked out her curtain whenever we came or left the house. She was soon telling people in the community that Lois was pregnant even before we knew that she was with child. Thank goodness that neighbor wasn't a member of the church.

David's favorite toy was a push-pedal car in which he careened around the sidewalk that circled from the front porch back to the garage at amazing speeds. He also used his car as a pulpit, standing on the seat at the front gate holding a songbook in his hands and singing at the top of his lungs every song he knew. He had obviously seen me lead the singing at church on Sundays and was simply following his Dad's example. People up and down the street told me they enjoyed hearing David sing.

Next to our parsonage was a four-unit apartment house. One resident was a heavy smoker. If David saw him coming up the sidewalk, our three year old would never miss the opportunity to tell him that smoking was bad. The man smiled at David and agreed with him.

The soundtrack of those years was a little ditty that exploded on the pop charts in 1950. David's grandmother bought him a child's record player that included several records. His favorite recording was "Hokey Pokey."

You put your right foot in,
You put your right foot out,
You put your right foot in,
And you shake it all about,
You do the Hokey Pokey
And you turn yourself around,
THAT'S WHAT IT'S ALL ABOUT!

The ironic thing was that our church discouraged dancing and the only song my boy wanted to sing was a song about a dance. David never tired of singing that song over and over.

The first year in Washington we decided that we would redecorate the house. The first project was to remove some garish wallpaper in the dining room. What a job! We used our Electrolux cleaner to wet the wallpaper which made it easier to remove from the wall. It was a hot job to do in the middle of winter. Lois went out on the front porch to cool off and a few days later contracted pneumonia. She was also three months pregnant. She was ill for two weeks, during which I finally completed painting the dining room.

I was taking 15 credit hours at the American University as well as keeping up with the work at the church. We had morning and evening Sunday church services in addition to a Wednesday night prayer meeting. Like my ancestors who worked more than one job, I was both full time student and full-time pastor.

There was always something humorous going on in the church to offset dealing with sour-faced Christians who had the capacity to drain any joy from the soul. For example, Irving was a 50-year-old bachelor who had never learned how to drive an automobile. He was a very timid man who had a government job tending boilers in a large building in town. He was trying to date a very nervous lady about the same age. Her name was Rachel. She also worked for the government. Rachel was from a very conservative Christian background—no make-up, no jewelry, hair in a bun, long sleeve dresses, very dour. She sang in a falsetto screech that was always off key. It reminded me of the sound of nails scratching on a blackboard. I tried to select hymns for Sunday worship that Rachel didn't know so she would not alarm any visitors who might be church shopping that day.

Irving confided in me that he wanted to date Rachel, but that he didn't have the courage to sit in the same pew with her. Rachel told Irving she would not date him if he did not have a car. So Irving bought a 1946 Nash and started taking driving lessons. Well, after several close calls and failing his driver's test three times, the driving instructor told Irving that he was simply too nervous to control an automobile. Irving wanted to give the car to me.

I was driving a 1946 Studebaker at the time, a far better car than his. I told Irving to think it over before giving me the Nash. Sometime later Irving came to me and said he was sure that he wanted me to have his car. I found a lady in our congregation whose husband had never learned to drive and who was happy to buy my Studebaker. Poor Irving never did get a date with Rachel and I always wondered why he was attracted to her. The only conclusion I could reach was the fact that love is blind. Both of these dear people continued coming to church, but I never heard either say more than hello to each other.

We were delighted to learn that Lois would give birth to our second child in July. We made arrangements with Dr. Linthicum, the same man who delivered David three years before. We visited his office in Rockville, Maryland regularly for prenatal care. Dr. Linthicum showed us the same care and compassion as we had received during David's birth.

Darlene was born on July 11, 1950, in Suburban Hospital in Bethesda. She was a beautiful girl who weighed 9 lbs. 10 oz. It was such a joy to take her home and then to the church so members could celebrate her birth with us. Ten days later we went to annual conference at the Spencerville camp where Bishop Charles Fairburn baptized her.

These were extremely happy days for us. On our final visit to Dr. Linthicum's office, I asked him what I owed him for all of his services. He paused for a moment and then answered, "Mr. Barnett, would $50 be too much?" I gave him the money, shook his hand, and thanked him for his kindness to us. We had no medical insurance at that time, and most doctors gave professional consideration to ministers. There was not a more compassionate man in all of the town of Rockville.

31

Electrolux

As had happened at Waynesboro, church attendance grew steadily under my leadership at East Washington. In the early 1950's people still had a "religious memory," that is, they knew what the church stood for and many had gone to church as children and teenagers. Back from the war and married with children, many of those GIs began returning to church as was expected of upstanding adults.

We frequently saw people converted in our evangelistic services. One Saturday evening I received a phone call from a lady who with her husband had come to Washington to sightsee and she wanted directions to our church so they might attend the next day. After I told her how to find the church, she proceeded to tell me about the large number of bars near her hotel. She was absolutely convinced that Washington must be a very wicked city. When I told her about the many converts God was adding to our church, she seemed shocked and surprised. Before she ended the conversation, she said that on second thought they would leave the first thing in the morning and return home. Washington was simply too wicked for her.

Harry and June Romesburg were two such converts. They became our best friends and staunchest supporters during my tenure at that church. Harry was my right-hand man. Seldom have I seen a couple grow in grace as quickly as they did. The Romesburgs had a boy David's age. Billy and David became close friends. David especially liked visiting Billy's house because the Romesburgs had a television in their apartment.

Harry was an airline mechanic for Capital Airlines at National Airport (what is today Reagan International Airport). Soon after his conversion, Harry told me that he needed to make something right; that some of the tools he used on the job did not belong to him. He wanted to return the tools, but he did not know who the owners were. He was serious about making restitution but didn't know how to go about it. Together we worked out a solution and Harry followed through. At work he called all the mechanics in his section and told them about his newfound life in Christ. He confessed that some of the tools he had were not his and that he wanted to return them. He showed the tools to locate the owner and told me later he felt a wonderful sense of release for having done it.

Harry had another confession to make about his past behavior that was beginning to interrupt his prayer life. He told me that during the days he had worked at a soda fountain in Uniontown, Pennsylvania, that he often helped himself to a milkshake and didn't pay for it. This was years ago. At first he rationalized that God certainly wouldn't expect him to make a ten hour round trip for such a trivial offense. But as he prayed, Harry could not escape that nagging sense of guilt. So, one Saturday, he drove to Uniontown and found the Italian owner of the drugstore. Harry explained that he had become a Christian and he wanted to make restitution for the wrong he had done.

"You don't need to concern yourself about those milkshakes," the drugstore owner told Harry. "You were a very, very good reliable worker. I thank God for what he has done for you, but please, don't you worry about it."

Harry said they sat down at the counter and had a milkshake together. The next morning at church Harry was all smiles. He testified to the congregation about his experience on Saturday, not to let others know how righteous he was, but to let others know how important it was for people to practice the New Testament teaching on restitution and seeking God's forgiveness. It was a powerful witness. Harry was a good man, full of the Holy Spirit and faith. We remained good friends for many years until he retired and moved to Florida.

Then, as now when church members purchase new furniture for their homes they frequently donate their old junk to the church. That's what happened when one lady gave an old-fashioned pump organ to replace the piano we used in the sanctuary. She considered this a worthy sacrifice to make to the church. After all, an antique dealer said that pump organ may have been worth as much as $10.

The only problem was the lady who played the piano for the congregation was so old and frail she didn't have enough strength to play more than a verse or two before becoming completely worn out by the constant pumping necessary to make the organ play. I got the bright idea that I could bring our Electrolux sweeper, reverse the hose to expel rather than suck air, cut a hole in the floor under the organ, and connect the hose to the bellows of that old reed organ. It worked! We had enough air to accompany an entire cantata if needed. But my solution created another problem. Whenever the organist turned on the switch to start the vacuum sweeper, it made considerable noise that was easily heard throughout the sanctuary. After services, visitors would shake my hand at the back of the church and tell me how much they enjoyed the service.

"But why does your janitor start running the sweeper in the basement whenever we start singing?" they asked.

So, the vacuum cleaner experiment, while efficient, proved to be quite embarrassing. The problem was solved when the older lady resigned and a much younger, stronger lady volunteered to be our organist.

We had a very special visitor almost every Sunday. I heard him coming before I saw him. He announced his presence by blowing a police whistle after getting off the bus in front of the church. Aaron Livsey was blind. The whistle alerted standers-by that he couldn't see. He had a handsome seeing eye dog named Gruff. Gruff led his master safely across the street, up a flight of steps, and into the church, always to the second pew on the left. People cleared the aisle when they saw Aaron coming. Gruff was never a problem during the service. Gruff usually slept during the sermon; sometimes he snored, or often he would look up at me behind the pulpit, not unlike several members of my congregation.

I will never forget the morning I preached a sermon on the healing of a blind man in John chapter 9. During the altar call, Aaron stood up and Gruff led him to the altar. He asked me to anoint him and pray for his healing. I anointed Aaron's eyes with oil. I wish I could report that he had the same result as the man in the Scriptures, but he wasn't instantly and completely healed, although the church and I were powerfully moved by his act of faith and surrender. Aaron told me at the door as he left that morning that he could see the outline of my head and shoulders in the bright sunlight through the doorway. For Aaron, it was a miracle.

In addition to all the preaching and teaching responsibilities at the church, I was also the janitor. The church did not own a vacuum cleaner so every Saturday I took our trusty Electrolux with all the attachments to the church. I never saw any paper scraps in the sanctuary because we had one dear old lady who was a kleptomaniac who gathered up all the scrap paper and stuffed it in her bag before leaving the building. It's true that God has a role for everyone in the church.

I was also responsible for the lawn and shrubbery on the property. Most Sundays I went to church early to rehearse my sermon. One morning I had the surprise of my life when I entered the sanctuary. There, covering almost every square inch of that church, was a carpet of dead bees an inch thick. I ran back to the parsonage to retrieve my vacuum cleaner and get rid of the bees before people started arriving. I collected three bags of dead bees. I later discovered that there was a large beehive in the attic and the bees were getting in via a vent pipe in the back of the sanctuary. Needless to say I did not rehearse my sermon that morning.

After I had been the pastor for several years, I decided it was time to get a complete treasurer's report. In all of our business meetings, when I asked for a treasurer's report, the treasurer would simply say, "All the bills are paid and we have a little money in the checking account."

At first I let it slide, but it had now been two years that I had been requesting a more detailed report and for two years the treasurer simply ignored my requests. I asked the treasurer if there had ever been annual audit of the books. She said, "No, never." Even though I had gotten rid of the hive in the attic, I knew I was dealing again with a queen bee.

As the pastor, I had the authority to demand to see the books, but remembering previous run-ins with powerful yet hostile churchwomen, I didn't want to push the issue. I didn't believe the treasurer was stealing any money, but I explained the problem to the conference superintendent. He said that an audit should be done immediately.

When I explained to the treasurer that the superintendent urgently demanded an audit of the books, she once again refused to comply. The next day I drove to her house. She was a government worker and not home during the day. I asked her husband if he would get the books and give them to me. He did.

When she got home from work and learned that I had collected the books to complete an audit, she was as mad as a wet hornet (I'm still thinking about those bees). She called me that evening to inform me she had talked to the superintendent and had filed charges of malfeasance of office against me in church court. It was true, for not long after the superintendent called to let me know the day and time the trial would take place before my congregation. If I was found guilty, I could forfeit my ministry credentials.

32

Trial

On a cool Wednesday evening in late summer Conference Superintendent Dewey Yale convened a meeting of the church to address the charges brought against me by the treasurer. I had notified the parishioners that the superintendent would be present to help the church resolve the conflict. A larger than average crowd of perhaps 30 people greeted each other and filed into church hall that evening. The superintendent had positioned a chair down front and to the left side of the auditorium. Everyone who entered that night sat on the left side, all but one. The treasurer was the only person who sat on the right side of the hall.

Superintendent Yale called the meeting to order, announced the reason for the convocation and outlined the procedures proscribed by the Book of Discipline that would be followed in dealing with the charges. When he finished this introduction, he lifted his arm to the lonely lady on the right side of the auditorium.

"You may begin," he said. The treasurer stood.

"Thank you, Superintendent," she said. "I want you people to know that Brother Barnett was out of his authority to come barging into my house and persuading my sick husband to hand over those books. My husband is an invalid and Brother Barnett frightened him."

Her husband had fought in the trenches during World War I and inhaled mustard gas. Although he was rational and could get around, he was unable to work. He was also extremely timid (something common to spouses of "queen bee" church members).

"He had no right to take those books," she said, shaking her index finger. "And so I have asked that he be charged with malfeasance of office."

She sat down. Superintendent Yale spoke. "You have heard the charges against your pastor. Is there anyone who wishes to speak in his defense?"

Hands went up, seeking permission to speak. One by one the members spoke of the treasurer's refusal to comply with the pastor's request for a formal report.

125

One lady said, "Brother Barnett is not of such a temperament to barge into any-one's house let alone to frighten or browbeat a sick man."

"Does anyone want to speak in defense of the church treasurer in this matter?" asked the superintendent.

The silence was deafening. After a few seconds, the treasurer jumped up from her seat and stormed out of the church saying, "It'd been better if I had stopped at a bar rather than come with this crazy bunch."

There was a hubbub of whispered voices and a few people even chuckled. Dewey Yale spoke for about ten minutes, explaining the rights and responsibili-ties of the local pastor when suddenly the back door was forcefully yanked open. Bristling with rage, the treasurer's 20-year-old son bolted up the center aisle, shaking his right fist in the air, and uttering vile threats. I was sitting in the sec-ond pew from the front on the left. The boy saw me and yelled in my face, "I'm going to get you for what you did to my mother." He concealed his left hand in his jacket pocket. Some of the men in the church said later they were quite cer-tain that he had a gun in his jacket. Whether he did or not, I do not know.

I said nothing to the boy, but just looked at him. He turned around and as quickly as he came, he was gone. The hall exploded with nervous conversation. No one chuckled. The superintendent asked for order. Some people didn't know who the young man was. I told the members how I had visited him in the hospi-tal just the previous month. He had a ruptured appendix and his mother couldn't tolerate seeing him vomit uncontrollably as he regained consciousness after sur-gery, so I held the pan to his mouth while he regurgitated.

"When he was feeling better," I told the congregation, "I had prayer with him and his mother thanked me for all that I had done for them."

Now he's threatening to kill me, I thought, but didn't say. This incident and others were teaching me that ministry wasn't about serving people because I wanted them to like me. I served Christ by caring for the needs of people I knew were precious to Him.

Would you be surprised to learn that the treasurer was the same lady who had greeted us so rudely at the front door the first Sunday we arrived at that church?

Dewey Yale concluded the meeting. "It's obvious you, the congregation, are in support of your pastor and that he has acted in this difficult situation both within his authority and in the spirit of a pastor. All charges are dismissed."

Lois had stayed home that evening with David and had missed the "big meet-ing." When I told her what had happened, she was genuinely frightened.

"I'm going to be afraid to open the door," she said.

I was so young and so focused on growing the church that I didn't think much about what had happened at the time. Looking back on that evening, if the congregation or Superintendent Yale had waffled in their support of me, it would have meant the end of my ministry. But I was young and strong. I had been through a world war and seen men wounded and die. I knew I could take care of myself. I wasn't afraid of anyone, but it bothered me that Lois was so distressed. When I left the house, she would say to me, "Be on the lookout for that guy."

The treasurer never returned to church while I was the pastor although she kept her membership there. She still attended camp meeting each year. I saw her in Spencerville the following summer. I approached her and calling her by her first name, I said, "I'm sorry for what happened. Is there some way we can be reconciled and put this behind us?"

She gave me that same icy stare that greeted us on the sidewalk that first Sunday.

"There's two sides to every story," she said and walked off in a huff.

The following years when I saw her at camp meeting I always made it a point to say hello, but her animosity toward me never thawed.

33

Graduation

David loved to go to the National Zoo in Washington. When Darlene was about a year old, we took her along in a stroller and spent the day laughing at the monkeys and marveling at the elephants. Another favorite family pastime was experiencing the airplanes at Washington National Airport. In those days you not only could watch the planes, you could hear them and feel them in ways which today would be unthinkable.

It's hard to imagine when today it may take an hour to find a parking spot in the monstrous traffic jams at Reagan International, but in the early 1950s we could park outside the front door in a large traffic circle in the front of the main terminal. Through the front doors, we entered the lobby whose far wall was glass from floor to ceiling. We walked to a door to the left and by depositing a dime in a slot, the door opened to an observation deck. From here we watched passengers board planes on movable stairs rolled to the side of the aircraft. Beyond the parked airplanes, airliners took off and landed on the runway. The largest planes at that time were the TWA Constellation and United DC Six. David and I stood not 100 feet from aircraft as they taxied in and out of the gates. We thrilled to hear the full throttled roar of the engines and struggled to keep our balance in the propellers' blowback. This seems so long ago, in the days before terrorists and personal injury lawyers made such intimate aviation experiences impossible.

Because David was so intrigued with airplanes, we decided to take our first airplane trip to Reading to visit my parents. The plane was a DC3. It was a short flight, probably about an hour, but David soaked it all in, amazed at the clouds and how the whole world suddenly shrunk smaller than the little village at the base of our Christmas tree. My uncle Melvin met us at the airport and drove us to Adamstown where my parents were living temporarily before moving to Ephrata.

Back on the church front, I learned that several ladies from our congregation were having regular prayer sessions about something that was very important to them. As their pastor, I wanted to know how I could help. Expecting news that someone was ill or had died or some other human calamity, I was dumbfounded to discover the subject of these ladies' fervent supplications to the Almighty was (promise me you will not laugh)…Lois' hairstyle.

The Free Methodist Church was a Weslyan-Arminian split-off from mainstream Methodism in 1860. Emphasizing John Wesley's doctrine of entire sanctification, Free Methodism was part of the American holiness movement that taught strict separation from mainstream culture in ways of dress and entertainment. During the first half of the 20th century, many Free Methodists in the pew were more likely to define themselves by what they did not do rather than by what they believed, much to the consternation of church leaders. As proof of one's holiness, Free Methodists didn't drink, didn't smoke, didn't go to movies, didn't buy on Sunday, didn't wear jewelry, and women were expected to wear their hair in a bun centered on the back of the head or a "rat" on which the hair was rolled. Among some stalwarts, Lois' curled coiffure that hung to her shoulders was deemed unacceptable, especially for a pastor's wife.

These dear old ladies were praying that God would convict Lois regarding her modern hairstyle. Lois didn't talk much in church as she was usually busy taking care of David and Darlene (there were no childcare facilities in our little churches). Then one Wednesday night at prayer meeting Lois prayed a deeply earnest and moving prayer. One of the ladies came to Lois after the service and apologized for the prayer group's judgmental attitude based on her hairstyle.

"Anyone who can pray like that won't become a better Christian with a new hairdo," she said. Those ladies were truly penitent and labored faithfully throughout my entire time at that church.

But that little incident was representative of a larger issue that affected not only my denomination but my own philosophy of ministry and vocation. What those ladies did was typical of quite a few Free Methodists before the war, particularly in the northeastern US. Spirituality was defined as separating one's self from what the church considered "worldly" but which most Americans probably accepted as pretty harmless (going to movies, wearing jewelry, and so on). The disciplines that Free Methodists had established for close-knit rural communities in the nineteenth century were being questioned more and more by a new generation of leaders like myself who had not only been to the far reaches of the world, but who had seen real evil in the suffering and the inhumanities of war. The denomination whose only qualification for ministry was a conversion story and an aptitude for public speaking began ordaining college educated men. By the 1950s a new breed of Free Methodist was emerging, one who was first "evangelical" and secondarily committed to the disciplines of holiness. It's not that this new generation wasn't dedicated to the church's founding principles or that we disbelieved or devalued Jesus call to "be holy even as your Father in Heaven is holy," but we knew lifestyle disciplines were the result of a changed life. Introducing people to Christ took priority over whether they went to movies or smoked or drank. Get a person in a right relationship with Christ and many of these lifestyle issues would sort themselves out.

My own situation reflected this new priority and was reinforced by the fact that I had not grown up in the holiness sub-culture. I had feet in two camps—my current church and my family's religious history and experience. Free Methodism had functioned in my life first by introducing me to a personal salvation and only secondarily as a lifestyle discipline.

I was a little different than many of my pastoral peers in that I seemed able to accept people as they were. I didn't see my role as an enforcer of church rules but as an encourager. And to a large extent I think this struggle between ardor and order characterized the struggle of Free Methodism and eventually transformed it. Eventually I would leave Free Methodism because of the narrowness of its vision and the paucity of compassion in the local leadership with whom I would labor. My ministry not only spanned the years of Free Methodism's transformation, but I believe embodied it.

One of the founding tenants of Free Methodism was "freedom of the Holy Spirit," as opposed to formalism and dead liturgy. But this freedom could be misunderstood and abused as I discovered with one of our new converts at East Washington.

Bob became a very enthusiastic Christian and expressed his gratitude to me by giving us a 14-inch floor model television set. David was truly excited with the gift. Not many months later Bob got mixed up with a group of charismatic Christians, and he told me that he had received the gift of tongues. The following week, as I was preaching, Bob stood up and came to the front of the church. He requested time to speak because he had a message from God. I told him that I also had a message from God, and since I was the pastor of the church, I intended to finish my sermon. I asked him to be seated. When he remained standing, Harry Romesburg came forward to escort him back to his pew. Bob was angry and he showed it. I finished my sermon that day, but Bob had completely disrupted the worship service. As the congregation filed out of the church, Bob greeted me by shaking his finger in my face.

"Barnett," he said, "the next time I get a message from God neither you nor Harry Romesburg will be able to stop me."

I said, "Bob, we will see about that."

The following Wednesday night, he came to a prayer meeting. It was our practice to kneel and pray in the pews. Soon after I invited everyone to kneel and pray, I heard Bob begin moaning and groaning. Suddenly I saw him stand and begin pulling and jerking on the end of the pew. He was trying to rip the pew from the floor. Others lifted their heads to witness the bizarre spectacle. Some of the women gasped in fear. Several men joined me in restraining Bob and we had to nearly carry him outside struggling and kicking. He threatened me again as he left, got in his pickup truck, and drove away.

But the incident didn't stop there. A few days later he drove up in front of the parsonage. Fortunately, I was home. I answered the door. He said he had come to take back the television set that he had given us. David could not understand what was happening. As Bob carried the TV out the door, David stood in the living room with tears streaming down his face. Although we could not afford to buy a television set, several days later I purchased a 14-inch table model television from a Dumont television store. David was ecstatic and became a very well behaved child. His mother rewarded good behavior with the privilege of watching TV. Of course, if he was disobedient in any way, he would not be permitted to watch the television. I can see in our own family how the baby boom generation would become so heavily influenced by television.

The four years I was the pastor at East Washington were certainly dramatic, but the conflict and craziness were soon forgotten. We enjoyed our children. David was very attentive to Darlene, who was of a completely different temperament than David. She was shy. I can't imagine Darlene ever telling our neighbor that smoking would send him to hell.

I finally completed my undergraduate studies at the American University. If I had to be completely undistracted, I did my serious study at the Library of Congress near the Capitol building. My major was history and my minor was philosophy. My parents came to the graduation exercises. My father and mother were so proud of me since I was the first member of my family to earn a college degree. Lois' parents babysat David and Darlene.

It came as a complete surprise at our 1953 annual conference when we learned I was appointed to my third church in Spencerville, Maryland. Some people thought it strange to send a city pastor to a country church. Spencerville was an older and larger congregation. The church building was being renovated, which I knew would mean a lot of extra janitorial work for me.

Once again I had to say goodbye to many Christian friends and converts who had never known another pastor. The children I had baptized and who had learned to walk and talk would grow up without me. When I visited the Phalens at their home, little Gail often answered the door. When she saw me at the door, she called to her mother, "Mom, it's Jesus, and he wants to come to see us."

34

Spencerville

Spencerville is now a suburb of Washington DC, but when our family moved there in 1953 it was farm country. The parsonage was a large four-bedroom house built before World War I. The rooms were spacious with large windows. With 1-1/2 baths, a large basement and attic, a walk-in pantry attached to the kitchen, we felt like we had moved into a mansion after living in the tiny parsonage in Washington. There was a big front yard, spacious back yard, a double car garage in the rear of the property, and a large garden plot that measured 80 feet by 80 feet. One of our members who owned a large farm supplied me with fertilizer in the spring before plowing. Someone from the church plowed and disked the garden for me. A teenager in our youth group brought a large water tank so I could spray insecticide on my crops and also water them in the dry summertime. I was so happy that at last I would be able to practice all I had learned about gardening from my father.

The house had been partially remodeled seven years previously. The plan had called for installing hard wood flooring, but for some reason that part of the project had never been completed. The wood flooring was stacked in the garage, taking up the space of a second car. Soon after we moved in, I let it be known that I wanted to finish the flooring project. A retired carpenter volunteered to help me install the oak flooring. It was a long, hard back-bending job. We covered the entire first floor, the front hallway and stairs to the second floor, and the hallway connecting the bedrooms upstairs. I could not work on this project every day because I had to write sermons, mow the lawn at church and the parsonage, visit sick people in hospitals, and supervise various work projects at the church.

The church had also been through a major remodeling project. The original wooden structure had been moved about 75 feet back from the highway and received a new brick exterior and steeple. Since much of the work on the church was performed by volunteer labor, Saturday was the big day when workers might be at the church all day long. After the last person left, Lois and I dusted and swept the sanctuary and the Sunday school rooms to make them ready for services the next morning. Sometimes we wouldn't finish until nine or ten o'clock on Saturday night. There weren't many volunteers who wanted to help with the mundane cleaning. Many times I would get home late and have to cut a stencil and mimeograph the church bulletin. Somehow we managed to do all that was required. We considered it part of the Lord's work and somebody had to do it. By the end of the first year all the remodeling work was completed.

The 1950s was a great time to be a preacher. Most people in the community went to church and most attended Sunday school as well. I taught an adult Sunday school class with an enrollment of 70 adults with an average attendance of nearly 50 people. Everybody appeared to be interested in studying the Bible. Free Methodist Churches sponsored Bible quiz teams for young people. The national church would announce the book for the year's Bible Quiz. It wasn't unusual for some team members to memorize entire books of the Bible. Contests were held at the annual summer camp meeting with the winner of the conference going on to compete at the national Bible quiz finals in Winona Lake, where the Free Methodist Church had its world headquarters. Bible Quizzes consisted of a quiz master who read questions. Each team was made up of three contestants with one alternate. The competition was to see who could get off their chair first to answer the question. Questions had point values based on difficulty and whoever scored the most points won. Jump judges determined who had been the first contestant to get off their chair. Eventually someone built an electrical contraption with switches that ran from pads on the contestant's chairs to a box with lights. The lights eliminated all doubt as to who had jumped first, second, third, and so on. It was quite exciting to see the teens as they developed finely tuned moves to tease that switch to trigger at just the moment the quizmaster finished asking the question. Our Spencerville team won conference Bible Quiz Challenges and went on to participate in national competition three or four times. David was on all of those teams; his future wife, Julie, was on the team from Columbus, Ohio.

We reported steady growth in attendance and church membership every year in Spencerville. We soon ran out of room to put the people. After a couple of years I started to promote an expanded building program. My enthusiasm for such a project was not matched by the older generation in my congregation. So year after year we squeezed more and more people into our small church like college students at the time competed to stuff people into phone booths and Volkswagens. It was not uncommon to have adults standing around the back and sides of the sanctuary for Sunday morning worship services.

When new people joined the church membership, the old guard was reluctant to share positions of leadership. Long-time members were delighted to see many new people they could enlist to do the work, but they were reluctant to include them in leadership positions. I was a more experienced pastor by this time and instead of forcing the issue as I might have done as a younger man, I accepted the challenge to help everybody understand each other and, with God's help and a great deal of patience, we managed to avoid the deeply divisive conflicts that had rocked my previous congregations.

Left to right: David, Clarence, Lois, Darlene at Spencerville, 1960

As the suburbs expanded from Washington, I had to manage the different expectations and values of both city people and country people. Take, for example, the issue of air conditioning. Many of the older members were farmers who didn't have air conditioning in their homes, and they saw no reason to have it in the church. Every year city folks expressed a desire to install a cooling system in the church and every year the long-tenured church board members would vote it down. Some summer evenings it was too hot to conduct the service in the church, so I would take the service outdoors on the front lawn under a large shade tree.

On one of those summer evenings, three young men saw our improvised open-air gathering, stopped their car by the road, and joined our congregation. After the service I invited them to the parsonage to enjoy some fresh watermelon. They told me they were students from a local Bible College. Before we had finished eating half of that cool, sweet watermelon, these young men started critiquing my sermon and charging me with an incorrect interpretation of the Scripture. They questioned me by asking if I believed in eternal security. I recognized the buzzwords of a different theological tradition than mine, and I knew no amount of theological conversation was likely to persuade either of us. So, I told these young men that I didn't think this was a good time or the appropriate place for a theological debate. I excused David and Darlene from the table as soon as they finished their watermelon.

"I think it's pretty rude for you to come to my house, eat my watermelon, and criticize me in front of my family," I said. "Your zeal for a theological position has ruined what might have been a pleasant evening."

I stood up and moved to the door as a clue that our fellowship was at an end. They got the message, thanked us for the watermelon, and left.

Lots of young adults came to our church and soon every Sunday school classroom was bursting at the seams with children. Perhaps the biggest event of the year was the annual Christmas program when every child was given some little verse to recite or part to play in the worship service. When Darlene was four years old she was given her first recitation. Lois directed the program every year. Darlene was a very shy little girl and did not want to get up in front of a whole auditorium of people. But her mother would hear none of that. Darlene looked palpably nervous when her turn came and she walked to the center of the platform. She took her spot and, like a little trooper, recited: "I'll do my best, the best I can, to live for Jesus, dairy show." She froze realizing she had gotten her words mixed up. Lois told her to start all over, "I'll do my best, the best I can, to live for Jesus every day; then Jesus will be proud of me, and God will love me too." A big smile of relief broke across her face as she walked off the stage.

How those children loved to sing, songs like, "Happy All the Time," "I have the joy, joy, joy, joy, down in my heart," or "Come into my heart, Lord Jesus." Frequently I would be very bold by asking the children for a selection. If a child wanted to sing, "Davy Crockett, King of the Wild Frontier" or "It's Howdy Doody Time," we would sing those songs to the delight of all the youngsters. It was great fun for me to teach the children many new songs.

One hot summer day I was trimming the long hedgerows at the church. A lady drove a big black Cadillac into the driveway and stopped near where I was working.

"Excuse me," she said. I turned off my electric hedge trimmer, tipped back my large straw hat, and walked around the hedge and came to the driver's side of the car.

"Do you do odd jobs?" she asked.

"Yes, ma'am," I replied.

"Well, you know, I see you cutting the lawn here and I really appreciate how nice and straight you've cut those hedges," she said. "I'm looking for a gardener to work for me and I'll pay you well."

As she talked, I was thinking how can I tell this lady that I'm the minister of this church? At that moment I certainly didn't look like a minister. While I was curious to ask what she was willing to pay her gardener, I thought it best to tell her the truth.

"You see ma'am, I'm the minister of this church," I said.

"Oh, I'm so sorry," she apologized with a surprised look on her face.

I'm sure in her world there was no way a minister should be cutting hedges.

35

Black and White

The longer one attends a particular church the greater the tendency to sit in the same pew year after year. In the eighteenth century churches capitalized on this strong sense of place by renting pews. This was one of the practices that led to the creation of the Free Methodist Church in 1860. The founders believed in free church pews, freedom of the spirit in worship services (as opposed to rote liturgy), and freedom from slavery, hence the name Free Methodist Church. The farmers in my congregation at Spencerville probably did not know that history, but they knew where they liked to sit in their home church.

One old fellow was a pig farmer who shuttled up the aisle every week to find his regular place at the end of the sixth pew on the left side of the auditorium. Most members knew not to sit there, so it was usually a visitor who would get a rather rude surprise if they happened to arrive before the old gentleman. He would slide into the pew, pretending he didn't see the person already seated there. More than once I watched him land in some unsuspecting person's lap.

Personally, I never realized how hard church pews were until I retired in 1989 and began attending Trinity United Methodist Church in Annapolis, Maryland where, yes, I sit in the same pew every week. However, I don't recall ever sitting in anyone's lap.

We made frequent short trips to my parents' home in the summertime. My brothers, Earl and Eddie, worked with my father. In 1959 he built a new home in Ephrata and opened a new, larger shop out on the main highway at the intersection of Routes 222 and 322. His company was called Clarence H. Barnett & Son. He named his second company after an 18th century religious building across the highway from his new shop called the Cloister. Cloister Services focused on residential plumbing work while the first company specialized in large commercial jobs such as schools, large factories, and nursing homes. My father was also an agent for a swimming pool manufacturer so they installed a swimming pool in the backyard of their home. David and Darlene enjoyed splashing around in the pool. Mom and Dad were always glad to see us. All the children, with the exception of my kid sister Edna who was in Oregon, lived nearby so when we showed up for a visit my brothers and sisters came to see us.

Every year I had a beautiful large garden. I set in telephone-size poles at either end of the garden from which I stretched heavy wire to support large plants. At harvest time I had four rows of plants eight feet high filled with lima beans. We enjoyed eating fresh vegetables all summer long and what we couldn't eat we kept frozen in the freezer. We canned tomatoes and string beans to keep us for the entire winter. If I had more lima beans than I could use, I took them to one of our church members who operated a roadside stand. Lima beans sold for five dollars a bushel and sometimes I would have three or four bushels to give him. When I gave my annual report at the conference, I generally concluded my report by saying, "I had many crops in my garden and I requested to return in order to harvest those crops." For eight years the bishop honored that request.

After the church remodeling project was completed, everything looked great except for a black drape that hung behind the pulpit. It had probably been given as a memorial gift but nobody could remember who purchased it. The black drapery looked terrible. After a funeral service one day, Mr. Pumphrey told me he wanted to buy a new drapery. If there was a death in our congregation, most members called on Pumphery's Funeral Home in Silver Spring, Maryland.

"What color would you like?" Mr. Pumphrey asked.

"What color would you suggest?" I asked, not confident in my interior decorating skills.

"It's your call, pastor."

"What do you think of gold?" I asked.

He told me that he would send an interior decorator to get the measurements and to decide on the material. I later told the church board that the matter was in the hands of an interior decorator. If I would have called a board meeting to discuss the matter, it would have taken three hours and probably no one would have agreed on the color or the material. After the gold drapery was installed I heard no negative responses.

Mr. Pumphrey also supplied the church with hand fans printed with religious pictures and a discreet ad for the funeral home on the front of the fan. Every Christmas season Mr. Pumphrey gave beautiful gifts to all the ministers in the area.

When children reached the fourth grade, they could enroll in an instrumental musical program in elementary school. David wanted to play the trumpet. After he proved that he could blow the trumpet, he was given a loaner trumpet to use in the school. We could not afford to purchase an instrument. One day I received a call to hold a seven-day revival service at an Evangelical Congregational Church in Reamstown, Pennsylvania, where my brother Earl and his wife, Berneatha, attended. The date was arranged, and I went to Earl's home to stay for the week. We had good services and the church paid me $95 for preaching. We decided that we would use the extra money to buy a trumpet for David and hoped that $95 would cover most of the cost. We went to a music store in Wheaton, Maryland where the clerk showed us a number of trumpets. When we found one we liked and asked how much it cost, it turned out to be exactly ninety-five dollars.

David was a happy, aspiring musician. He blew that trumpet throughout our large house and progressed rapidly. Soon he was a good player. The music teacher made rounds to a number of elementary schools, so by the time the students reached junior high school they could play well.

When Darlene reached the fourth grade she started private piano lessons with Lois' Aunt Naomi Diddle who lived in Rockville, Maryland. Soon David was taking lessons as well. We already had a piano where Darlene and David could play whenever they desired. Lois took the children for lessons for three years.

Because Spencerville was a rural area, David and Darlene had no playmates close by. They learned to entertain themselves by making their own games. While waiting for Darlene to finish her piano lesson, David learned from Naomi's son, Freddie, how to make spinner games with a piece of plywood, nails, and safety pins. David created his own baseball board game with four or five spinners (safety pins). Around each spinner would be various blocks indicating balls and strikes, outs, home runs, triples, doubles, singles, foul balls, and errors. David constructed a whole league of teams. He played the role of an announcer on radio. If you listened to him you would swear that he was broadcasting a real game. There seemed to be no limit to his imagination.

Darlene played more quietly, but if I walked by her room I could hear her carrying on lively conversations with her dolls. I think she had every doll that had ever been given to her as a child. Once I was the featured speaker at a Sunday School Convention for Free Methodists from Oil City, Pittsburgh, and the Maryland-Virginia Conferences. The meeting was scheduled over several days so I stayed in the home of a very prominent family in Oil City. When my hostess learned that I had a daughter who loved dolls, she gave me a large life-like doll about 30 inches tall. Darlene treasured that doll. She would sit and talk to it for hours.

Darlene and David played well together most of the time, but if David teased her or disturbed her meticulously arranged toys, she became anything but shy.

One Sunday evening we were invited to the home of some church members following Sunday services. David was teasing her and Darlene responded by hitting him on the head with a baseball bat leaving a large black and blue knot David says is still there to this day.

When David entered junior high school, he stopped taking piano lessons and began organ lessons. He had an excellent teacher, Marvin Fuel, who came to the church for a thirty-minute session every other week. Mr. Fuel really inspired David who practiced for hours and hours at a time. He went to the church to play the Hammond organ after Sunday lunch and wouldn't stop until I went around 5 p.m. to tell him it was time for supper. It wasn't long before he could play better than the two church organists. One of our organists told me she did not play hymns written in sharps.

In a year or two David taught me many solos that I have sung for many years. His teacher had a friend who wanted to sell his organ. He believed David had real gifts and thought David needed a better instrument to challenge him. The only problem was the man wanted thousands of dollars for his instrument.

Both David and Darlene were very musical. In high school David volunteered to learn the baritone horn, which he played until his senior year when he took up the tuba. He took a class in pipe organ at Indiana University. Darlene also played the piano and organ. Not only did David and Darlene accompany my singing at church, but many evenings our family would sing songs around the piano or the organ. It is impossible for me to express how very proud I am to have musically talented son and daughter.

Naturally I had hoped that David would follow in my footsteps and show an aptitude for playing baseball. When he was in the fifth grade, I signed him up to play in little league. He enjoyed wearing the red and white Wildcats uniform more than he liked actually playing the game. He played right field. David was smaller than most the boys in his class. He confided in me that he was afraid of being hit by the ball when he came to bat.

"Do you see how big that 12-year-old pitcher is there on that mound?" he said.

"Don't be afraid to swing at the balls over the plate. Just keep your eye on the ball," I coached.

"I hope I walk," he said. "That's the only way I'll get on base."

David had a perfect batting record—he never got a hit, but he did walk several times. We played catch in our backyard. I threw curve balls so he could see how the ball breaks. I didn't do that very long, however. I threw a curve; the ball glanced off David's glove and hit him on the cheek resulting in a black eye. His mother scolded me for doing such a stupid thing. David played only one year in the little league. He was more comfortable playing softball where he was an average player. Baseball was not a big thing with him like it was with his father.

Our church had a softball team that played almost weekly against other church teams in our community. For some reason the retired carpenter who helped me lay that hardwood floor in the parsonage thought playing softball was sinful. As he was leaving church one Sunday he said, "If you don't quit playing softball, I'm going to leave the church."

I said, "Now, Mr. Boswell, you don't want to do that. I'm just having fun playing with the young people of the church. I don't see anything sinful about that".

"You better quit or I'm leaving," he insisted.

Well, I didn't quit and he left. I learned that he had begun attending a Brethren Church, and it so happened that the first week he attended there, they played a softball game with our team. I would stop by his house occasionally to let him know that I still loved him as a Christian brother. I don't recall that he ever returned to worship as long as I was the pastor. I hated to see him leave our fellowship over something I considered so trivial.

One evening I was approached by several adults who were the parents of small children. They wanted to talk with me about a problem that was developing outside the church building on Sunday nights. It seems David, who was probably ten years old, was telling scary stories to the children while the parents visited in the church.

"It's nice that David entertains them," they said, "but he's frightening them so badly they can't get to sleep."

About the same time his fifth-grade teacher called Lois to inform her that David was clowning around too much in class. Lois told the teacher that she would come and sit in the class and that would take care of the problem. The teacher never had to call again. Apparently David got the message.

When Darlene was in the sixth grade, she was made patrol guard on the school bus. She was given a special shoulder and waist belt to designate her authority. She was careful to be sure it was safe for children to board and exit the bus. One day she came home crying because an African-American girl who lived on Batson Road accused Darlene of being partial to white children. Darlene was very upset because she had never shown any partiality.

These were the early days of racial integration in the schools. We had many problems with race relations in the high school. The principal called area ministers to the school one day and pleaded for our help in trying to reconcile the races. He suggested that we discuss the issue in Sunday school classes and that we would preach against bigotry in our services.

We had no African-American families in our church. At that time they were colloquially referred to as "coloreds" and the more politically correct, socially acceptable term of respect was "Negroes." One Sunday six African-American adults visited our church. They all sat together in the last church pew. I saw them, went to where they were sitting, introduced myself, shook their hand, and welcomed them to our services. This must have been an unprecedented act because our members were shocked to see them there. As they entered the church, they turned to look back over their shoulders at the visitors and then began speaking to each other in agitated whispers.

"What are they doing here?" one man asked me.

I said, "I'll tell you later." At that time many black leaders were encouraging their people to visit white churches to learn how they would be received. I'm sorry to say that most people in my congregation were not happy to see them in their church. We managed to be civil during that service, but most were glad they did not return.

About the same time David had befriended an African-American boy who lived about a half-mile away. He invited Eliot to get off the school bus at our house and play after school. Later, after I drove Eliot home, I had a tough task of trying to explain to David why he should not invite Eliot to stay and play another time. The church members would be shocked to see Eliot in our front yard and they would not hesitate to make trouble about it. It was difficult to know how to respond to the deeply entrenched racial divides that existed in that part of the country in the late 1950s and early 1960s.

On a lighter note, Darlene attended an after-school meeting of the Loyal Temperance League, a program to teach children the dangers of alcohol sponsored by the Women's Christian Temperance Union. The children made crafts and sang songs. One of the choruses was "We will turn down our glasses when pours the red wine." I had started wearing eyeglasses about this time. I came to supper table wearing my new spectacles. Darlene looked at me and said, "Daddy, turn down your glasses."

That was how it was with trying to change people's thinking on race. They heard the biblical words that "in Christ there is no male or female, slave or free," but they had a hard time understanding what the message was really about.

36

Expanded Ministry

In the Spencerville congregation we had a distinguished old man who was a floor-walker at the Woodward and Lothrop department store in Washington, DC. He was a very friendly man who could talk a mile a minute. The congregation elected him as "class leader," a position which meant that he led the midweek prayer and testimony meeting. He had people sing several hymns, read the Scripture lesson, and then he talked and talked and talked some more. About ten minutes before the end of hour-long meeting, he would look at his watch and then say, "Ok, folks, let's have some popcorn testimonies," meaning he wanted everyone to give a short statement regarding their spiritual condition. J. W. Ayres was a good man filled with the joy of Christ.

David and Darlene were always happy to discover that I had a wedding scheduled at the church because it meant we would be privileged to eat out a few days later. Going to a restaurant was very special for our family. We might go to the Hot Shoppe restaurant either in Bethesda or in Silver Spring. We could only afford the luxury of eating out if I received extra money. Sometimes the bride or groom would call the parsonage.

"May we stop by the parsonage and get married tonight," they would ask. There was no premarital counseling in those days. Our living room was pretty much off limits to the kids because we had to keep it presentable for a marriage at a moments notice. When Darlene was little, she reminded us, "We cannot eat in the divving room." Weddings in the parsonage usually netted a smaller honorarium, which meant the family went to McDonalds instead of the Hot Shoppe.

Our family budget was very tight. We tried extremely hard not to complain about money within earshot of the children, so David and Darlene didn't realize that we were living on every penny I made. We seldom had money for anything extra, but we always had enough for what we really needed. During our later years in the ministry our financial situation improved considerably. But there was a saying that too many pastors reported hearing their members pray, "Lord, keep our preacher humble and we'll keep him poor."

I was kept very busy with a growing Sunday school and church. One of the big mistakes I made in my early ministry was thinking a church could not go forward unless I was pushing it. Consequently we had not taken a vacation in five years. The only Sunday I had missed was the one when I held a revival service at my brother's church in Pennsylvania. I had to have my tonsils out. I was careful to schedule my operation on Mondays so I could be in church for Sunday. I didn't sing that Sunday. Later I had surgery for the removal of an infected appendix. I couldn't stand up straight the following Sunday, but I was there.

Not long after that, the Sunday School Superintendent, Beulah Moore, called me to the front of the congregation. She said the board had voted and wanted me to make pastoral visits on our members who spent the winter months in Florida. She handed me an envelope with more than enough cash to cover our two-week sabbatical. We enjoyed that time off so much and thereafter took a vacation every year.

We were honored to have a very distinguished medical doctor in our community. During his medical practice that spanned more than fifty years, he had founded Montgomery General Hospital in Olney, Maryland. Dr. Byrd was surely good to our family. He never charged us a penny for all his services including surgeries in the hospital. He made frequent house calls when our children were ill. He was a personal confidant to me. One day he told me that my church members healed well. I told him it was because they lived right and they also died well.

"You're right," he said with a smile.

While I was the Pastor at the Spencerville church, I was also the conference Sunday School Secretary. I promoted the work of the Sunday Schools in the thirteen churches in our conference. I trained Sunday school teachers, and was a resource for ideas and programs to advance church attendance and to improve church buildings. In my annual report, I gave special recognition to churches that were growing. Every year I nominated the Conference Sunday School Teacher of the Year. The Spencerville Church had the largest Sunday school in the conference. Churches reported to me every month so I knew what was happening in all of the churches. My work as Sunday School Secretary came to the attention of the denominational General Sunday School Secretary, Royal Nelson. He contacted me in 1962 and asked me to pray about coming to the church's world headquarters in Winona Lake, Indiana, to be his assistant and to edit the Sunday school monthly magazine for the entire denomination. I was completely surprised because I had never given a thought to a national ministry. The job included giving Sunday school workshops and speaking at annual conferences; in short, doing all the things I was doing in my little conference around the United States.

As flattered as I was to be recognized and offered the position, I had a tough time making the decision. I knew I was called to be a pastor, and the thought of leaving pastoral ministry to become a headquarters administrator was complex and difficult. David was entering high school and Darlene was beginning junior high, so if ever there was time to make a move, as far as my family was concerned, this was about as good as the timing would get.

I went to Indiana and talked with Reverend Nelson as well as several other church leaders who encouraged me to make the move, citing it would give me an expanded ministry. I prayed about it often, but still could not get a sense of peace of about what I should do. I wondered how Abraham could pack up his family and his belongings and just set off trusting God. I also was being called to leave my home, but I wasn't sure if it was God calling. After several months of this agony, I placed the matter in God's hands, called Reverend Nelson, and told him I would accept the offer to be his assistant.

No sooner had I hung up the phone, when I was flooded with doubts and anxiety. I thought about all I would be leaving behind—a lovely large house, a wonderful congregation, a great garden, nearby family relatives, and a host of friends both personal and professional throughout the Maryland-Virginia Conference. I knew what I had, but it was the lure of what lay ahead that moved me to say "yes." I dreaded having to tell the people with whom I had labored for nine years that I was leaving.

But two weeks before annual conference I told the people in my congregation that I was leaving to accept the invitation to work at headquarters. Of course, they were shocked and very sad to learn the news. One of my dearest members felt so betrayed by my leaving that he broke off our friendship. It wasn't until several years later that our close friendship was restored. Sensing my pain, some members encouraged me to write and tell the people at headquarters that I changed my mind, but there was really no way I could do that.

I thought those two weeks would never pass. We made arrangements to rent a U-Haul truck and with the help of Lois' brother, Jack, we packed up all our belongings and furniture except our large freezer. We had already filled the truck and had to rent a trailer to get all of our stuff ready to move. As our little caravan of cars and trucks pulled out of the driveway of our home in Spencerville, we were all very silent. It was the end of an era and another was beginning far to the west.

37

Winona Lake

Before leaving Spencerville, I had made arrangements with a realtor in Indiana to rent a home on what was known as The Island in Winona Lake. The drive to Indiana took twelve long hours. David rode with me in the U-Haul and Darlene traveled in the car, which Lois drove. As we pulled into Winona Lake, we couldn't wait to unpack the beds and get a good night's rest. When we pulled up outside the rental house, imagine my surprise to find people living in it. We double-checked the address to be sure we were at the right place. We had not made a mistake, although it was apparent someone had. In all the times Lois and I had moved during the war and afterwards in college and in my church work, this was the first time we had arrived in a new place and didn't know where to go.

I found a telephone and contacted the realtor. She gave me a long cock-and-bull explanation of a communication mix-up. Then she informed me that her brother who was an officer at the headquarters just so happened to have recently completed building a house in town. She gave me his number and after a few phone calls, we made arrangements to move into his house temporarily. In a few days we finished unpacking the truck and the trailer. Our relocation crisis was over and now we would adjust to the idea of being Hoosiers.

Since the 1920s, Winona Lake had become a more or less permanent Christian campground. The famous Billy Sunday made his home there and had preached in the large wooden tabernacle named for the baseball player turned evangelist. Homer Rodeheaver established his gospel music publishing house there. In addition to the Free Methodist Church, many other groups met in Winona Lake including Youth for Christ, Jews for Jesus, and many missionary organizations. Of course, most of the activity took place in the summer. During the brutal northern Indiana winters, the village was left pretty much to the locals.

The Free Methodist Headquarters building was located at the top of the 9th Street hill. A long tree-lined drive made a hairpin turn at the front steps of the stately building that had once been a college but which had been the church's administrative offices and publishing house since the 1930s. There I met Reverend Nelson, who welcomed me warmly. I was shown my office down the hall to the left. I was told where I could find materials I needed and immediately I started work on the next issue of The Sunday School Journal.

Lois worked as a proofreader for all our publications. We registered David and Darlene for school in nearby Warsaw, changed our automobile license plates, got Indiana driving licenses, and did the million and one other things that are necessary when taking up residence in a new state.

The Winona Lake Free Methodist Church was large and had a great Sunday school program and dynamic youth organizations. We made friends with the fellow workers at headquarters who attended there. I was familiar with the names of these people; Myron F. Boyd, the voice of the denomination's international radio program and later bishop, Lloyd Knox, the church's publisher, Don Joy, a wonderful writer and thinker, Bishop Fairburn, a great chronicler of the church's history, Robert MacDowell, the young, exciting head of Free Methodist Youth, Clyde VanValen, Franklin Todd, John Benson, and so many other leaders in the church became our friends. It was a rich environment of theological ideas, creativity, and, for the most part, exceptionally competent people.

Winona was only one of three lakes in Warsaw. The waters teemed with bass and bluegill. Soon after we arrived in Winona Lake, I bought a 16-foot rowboat with a one and a half horsepower Johnson motor, which was excellent for trolling for fish. Darlene was a good fishing partner; however, she didn't like getting her hands dirty so she would never bait the hook or take the fish off the line. But she enjoyed riding slowly along the lake, trailing our lures from the back of the boat. We caught many small-mouth bass weighing between one and two pounds. We ate a lot of fish at suppertime in our house.

Once I went fishing with Lois' brother, Jack, who had come to visit us. I caught a large gar fish which I landed in the boat. Nearly a third of the length of that fish was its head. Its eight-inch snout was filled with razor-sharp teeth. Inside our rowboat, the fish thrashed and snapped its jaws wildly. Our arms and legs were flying all over the place trying to keep from being bitten by this large fish. Finally, Jack lifted one of the oars from its place and hit the fish on the head, stunning it so that I could cut the line. We took the gar fish home to show the family and then discarded it.

Lois went out with me in the boat sometimes. While I fished, she worked crossword puzzles. She never took a line.

The small motor worked fine, but one day I was fishing at the far eastern side of the lake when a storm came up suddenly. I headed for my dock in the canal that connected the two ends of the c-shaped lake (and which created The Island). When I rounded the point near the seminary camp (what is today the city beach), the wind hit my little rowboat head-on full-force. Sitting up in the boat, I was acting like a sail and the wind was pushing me back, preventing me from making much headway. I revved the little motor to full throttle, and I leaned down in the boat. Wind-whipped waves were breaking into the boat. I hung on and hoped I wouldn't be swamped. Finally the wind slackened and slowly I made my way into the canal and to the dock. I was soaking wet, but none the worse for wear.

That dock reminds me of one of our first trips to Winona Lake for the denomination's quadrennial General Conference. Darlene was about five years old and we had rented a cottage across the street from the dock where I tied up my rowboat. It must have been after a Sunday service because the family was all dressed up. We were walking back to the cottage when Darlene decided she would walk out on the little dock to peer down into the water of the canal. She lost her balance and tumbled off the end of the dock into about three feet of green water filled with seaweed. We ran to the dock to fish her out of the canal. She floated to the surface with her eyes wide open, her pretty dress and hair draped with seaweed. I pulled her out of the water and quickly got her to the house and a shower. It was a terrible moment, but in the years that followed, the episode provided the family with one of its great stories of tragedy turned to joy. David regaled anyone who would listen with the story of Darlene emerging from the clutches of the deep, wide-eyed and draped with seaweed.

After school started in September, we got into a pleasant routine. It wasn't long before we all discovered we were pretty happy in Indiana. We had come a long way from that first day when I was so doubtful that I had made the right move.

There were only two drawbacks. One, we were more than 600 miles from our extended families in Maryland and Pennsylvania. Two, I missed being a pastor where I had close contact with many people every week. I really missed making hospital visits and conducting funerals. I missed preaching two times every Sunday. After I got settled into the new job, I began accepting teaching and preaching assignments in district and conference meetings. I soon learned that my new position required that I travel throughout the country and Canada. If my speaking engagements were more than 150 miles away from home, I took a train from Warsaw to Chicago and then flew from O'Hare Field to the destination. I had one or two trips every month.

After several months we relocated to another house on The Island in Winona. It was closer to headquarters and to the church. The house had a huge living room and dining room, which was its most attractive feature. The rest of the house was little more than a winterized camp meeting cabin and left something to be desired (heat usually).

About that same time I purchased a lot on 12th Street where we planned to build a new home. Lois' father and mother came to visit us and together we cut down a large tree in preparation for the construction. We built a modest three-bedroom house with a full basement. We moved in very close to our first anniversary of landing in Winona Lake. We had outstanding neighbors: Bishop Walter Kendall, Mission Secretary, Byron Lamson, and church treasurer Alfred Hill.

It was the house on the north side of our lot that almost made us wonder if once again we had done the right thing. Shortly after I purchased the lot but before the house was finished, the lady who lived in the pretty brick bungalow was found murdered in her garage. As you might imagine, there weren't many murders in the religious village of Winona Lake. Mrs. Bolinger worked at the FM publishing house, which was right across the street. When she didn't show up for work that morning, her boss went to check on her. He knocked on her front door. When she didn't answer, he looked in the windows of her garage door to see if her car was there. That's when he saw her sprawled on the concrete floor in her bathrobe, lying in a pool of blood. She had been stabbed repeatedly. The horror of that sight was surpassed only by the agony of learning several days later that it had been his son who murdered Mrs. Bolinger in a failed robbery attempt.

For a long time, the little red brick house on 12th and College Avenue was known as the murder house. But by the time our place next door was finished, life had returned to normal.

As I traveled around the country visiting churches it didn't take me long to learn why so many FM churches were small. Here's one typical example. I was in Minneapolis, Minnesota to speak at the local church. The pastor met me at the airport. On the way to his house I inquired about how things were going at his church.

"Things are going well," he said.

"How long have you been the pastor here?" I asked.

"I'm starting my sixth year," he replied.

When I entered the church that evening for our service, I noticed the Sunday school register where worship and Sunday school attendance was posted. The previous week he saw 26 people attend Sunday school. So, here was a handsome, middle-aged preacher who thought having 26 people in Sunday school qualified as things going well. I couldn't believe it.

When I was in Washington, a young man in my congregation told me he believed God was calling him into the ministry.

"Pastor, I don't want a large church," he told me. "I'll be very happy with a small congregation." Maybe he thought he was being humble.

"Dream, man, dream!" I said.

I had gone to small churches, but I never wanted a church I pastored to remain small. If a church I pastored for six years had only 26 people in Sunday School, I would have considered my work there a failure. But I found the attitude of that Minneapolis pastor in every conference of the denomination. Years later when I could have been elected Conference Superintendent, I declined the office. Actually, the truth is I "chickened out" because I could not imagine what I would do with such pastors if I were their superintendent.

I learned an important lesson in the process of building a home. Every day I would stop by and carefully note the progress that was made in the building project. It was exciting to see the house nearing completion. Finally the day came when the realtor handed me the keys and said, "It's yours." Suddenly I didn't feel as excited as I did several days earlier, anticipating this day. So the lesson I learned is there's usually more joy in anticipating something then there is in actually receiving it.

I always wanted to have a birch tree in my yard, so I bought one and planted it in my new front yard. Whenever I traveled to a different state, I looked for a rock to place in the flower beds in the front of our house. I looked for rocks in mountain streams or on a lakeshore.

We wanted a full-size basement not only for the storage space, but also as a shelter during a tornado warning. Springtime in Indiana is notorious for tornadoes. It seemed we would have a tornado scare every time I was away on a trip. David was in college, so when the skies turned that awful greenish black and winds grew suddenly still, Darlene and her mother would go to the southwest corner of the basement and huddle in the corner. Lois was terrified of the storms. Darlene would put up a brave front to help calm her mother, but all the while Lois knew that Darlene was just as frightened as she was. Once a tornado ripped off the treetops in our yard but none ever touched down in our community, although one did touch down about six miles from our house.

The most challenging part of my new work was writing the monthly editorial for the Sunday School Journal and meeting press deadlines, which were as solid as the Rock of Gibraltar. I wanted to provide helpful and inspirational articles for Sunday school superintendents and teachers in 1,200 Sunday schools across the United States and Canada.

I developed a Sunday school program called "Focus" that helped churches address five areas for a growing Sunday school. Each quarter pastors were requested to send in a report on these five action items. Number one was evangelism. In this section we shared ideas for Sunday school outreach and growth. The second Focus was Growth. We asked pastors across the US and Canada to send us their quarterly average attendance in both the Sunday school and morning worship. Focus number three was Teacher Training where we stressed the importance of continuing education for Sunday school teachers. Our department created a certification program that involved completing work on five books on the subject of Christian education. Focus number four was Individual Attention. We stressed the importance of having a personal knowledge of all of the students in one's class and finding ways to give them recognition. I wanted to remind teachers that we teach students and not lessons in our classes. Focus number five was General Improvements. Churches earned points in the program if they upgraded their Sunday school or church facility.

Every quarter we published the 25 leading Sunday schools across the denomination. We asked people to send us success stories, which we printed in the Journal. Sometimes I used articles submitted to us from freelance writers who received a small price for the material. But most of the articles were written by Reverend Nelson and me. I worked with Sunday school leaders from other denominations to develop enlargement campaigns.

38

Road Warrior

My boss, Royal Nelson, resigned to return to California where he was elected conference superintendent. After serving as his assistant for two years, I was promoted to the office of General Sunday School Secretary. Now I had to find an assistant. I called Reverend Philip Myette from New York to come to headquarters. He accepted the offer and with his wife Lois came to Winona Lake about a month later.

Whenever we had a mailing to all of our churches, David and Darlene helped us stuff envelopes and prepare the letters for mailing. David used to get quite a kick out of the strange names on our mailing lists.

David and Darlene did well in school. David was active in speech tournaments and always had a part in the class plays. While he continued to play in the band, he also joined the choral music program. Darlene, too, was active in her school's choir. One day Miss Voiral, the choir teacher at Warsaw High School, called Lois to tell us that David had signed up for speech, band, and chorus and students were only supposed to be in two classes. The concern was that extra-curricular activities could impact the student's grades. But David was allowed to participate in all three programs. I might have been the General Sunday School Secretary, but I think more people knew me as Dave Barnett's father.

In my new assignment, I was expected to spend more time traveling throughout the denomination. In addition to my work with Free Methodist Sunday Schools, I assumed a key leadership position in The National Sunday School Association, which reached its zenith during the 1960s. The National Sunday School Association was made up of 40 denominations. The NSSA convention lasted three or four days and brought together 6,000 to 8,000 teachers and Sunday school leaders together from all around the country. They came to attend workshops and hear inspirational messages. I was the secretary of the executive committee of the National Sunday School Association for several years. I also served on a commission of that organization made up of all the denominational

Sunday school secretaries. We held an annual meeting where we planned programs and published books for the use in the member denominations throughout the country. All of these responsibilities meant that I was away from home nearly half of the time for about four years. Often I would be away only over a weekend, but occasionally I would be gone the entire week.

When I arranged a trip to a particular conference, I would visit five or six different churches. Each church usually served an evening meal. Most of the time, the menu was ham, green beans, and scalloped potatoes. I like all three dishes, but when it was time for the meeting to begin I would be so thirsty that I had difficulty speaking.

I made several trips to Canada in the fall, but I forgot that winter comes early in Canada. It snowed every day I was in Saskatchewan. While there I made my first ever visit to a curling parlor. No, I did not get my hair curled. Curling is the game in which men with brooms assist a large stone to slide down an ice lane. The curling parlor is a large building something like a bowling alley where the entertaining games are played. It's very popular in Canada.

Back home David as a senior in high school entered an annual speech contest sponsored by the American Legion in the state of Indiana. He competed with winners from other schools in the district and emerged as the winner. The competition continued to other districts until four statewide winners were awarded four-year scholarships to Indiana University. The finalists went to Terre Haute, Indiana for a televised playoff contest. As we drove to the studio, I could not tell who was more nervous at that time David or me. David actually tied for second.

On Memorial Day the American Legion sponsored a parade that started in downtown Warsaw and ended at the city cemetery near Pike Lake. David rode in a car with the Legion officers at the head of the parade and delivered a speech at the veterans' circle in Union Cemetery. We were very proud of David. We saved the write-up of the event from the local newspaper, which featured a picture of David standing in the car.

The Westminster Hotel is another Winona Lake landmark. It was the scene of many social events, including fashion shows from the local school of photography. David played the piano at these gatherings and earned some extra spending money while he was in school.

I had a frightening experience about the time David graduated from high school. We drove David to Bloomington for his orientation to Indiana University. I began to experience pain in my right armpit. It turned out that my lymph gland had swollen to nearly the size of a golf ball. When I returned from the University, I went immediately to Dr. Arford, who sent me to Saint Joseph Hospital in Fort Wayne. There the surgeons removed the gland and tested it for cancer. We were relieved when the report indicated no malignancy. An inflamed lymph vein from my armpit to my wrist also had to be excised and tested. The vein was about the size and texture of the "E" string on a guitar and was restricting me from straightening my arm. Six months later the doctors tested my lymph glands at the base of my neck and also took some bone marrow from my sternum. Thankfully, all the tests were negative for cancer.

I never thought of myself as a silly or a frivolous person but God has blessed me with a good sense of humor. Someone once said that a sense of humor is like springs on a wagon; it cushions a lot of jolts in life. When I was going through all the cancer tests, Lois was having a lot of female health problems. It so happened that both of us were scheduled for brief stay in the Parklawn Hospital in Fort Wayne at the same time. We asked if we could stay in the same room. Although it was not common practice for a man and a woman to share the same room, our request was granted. During the evening prior to our surgeries, various nurses stepped in the doorway. When the nurse who came to prep Lois saw me, she said, "Oops, wrong room!" and left. A few moments later she returned with a surprised look on her face.

"What's going on here?" she asked. We all had a good laugh and I explained the situation to her. When the male nurse appeared to prep me, he stepped into the doorway, saw Lois and said, "Oops, wrong room!" He checked his records and saw he was in the right room.

"Are you Mr. Barnett?" he asked.

"Yes," I responded.

"Do you know this lady?" he asked suspiciously.

"No, I've never seen this lady before in my life," I said.

Double-checking his records he murmured, "What's going on in this place?"

I started to laugh and I told him we were married. He laughed with us as he got his razor and prepped me for surgery.

Throughout that entire evening different nurses would do double takes in the doorway. Both surgeries turned out well.

39

Firsts

Lois and I had been married 20 years before we had our first major disagreement. It involved where David would attend college.

Many students in the Free Methodist Church attended one of several Free Methodist colleges. Roberts Wesleyan, from which I had graduated, was in New York. Seattle Pacific was a popular destination for west coast students. But the church college closest to Winona Lake was Greenville College in Greenville, Illinois. Lois thought David should go to Greenville, and I wanted him to take advantage of the full-ride scholarship he had earned to Indiana University. I recalled that I lost almost a year of credits when I transferred from Roberts College to the University of Virginia. I was concerned that David might face similar problems if he pursued advanced degrees, which I was almost certain he would.

David refused to go to Greenville, even though some of his closest high school friends from church were going there. He wanted to go to Indiana University. It took us a long time to resolve the immediate conflict, but Lois continued to believe that David needed the influence of a Christian college.

When David left home for college, I really missed him. I missed him asking for the car keys, playing the organ, watching him come and go through the front door; I missed him walking with us to church and sitting in the church pew singing bass beside him.

After completing his sophomore year of college, David decided he was going to marry his high school sweetheart. Since he was not yet 21 years of age, the state of Indiana required a parental signature in order to get a marriage license. Lois thought he was too young and so she refused to sign. He reminded Lois and I that we were both under 21 when we were married. I remembered how much I loved my high school sweetheart and how much I wanted to be married. These strong sentiments led to our second disagreement since our marriage. My head agreed with Lois, but in my heart I wanted to sign and give David my blessing. Eventually, my heart won over my head. David married his high school sweetheart, Sue Quillen, and they moved to Fort Wayne, where David attended and eventually graduated from the Fort Wayne campus of Indiana University.

Darlene was a good student. She spent more time studying at home than David. She played the organ and helped me learn new hymns and spiritual songs. I loved to sing duets with her. She and her mother sang beautifully together. We were a singing family who sung in church choirs and have been involved in church music all of our lives. Darlene and David are both organists in their respective churches today.

Darlene was faithful and diligent as a child in her practice sessions at the piano. She set the timer on the kitchen stove and would not stop practicing until she heard it ding. But when her time was up, she stopped playing immediately regardless of where she was in the piece of music. When I asked her why she didn't finish the music, she told me she only had to practice for thirty minutes.

After Darlene had been playing for several years, she told me about a classmate who could not read music.

"Dad, can you imagine! She can't read notes."

Music was such a part of our family and her personal history, Darlene thought everybody could read music. One summer when she was in high school, a member of the Canadian Parliament who was a Free Methodist invited me to bring my family to his cottage on one of the beautiful lakes beyond Sault Ste. Marie. He said the cottage had plenty of room. A colleague at church headquarters, Reverend Roy Howell, and I had been requested to come to Canada for a Christian education workshop. We arranged the time for the workshops, and when we finished we spent a week with Roy and Iva Howell in the cottage located on Lake Wakomata. The lakeshore was rimmed with beautiful birch trees. We had a large motorboat and some fishing rods, which we used almost every day. Darlene enjoyed driving that boat while we fished in the crystal clear water. We didn't catch many fish but Roy and I enjoyed wetting the line and relaxing in the perfect June weather.

Late one night in early January, 1968, I received a phone call from my brother Earl. Struggling with his own emotion, he told me our father had died following prostate surgery two days earlier. I was shocked. I didn't even know that Dad was hospitalized. I felt like I had been shot and sustained a serious wound to my heart. I couldn't sleep that night. I tried to acclimate myself to the fact that my father was really dead. My heart went out to my dear mother and I cried as I thought about her.

In the morning I called my office and told them I would be away for a week to attend my father's funeral in Pennsylvania. We packed our suitcases in the car, and headed for Pennsylvania Dutch country, specifically to the town of Ephrata. The weather was cold, the ground covered with snow all the way home. The roads were clear, so we had no difficulty driving. Twelve hours later we arrived.

My mother appeared to be in shock. She said very little except that she was very glad to see us. She knew almost no details of Dad's death. If she did know, she chose not to speak about it. When we went to the funeral home for viewing, she did not go up to the casket but chose instead to sit at the far end of the room. Since Dad was a longtime businessman, we had arranged viewing in two funeral homes, one in Ephrata and the other one in Wernersville, not far from Haines Church were Dad was buried the following day.

He was buried on a very cold and windy day. More than a foot of snow covered the ground at the cemetery. The people who attended the funeral service stayed in the church. Only the pallbearers, the funeral director, and the cemetery workers withstood the biting cold as the casket was placed on the catafalque above the ground. My Dad is buried not more than fifty yards from his boyhood home.

The committal service ended quickly and then the family shared a meal together following the burial that gave us time to visit with relatives I had not seen in years and years. We stayed with Mom for several days and then returned home to resume our tasks. 1968 was a year filled with numerous events, some were very sad and others were very exciting, not the least of which was resigning my work at church headquarters as the Sunday school director for the denomination to return to pastoral ministry. Here's how that happened.

After Darlene graduated from high school she made plans to attend Greenville College in Greenville, Illinois. The state of Illinois paid the tuition for students whose parents earned less than $15,000 a year. We easily qualified for assistance. That summer I decided it was time for me to terminate my work at headquarters. I was also concerned that Lois would be left at home by herself while I was traveling and that idea did not appeal to me. I made my intentions known to my supervisors. After my current commitments were done in mid-September, I wanted to return to pastoral ministry. I received a call from the superintendent of the Illinois Conference that a pastor was needed at the church in Decatur, just 90 miles north of Greenville. I committed to accept that appointment.

40

Decatur

The only house I ever owned had been in Winona Lake. Although I was happy to be leaving headquarters, I missed the lifestyle we had developed during those wonderful years.

We moved to Decatur, Illinois the first of September in time for Darlene to enter college. I had purchased a 1964 Oldsmobile Cutlass before we moved from Winona Lake. The plan was that Darlene would take the Cutlass to college. Soon after we moved Lois and I drove in our Olds 98 to Los Angeles, California, where I had assignments at the National Sunday School Association Convention. Darlene left for college at about the same time. Ten days later, Lois and I were back in Decatur to begin my work as pastor of the Decatur Free Methodist Church.

I did not transfer my conference membership at that time. I was still a member of the Wabash Conference from my days in Winona Lake. But Decatur was one of the largest churches in the Illinois Conference and by the end of my first conference year it occurred to me that some of the preachers resented the fact that an "outsider" had been appointed to one of the largest churches. My conference membership was becoming a political issue among my peers. There was no open hostility but I was aware of their feelings. The congregation was very supportive with my leadership during the two years I was their pastor. I was happy to be home every night with Lois.

The Decatur church building was an old downtown church, just one block from the main downtown shopping area. The large parsonage was adjacent to the church, which occupied one half of a city block. Our 1964 Olds 98 would almost fit into the terra-cotta block garage behind the parsonage. I cut the surface of one of the terra-cotta blocks so I could close the garage door, which fit up against the rear bumper of the car. We parked the small car in a doctor's office parking spaces around the corner.

The parsonage had four large bedrooms on the second floor; the spacious living room had a beautiful fireplace. The old brick church featured a large tower and stained glass windows. The sanctuary had two aisles between curved pews and inclined down ever so slightly to a large rostrum with a beautifully bowed communion rail. A choir loft to the right of the pulpit contained a large pipe organ in excellent condition. Although Free Methodists are known for their great singing, for some reason the Decatur congregation had a small choir. When Darlene was home from college on weekends, she and Lois added significantly to the effect of the choir.

The church office was on the second floor of the building above the Sunday school rooms. The Decatur church had a strong Sunday school. Many young adults moved to Decatur from smaller towns within a fifty-mile radius of the city for better job opportunities. Firestone made tires there and a large soybean company named Staley's employed many people. When the winds blew from the east, a terrible odor infiltrated the city.

On special days such as Easter, Mother's Day, and Christmas, when most churches have their largest attendance, we had our lowest attendance because our many young families from the surrounding towns would go home to visit relatives. The church members were friendly and they responded well to my leadership. Some members took me to Cardinal baseball games in St. Louis. Others had memberships in the YMCA and invited me to go swimming with them frequently.

Darlene came home from college every week. She complained about living in a dormitory with a bunch of sloppy girls. Darlene was a very neat and organized person. When her neatness compulsion got too strong, she found herself picking up clothing all the time. It got so bad she wanted to quit college, but we insisted that she continue. A month after school started we received a call from her advisor telling us that Darlene was very homesick. We persuaded her to finish the first semester at Greenville. That winter she moved home and attended Milliken University, located three blocks from our home in Decatur. Her boyfriend, Ron Stafford, drove from Muncie, Indiana, to see her. He was a student at Ball State University. Darlene was very happy to be home.

The pastors in the Decatur Ministerial Association sponsored a Billy Graham Crusade with one of Graham's associate ministers, the Reverend John Wesley White, as the evangelist. It was called the Golden Prairie Crusade and it lasted for ten days. All the components of a major Crusade were employed. George Beverly Shea sang every night, attendance was good, and we believed there were excellent results with a good number of persons who professed to be converted to Christ.

I think we had more needy persons in Decatur than any place I ever lived. Since the parsonage was located next to the church, we frequently had beggars knocking at the door looking for help. I heard some of the strangest requests and hard-luck stories. I thought that the church was advertising in a beggars' magazine. Of course, the most frequent request was for money; money for bus fare, money to buy gasoline, money to buy food for babies, and many more requests. Often an old car loaded with dirty infants and babies stopped out front, the man stayed in the car while the woman was sent to the door to ask for money. Single men sometimes asked for a pair of socks or a razor blade, or maybe a sandwich, or money ostensibly to call his mother to tell her he was well.

One old pro came into the rear door of the church, up to our offices. He walked right past my secretary directly into my office. He proceeded to tell me that he had to get to Taylorville right away and would I take him there. I told him I could not do that. He continued to plead with me, but I was suspicious of what might happen if he and I got alone in my car. As soon as he left my office I called my friend who was pastor at the large Methodist church three blocks away on Main Street. He told me the fellow had been in his office making the same request a few minutes earlier. He told me he had the same uneasy feeling regarding the man. That evening the newspaper reported the story that a driver was injured when a hitchhiker had beaten him and stolen his car. I couldn't determine if that thief was the same fellow in my office or not, but I'm pretty sure it was.

Darlene was home alone much of the time. We urged her not to open the door to strangers. She had grown up in Winona Lake and could not imagine that anyone would harm her. We were shocked when one day we learned that she had opened the door to a man who requested a razor blade. A razor blade! She naively asked him to wait until she went upstairs to the bathroom and got one of my razor blades, wrapped it in some tissue, and took it down to the door where he was waiting. How good of God to protect her.

Here's another true story of God's providence. In 1969, David graduated from Indiana University. That was the height of the Vietnam War, and healthy college graduates were being drafted. David was trying to enlist in the Air Force in Fort Wayne where he lived, but he was told that there weren't any openings. On one particular Sunday, an Air Force officer came to a morning worship service in Decatur. As we sometimes did, we invited him to the parsonage to have lunch with us. Our conversation included us telling him about David's situation. The officer listened and then said he could take care of that for us. Within a couple of weeks, David called us to let us know he had received a letter telling him that he had been accepted in the Air Force.

The Scripture tells us that Abraham entertained angels unaware. I believe that officer who sat at our table on Sunday turned out to be an angel. We never saw him before or after that Sunday. What do you think?

David signed up with the Air Force that summer to have a choice of duty assignment that he might not get if he allowed himself to be drafted. He reported for basic training in September, 1969. It was difficult for me to accept the fact that David was leaving his wife and home to enter military service. I relived my own experience, remembering the pain and anxiety of going off to war.

The New Madrid fault runs through southern Illinois. On Nov 9, 1968, an earthquake centered about 135 miles south of us in Mt. Carmel, Illinois, shook the Midwest. It was measured a magnitude 5.5 on the Richter scale. I was in the basement of the parsonage when I felt the earth tremble and heard the dishes rattle in the kitchen. It lasted only a few seconds. I inspected the house and found no damage. I went next door to the church to check with my secretary, who told me everything seemed to be okay, but she did hear some glass breaking. I went into the sanctuary to check the stained-glass windows and everything looked fine. When I went outside and looked at the glass windows high in the church tower, sure enough several of them were gone. That was all the damage we sustained from the earthquake. Lois was working at the school board office at that time and they suffered no damage at all.

Darlene announced that she and Ron were planning a wedding for June 6, 1970. Months earlier Ron had asked for my permission to marry Darlene, and I said yes. No father is happy about losing a daughter who had given so much evidence that she loved her home, but Ron had demonstrated his love for her, so we looked forward to welcoming Ron as a son. Darlene and Lois talked about the wedding for months; maybe it was an entire year. Both Darlene and her mother are "list people" so you can imagine how many lists they made to arrange all the details of the wedding. They purchased dress material and patterns were sent to the maid of honor and to all her attendants. The girls were asked to make their own dresses. There were lists for flowers, wedding guests, family relatives, wedding rehearsal guests, reception, food, and lots more. Most of the wedding party came from Indiana, Pennsylvania, and Maryland. David and his wife came from San Angelo, Texas where he was in Security Service School. Sue had a tough time getting into the dress since she was four months pregnant.

But all their planning resulted in a well-executed, large, beautiful wedding that came off without a hitch. As difficult as it had been when David left home, it was even harder for me when I saw Darlene and Ron drive away for Indiana. I was very pleased that my brother, Earl, had driven our mother to the wedding. It was the first time we had seen her since Dad's death. There is a rhythm to life that is always moving forward to tomorrow. Our sorrows at the time of death lead to the joys of a wedding. There's a sense in which all that we have and all that we ever hope to have is somehow wrapped up in our children. Parents make an investment in their children. If you live long enough, you learn whether you made a good investment or not. We had uprooted our lives and moved to Winona Lake, largely for the benefit of our children and the payoff has been the enrichment that Ron and later Julie, David's faithful wife, have contributed to our family. They have given us five grandchildren and five great grandchildren and we pray to God for many more.

I made many visits to the elderly and sick members of my congregation. Next to preaching I enjoy the ministry of visitation most. Those events are not always serious and sad. I was making a hospital visit to one of my members who was in a semi-private room. The roommate was a total stranger. It's not unusual for the other individual to get involved in conversations I might be having with my parishioner. But on this day, visiting an elderly lady from my church, the roommate was doing all the talking. She didn't know I was a minister until I told her that I was a pastor of the Decatur Free Methodist Church. That was all she needed to know. She started telling me about something that happened more than forty years ago in a Free Methodist Church somewhere, but she couldn't remember what she was upset about. When I asked her if she had been to any other church since, she told me that she had not. Naturally, I invited her to come to our church when she recovered from her illness. Her response was simply, "I don't cotton to Free Methodists."

"What do you mean?" I said. "I've never heard that expression before—you don't 'cotton' to Free Methodists."

"You know," she said somewhat exasperated, "it's just plain English."

My church member got the biggest kick out of her saying that and soon all three of us had a great laugh together. When I concluded my visit, I prayed for the recovery of my church member and I included her name in my prayer.

"Thank you, Pastor," she said. "Thank you."

Another time I was visiting an elderly man who had an interesting roommate and once again the roommate got included in the conversation. When I asked him his age, he gave me a number that would have made him born in the 1850s.

"Do you remember when Abraham Lincoln was President?" I asked.

He simply answered, "Prit'ner." I never heard it before or since pronounced the way he spoke it. In case you don't know what he said, he stated he was "pretty near" old enough to have known Abraham Lincoln.

I regularly visited a group of men who lived in nursing homes throughout Decatur. In spite of their debilitating illnesses, these men were very alert. They told me that the government was paying doctors and nursing home operators for many services that were not given. Doctors were charging for visits they never made and nursing homes were charging for physical or voice therapy that was never received. I knew these men would not lie to me, so I decided to look into the matter if for no other reason than to put the men at ease.

I asked the various nursing home administrators about the complaints. They told me the patient had to be mistaken, that he didn't remember receiving the therapy or seeing the doctors. Administrators at all the nursing homes told me the same thing—patients forget.

I became concerned about such blatant fraud, and I wondered if I might do more good for people working for the Department of Health and Human Services in Washington, DC, tracking down on this abuse. I became curious enough to take a civil service exam to find out if I qualified for such work. I was given a GS12 and advised to go to Washington for some interviews. I was sent to two different offices in Washington, but there were no openings at that time. I'm not sure I would have accepted a position if one had been offered. But I did want to explore the possibilities for a change.

I never talked about this to anyone, but somehow the assistant treasurer at church headquarters started a rumor that I was leaving the ministry. Now I understood why my conference superintendent never responded to my request to be appointed to a church in the Wabash Conference. Apparently the rumor did not reach as far as the superintendent's office in Illinois. I was disappointed that the assistant treasurer had spread a false rumor. He could have easily checked with me to verify the story, but he didn't.

But Lois and I were ready to leave the Midwest. Our children were both grown and gone. The unexpected death of my father and my distance from what had happened still tore at me. My Mom and Lois's parents back East were getting older, and we sometimes wondered what in the world are we doing way out here in the Midwest.

I may have been in too much of a hurry to get back to what I considered "home." I contacted the superintendent of the Maryland-Virginia conference and requested to be considered for an appointment. To my surprise, he told me the only position available for me was the Layhill Free Methodist Church. This place was such a dump the parsonage didn't have suitable drinking water. I had already informed the Illinois superintendent that I was planning to go back East, so we were stuck between a rock and a hard place. We made plans to go to Layhill

Church and live with Mom and Pop Weinel in Rockville, Maryland while drinking water was piped into the Layhill parsonage. Some people in the Maryland-Virginia Conference were outraged that the superintendent had not offered me a better appointment. Had they known I was returning prior to annual conference, they wanted to put forward my name to become the conference superintendent. I don't believe I would have accepted for the reasons I've already stated. We loaded up a moving van and left Decatur the last week in July 1970 much to the disappointment of most members of that church.

41

To Jilly from Pop-Pop

Lois and I moved in with the Weinels until city water was installed in the Layhill Church parsonage. I had to eat a lot of humble pie during those months. I had been elevated to one of the top leadership positions in the denomination for more than six years, had served one of the largest Free Methodist churches in Illinois, and was coming back to my home conference to pastor a rough and tumble country church that was being choked by suburban sprawl. My $50 a week salary was insufficient, so I got a full-time editorial job at Vitro Corporation, a company that printed countdown manuals for firing missiles on atomic submarines. It was sometimes very interesting work that required a security clearance, but at other times was quite boring.

Members of the Layhill Church were happy to welcome us, and we appreciated their generosity. Unlike the Decatur church, these people were great singers. The church was probably best known as the home church of a gospel singing quartet, The Shorb Brothers. They traveled through the country for many years.

Shortly after arriving, I organized a youth folk singers group. I played the guitar. It was great fun because they were terrific singers. Some members of the group were the children of Hubert Shorb, the tenor in that male quartet. His kids loved music having been exposed to it in such a rich family tradition and they enlivened our folk group considerably.

The water situation was finally rectified and we moved into the parsonage in the fall. Lois got a job as a librarian assistant in an elementary school about a mile from our house. The parsonage was a modest but comfortable place with four small bedrooms, two on the second floor and two on the first floor. I used one of the rooms as an office. The basement of our house was used for Sunday school rooms on Sunday morning.

The church was a wooden structure, built when Layhill was a sleeping country crossroads in the last century. What had been the main street of that old town was now a busy two lane road and the front door of the 25 x 45 foot wooden church was no more than five feet from the side of a very busy road. It was an extremely dangerous place. Walking inside the church was like stepping back 100 years. I suppose antiquarians would have loved the rustic charm of the wooden floors, but it was all wrong for the young families that filled the former farm land with starter homes and split levels. In later years the congregation greatly improved their facilities. But when I was there in the early 1970s, I wouldn't have thought there was enough land to erect a new building.

We were still living with Lois' parents in Rockville in the late summer of 1970 when David and Sue stopped for a brief visit. They were on their way to England, where David was to be stationed at Chicksands Royal Air Force Base about 40 miles north of London. Sue was pregnant with Jill who would be born in London October 27, 1970.

We waited anxiously to see pictures of Jill. The months seemed to whiz by, and every month or two we received pictures and audio cassettes of Jill from the little village of Stotfold where David lived. This increased our desire to fly to England as soon as possible. When the school term ended where Lois worked, we made arrangements to fly to England. David secured a two-week leave from base and he took us to London and many other places to sightsee. The third week Lois and I set off on our own to tour several cities traveling on double-decker buses throughout the countryside. We returned to David's house the last few days in England. By this time I was getting used to driving on the "wrong" side of the street. But we had to return home in time for the annual conference session in Spencerville.

On the occasion of Jill's first birthday, I wrote the following letter dated October 27th, 1971.

Dear Jill,

It is difficult to accept the fact that you will never remember some things that your Pop-Pop shall never forget. The joy we felt when we learned of your arrival was not diminished by the fact that you were on another continent of this world. The miracle of your coming to us quickened my faith in the beneficent Creator. Surely God is good, I thought as I broadcast the joyous news of your arrival. You have no idea how anxiously we waited your first pictures which arrived some weeks later. How eagerly we listened to the cassette tapes for your bright, shrill sounds that helped us to feel the role of grandparents. Our trips to the department store where we carefully selected colorful and cute clothes also helped us to realize that we had a little angel in England. Other pic-

tures arrived and we knew that if we did not get to England soon we would miss seeing the most important event of 1970.

You will never know how anxious we were to see you and to hold you. We counted the days until our heavenly Father made it possible for our dreams to come true. It is hard to describe the sheer, pure joy I felt just to be with you, your Daddy and Mother on that bright August day in jolly old Stotfold. Dreams had become a reality; you were all your Pop-Pop had ever imagined and more. Your flashing black eyes and deep right dimple never came through in your photos. Feeling your chubby arms and rubbing your button nose surpassed any picture and sound no matter how delightful and revealing. What a day, you were beautiful and how we loved you. You won't remember how your Pop-Pop tried to cram nine months into three weeks; however you made it easy by not being a bit strange toward your foreign invaders. From the very first day, we made up for lost time by traveling together throughout your house and yard, especially the backyard. You will never remember the fun we had peeking into windows and laughing at Jill's reflected image. We enjoyed watching birds and pigeons pierce the sky and then land on rooftops or Mommy's clothesline and Jill's backyard fence.

You won't remember our daily strolls through old Stotfold, and how we sang together always singing your song. Your neighbors surely must have noticed how proud I was to be your Pop-Pop. Stevenage and Letchworth will be remembered always as places we invaded crowds of shoppers with you leading the way in your GI stroller with its one Pop-Pop horsepower. It was shoes for the family at Stevenage with you coming home with a smart red pair of sandals. You won't remember the fun we had another day getting acquainted with a black and white bear and her cub in the Letchworth arcade. We didn't care how long it took your mother and grandmother to shop for family members back in the United States, the only thing important was that we were together. Someday you will see your Pop-Pop's pictures which partially tells the story of our three wonderful weeks with you. What they don't show are the things your Pop-Pop will try not to forget; the glee in your eyes while eating ice cream, your tense amazed look when drinking Coke, your determined expression when tearing Pop-Pop's glasses from his nose, your stretching to touch the chandeliers at Woburn Abbey, orange, white, and red peace roses in your front yard, your chewing on straps, any kind of strap, playing peek-a-boo to windows and around doorways, under the blankets in bed, your morning chatter in bed that made getting out easier for your Pop-Pop than anything I can remember. Jilly, you not only got into my hair and my pockets, you got into my heart.

Now we are back to the picture waiting stage until once again we shall have the opportunity to enjoy the pleasure of your company or until we receive your year-old studio photo. Your Mom-Mom and Pop-Pop will continue to get out the projector and flash your picture on the walls of our home. We will look for-

ward to the time when the sound of your laughter will vibrate throughout this house and when we can eat ice cream together and go for a ride and walk together and sing. One year old—what a wonderful age, Jilly. Your Pop-Pop has been there 47 times. You will never remember your first year, your Pop-Pop will never forget.

Happy birthday, Jilly,
Love,

Pop-Pop

42

Layhill

When we attended the annual conference in Spencerville, many old friends, preachers, and lay people alike sincerely welcomed me back to the conference. I was never quite sure the superintendent was as glad as others. He knew that some of the lay people were promoting me to be the superintendent. He was my successor when I left the Spencerville church to serve at headquarters. But he was always cordial and friendly.

I do not recall anything significant about that conference, only that many of the people there seemed out of step with the contemporary world and not current in their thinking. They appeared to be stuck in the past. In fact, it was as if the decade I had been gone had never happened. Nothing had changed.

My second year in Layhill we reported a slight gain in Sunday school attendance as well as church membership. The people were pleased with my preaching and leadership. Although our attendance suggested that we should consider building a larger church, I made no effort to promote a building program because I did not think we had sufficient land and we certainly did not have money. Besides, I could not see myself there for the long term.

About halfway through that year I learned that Lois's uncle, the Reverend James Diddle, planned to move to Florida, where he had been asked to serve as the conference superintendent. He was the pastor at a new Free Methodist church, Roberts Memorial Church. They were a smaller congregation, but the facilities were first rate, much better than we had at Layhill. I suggested to the superintendent that I would like to devote my full time to pastoral work and not have to continue my employment at Vitro and suggested he "yoke" the two churches. I felt I could easily pastor both congregations which, together, could support a minister with a more livable wage. Since the two churches were only three miles apart, the superintendent was open to the idea. He approached the congregations with the proposal and eventually they agreed to the plan after some details were worked out.

In the late May, Lois and I drove to Muncie, Indiana, where Ron was graduating from Ball State University. When we left on this trip, we understood that at upcoming conference, I would be appointed pastor of both churches. However, when we returned home several days later, I discovered to my shock and dismay that the superintendent had contacted a young man graduating from college in Harrisonburg, Virginia, and offered him the Layhill church with the idea that I would be appointed to the Roberts Memorial Church. I called the superintendent and told him I considered this action a double-cross. The superintendent did not agree. He said that he met with my board members while I was away which, by the way, was in violation of Church Discipline, and asked them their preference. Once again the superintendent had put me in a difficult situation; the first time by appointing me to the unlivable Layhill situation, and now by weaseling out of a commitment he made with me and blaming it on the people from Layhill. I learned later from the Layhill people that the idea was entirely the superintendent's preference, not theirs. The superintendent and I never had a fallout over this, but he knew he had broken a promise which was wrong. Right then I believed he would be happy if I was out of the picture. It gives me pain to write this about a Christian brother.

At conference time I was appointed to Roberts Memorial Church. The young people in the folk singing group at Layhill were the most disappointed to see me transferred to another church. The folks at Layhill were good people who supported my leadership the two years I was their pastor. I don't know what arrangements were made to support the young man who followed me as the pastor.

It was at this time that I began to seriously question my future with the Free Methodist Church. I began to think and pray about moving my ministry credentials into a larger denomination where I could make a fresh start and still be close to our aging parents in Maryland. I thought that I would probably need to look into upgrading my education if I was going to have a chance competing with younger men for churches.

Here's an example of the kind of decision-making that passed for leadership in the Maryland-Virginia Conference of the Free Methodist Church. The Roberts Memorial Church had been located in the city of Washington, DC, for many years. Like many congregations at that time, the Roberts Memorial Church decided they wanted to get out of the inner city and move to the suburbs. For reasons unknown to me, the church was moved out to Fairland, a community within two miles of Spencerville and about three miles from Layhill. They could have combined these three congregations and had a dynamic witness in the northern suburbs of Maryland. Most of the members of RMC were retired government workers who still lived in the city and didn't like commuting. So Sunday attendance at the new colonial brick church was small.

The parsonage was a very large house with all of the amenities that one could ever desire, but once again the pastor was the church janitor. I was paid $90 a week. Lois continued working as a librarian assistant while I resigned my work at Vitro Corp. I decided I would go to Wesley Theological Seminary, where I began work on a Master of Divinity degree. I took nine credit hours of study, which I really enjoyed. It felt good to be back in school. I was where I should have been twenty-five years earlier. My superintendent warned me that if I went to seminary, those teachers would ruin my faith. I couldn't believe his hubris and disregard for learning. He wasn't concerned about me. He had a slot that needed filled and that's all I mattered to him. I often regretted that I allowed him to persuade me to take a church after two years of study at a church college. However, I gained a lot of practical experience that put me miles ahead of my classmates in seminary. I finally concluded that all things do work together for good to those who love God.

That autumn I contacted several district superintendents in the Baltimore and the Virginia conferences of the United Methodist Church to explore the possibility of transferring my credentials to either. Each superintendent expressed an interest in me coming to their district. I told these men I was obligated until July of the following year. The Baltimore superintendent took me to Cumberland, in western Maryland, where a church would be open next year. I didn't think being 100 miles away from seminary would be a good decision, so I declined consideration for that church.

That next spring a United Methodist pastor friend urged me to contact the Alexandria District Superintendent, who arranged for me to come for an interview. The Virginian told me to plan to transfer. He promised me an appointment in the Alexandria District. A few weeks later, the Baltimore superintendent called back with an offer to pastor a church closer to the seminary. I remember thinking how strange that United Methodists were making numerous offers to me and the denomination I had served for twenty-five years could not find a church that paid a living wage.

Back at Roberts Memorial, we had no church organist so Darlene and her husband Ron came to Fairland every Sunday to be our organist. Ron had taken a teaching job in the public schools of Annapolis. It was about forty-five miles from Annapolis to Fairland, and Darlene received no compensation for her services for the entire year. We were happy to have them every Sunday to enjoy a good meal together. She was an excellent organist. I taught an adult Sunday school class that year, but not much happened during the weekdays at that church. The routine of church work and school kept me very busy as I looked forward to transferring to the United Methodist Church.

Many Free Methodist colleagues have asked me over the years why I changed my denominational affiliations, especially since Lois was a fifth generation Free Methodist. I have tried to answer that question candidly in these pages. Put simply—I saw no future in the Maryland Virginia Conference of the Free Methodist Church. I had already served the largest church when I left Spencerville for church headquarters and I certainly did not want to serve as the superintendent. I maintained cordial relationships with the people and the preachers in the Maryland-Virginia Conference. We continued attending evening services at the Spencerville camp meetings for many years.

After having served twenty-five years as a pastor and administrative officer in an "establishment evangelical" denomination, I transferred in 1973 to the United Methodist Church. The basic reason for my transfer was that I was no longer compatible with the views of those in leadership at the conference level. Let me hasten to say that I never had any major conflict with the doctrinal statements of that former denomination. My unhappiness stemmed from the fundamentalist interpretations of those doctrines and from the attitude of leaders that looked for answers to the complex problems of humanity by the simplistic assertions that all that was needed was an "old-fashioned revival."

After two district superintendents had assured me that there was a place for theological conservatives in the United Methodist Church, I accepted an appointment as the associate minister of St. Paul Church in Woodbridge, Virginia. My transfer to the United Methodist Church did not change my style of ministry; it provided me a much larger field of service

In July of 1973 I attended the Maryland-Virginia annual conference, gave my report, and then requested a letter of transfer to the Virginia Conference of the United Methodist Church. No one was surprised at the Roberts Memorial Church when I left after just one year. It was difficult to leave the conference, but I felt it was something that I had to do. I was greatly relieved when Pop Weinel gave me his blessing. My last sermon to the people of Roberts Church was filled with expressions of gratitude for their support during my tenure as their pastor. They knew why I had to move on and none ever spoke unkindly about my decision to transfer.

43

"Our Heavenly Mother"

Following my last Free Methodist conference I drove to Woodbridge, Virginia, a suburb of Washington, DC. St. Paul United Methodist Church was a 1,600 member congregation led by Senior Pastor, the Reverend Roy Everett. He and the congregation's lay leader, Joseph Dunivin, and I had a fruitful discussion in which I shared my experience as an elder in the Free Methodist Church. My duties as associate minister were outlined for my ministry at St. Paul. We all had positive feelings regarding working together. Before I left the interview, I gave them all the necessary information to contact me. They said they would let me know their decision soon and when I returned home, Lois said Reverend Everett had already called to tell me that I was to be the associate minister at the church. I was given several weeks to consummate the move.

Our parsonage at Woodbridge was completely furnished. We were asked to use their furnishings, so we kept only a few choice items of our furniture and sold the rest. I placed an ad in the paper; Lois could hardly bear to see our furniture sold. Before she left for work she said, "I hope you sell everything while I'm away at work."

Some of our living room and our dining room furniture was only a year old. Everything was in excellent condition. Fortunately, somebody responded to the ad in the paper, came to the house, and bought all of the furniture in one day. We packed the few things left over and moved to our new place in Woodbridge. We lived in a Cape Cod style house with two bedrooms upstairs and a bath and bedroom on the first floor. A full basement provided some space for our personal things.

Shortly after getting settled, it was time for me to register at Wesley seminary and arrange a schedule of classes for the semester. My advisor at seminary told me I could do some personal study that would diminish class time given my twenty-five years experience and some earned credits with excellent grades. He advised me to do some personal study in which I could earn as many as thirty credits for graduation. The professors made up a list of fifteen or eighteen books for me to read in a semester. At the end of the term I was given a three-hour written exam. I read books and made copious notes, which became a great resource when I wrote my final Church in Ministry paper, worth fifteen credits. One other man and I were the only two students who utilized this program before it was discontinued.

It was during this time that the women's liberation movement had taken root women started showing up for the first time in seminaries. The young female enthusiasts took every opportunity to correct anyone who used a male reference when referring to God. I thought it the height of rudeness when one of these feminists would interrupt an older professor who would nearly swallow his dentures if caught using the pronoun "He" when referring to God. If he started to speak in class, the female students focused their eyes on him, waiting to pounce on the poor soul if he forgot to be politically correct. This feminine elitism reached its nadir when one woman was asked to pray.

"Our Heavenly Mother," she began to a chorus of groans from the less revisionist male seminarians in the classroom.

Women were suddenly being fast-tracked to become leaders in district ministerial associations Women seemed anxious to fill a slate of officers and many men were happy for them to assume the burden of leadership. Soon our conference found it necessary for some reason unknown to me to have at least one woman district superintendent in the conference. Women were quickly elevated to conference leadership positions. One lady, who filled the pastor's position after her husband died, was appointed pastor of a rural black community church for several years. Then she administered a mission in Richmond. Several years later, feminists in the conference started to promote her as a candidate for Bishop. When she did not get elected in the Southeast Jurisdiction, she moved to California where she was finally elected to the office of Bishop. It was unprecedented in my experience and in that of my Methodist colleagues that an individual could be elevated to the Bishop position with so little experience.

By the time I graduated, the trends were clear. There were as many women as men entering seminary. It was not uncommon for both a husband and wife to be ministers. This created a huge conundrum for district superintendents tasked with placing these couples in churches following graduation. Another new practice facilitated by the growing feminist culture was the practice of married couples retaining their last names or assuming a hyphenated identity. It all seemed so pretentious and silly to me, but then I have never been politically correct.

I'm sure I speak for many men of my age and generation who find it very difficult to realize that women's liberation has brought us to the point where men and women fight and die side-by-side in the military. Each generation must find something against which to rebel and shock their parents. The traditional roles for husbands and wives that provided such a solid foundation for the newly-weds of my generation was being made obsolete for many by affluence and self-centeredness. I find myself sometimes trying to keep up with the change, but really, I think I've reached a stage where I have no desire to change. It is one of the rare privileges of age.

The breakdown in traditional family roles and values touched our own family. In 1973, Sue divorced David. Although we don't know all the details, it was a painful time for us all.

The early 1970s were a time of great upheaval in the church and in society. Campuses swarmed with students and activists protesting the war in Vietnam. Students said don't trust anyone over 30. It was a children's revolt that captured the evening news night after night. This behavior appeared almost traitorous to those of us who had fought in World War II. My heart ached as I saw how returning fighting men were scorned by longhaired, selfish brats who never worked a day in their life. This old soldier was ashamed of the hordes of this country's youth who seemed to be learning how to protest but not much more.

Several ministers in our district chose to join the protesters, but I did not understand how they could leave their pulpits and join the ranks of people who showed such blatant disrespect for the country and for those who were making such sacrifice to serve the country. Someone once asked me if I would ever march in a protest.

"No," I answered facetiously. "I never took that course in seminary."

During those confusing days I was speaking to a church group, expressing my thoughts on protesters. I made it clear that, while I fought for the precious right of Americans to protest unjust government policies, I told them not to expect to ever see me with an antiwar placard in my hand. One woman got up and walked out of the church, which was okay with me.

I couldn't help but recall my own homecoming after fighting overseas. People celebrated my return. But patriotic citizens seemed to have all but vanished. During the Vietnam War, I felt that patriotism was dead. Theologians were proclaiming God was dead. I was one evangelical who would say to my revisionist colleagues in those days, I know God isn't dead because I was talking with him this very morning. People have a right to choose to be wrong.

I was astonished by the number of my classmates in seminary who did not believe in the divinity of Christ nor in most of the doctrinal statements in the United Methodist Church. Some were persuaded by their studies to reaffirm orthodox faith, but others seemed more interested in avoiding the draft than preparing to actually serve the Lord in full-time ministry.

Theological confusion reigned among many of my professors as well. However, my advisor and teacher of systematic theology, Dr. James Logan, was an excellent role model. He was a Wesley scholar and I took many classes from him. Dr. Roy Morrison was a brilliant black professor who taught philosophy courses. Dr. Morrison was about my age and as he talked with me personally about certain subjects I became convinced that we had much in common. I went up to him after class one day and told him as much.

"Mr. Barnett," Dr. Morrison smiled and said, placing his hand on my shoulder, "our childhood days were nothing alike. It's true that we both came from poor beginnings, but you were never black."

The Congress had done away with segregation, but we still had a long way to go with integration and Dr. Morrison would not let you forget it.

For the last twenty-five years of my ministry my strongest competitor was not the pastor down the street, but the religious hucksters who peddled their wares every Sunday morning on television. It's impossible to overestimate the influence television has made in American culture. How did we ever manage to get along before we had computers? Someone has correctly stated that we have become a nation of technological giants and moral midgets.

44

Another Wedding, Another Father

Woodbridge was the largest church in which I had ever pastored. Its 1,600 members were more than all the Maryland-Virginia Free Methodist churches combined. My duties as an associate pastor were varied and exciting by the sheer number of people. I was given the opportunity to preach one Sunday a month; the other Sundays I was worship leader in all of the Sunday services. My primarily responsibility was to follow up on all the church's visitors to church, sometimes numbering twenty people or more. I attempted to contact them all the week following their initial visit.

It was not uncommon to receive thirty new members every month into church membership, however since many of our members were military families, we were constantly transferring members to other churches.

My other chief duty was calling on the sick and the shut-ins who could not attend church services. I made regular rounds at Potomac Hospital in Woodbridge as well as other hospitals in Alexandria, Washington, DC, Quantico Marine base, and other military bases in the area. Many of the members of the church were active or retired military living on those installations.

I also worked with the youth of our church. Given the success I had enjoyed with the folk singing group at Layhill, I organized a similar group at Woodbridge consisting of twenty-five singers and five instrumentalists. I played guitar along with them. We sang virtually all the songs in the "Sing and Celebrate" song books. The group sang once a month in congregational worship. We also presented programs in neighboring churches. Those young people were such a fun group.

Associate Pastor, Woodbridge United Methodist Church

I taught short-term adult classes in Sunday school as well as leading the six-month confirmation class every spring. Confirmands were received on Pentecost Sunday. This ability to shape the religious thinking of young people and watch them unite with the church was deeply meaningful for me.

St. Paul Church operated a day school that met in our church building. I was frequently invited to speak in their assemblies.

Ministers in Woodbridge had a very active ministerial association. It provided a chaplaincy service on a rotating basis to the local hospital. Pastors served for one week at a time. The rotation worked out so that a minister would serve about twice in a quarter. I enjoyed the work of chaplain. The hospital had an in-house television channel that presented a half-hour worship program Sunday morning.

I usually received very good feedback from the times I appeared on the program. New members were brought into the church resulting from my ministry as a chaplain at the hospital.

I was taking nine credit hours at Wesley Theological Seminary. The senior pastor at Woodbridge was a very fine man who treated me as a true partner in ministry. Roy Everett recognized that even though I was an associate and a student, still I had as much experience in ministry as he had. We shared equally in conducting weddings and funerals. It was not uncommon to have three weddings on a single Saturday. Large weddings were held in the sanctuary that seated 800 people while smaller weddings for smaller groups might occur in the chapel that seated 75 people.

I fit into a partnership with Roy Everett like an old shoe. We met on Sunday morning to anticipate the activities for that day. On Monday morning we evaluated the worship services and coordinated our work schedules for the coming week. I was free to develop my own schedule, but apprised him of any information I might encounter regarding any members of the church.

Unfortunately the following year, Roy was transferred to the Springfield church about ten miles up Route 95 from Woodbridge. We were still in the same district so I saw him frequently. Several years later, Roy was appointed district superintendent in the Staunton District of the conference. He tried to get me a church in his district, but he was tragically killed in an automobile accident on Route 11 returning home from a wedding.

The lay people at St. Paul Church gave Lois and me a very cordial welcome. We became great friends with Joe and Dot Dunivin. St. Paul Church had a program called Fellowship Friend that paired up new people in the congregation with long-term members. The program was designed to help new people integrate into the life of the church. Dot was Fellowship Friend to Lois. Lois joined the choir immediately and also attended a large adult Sunday school class.

My first year at Woodbridge witnessed some very important events for our family. Early in 1974 David and Julie came to Woodbridge to announce their engagement. David said he wanted Julie to have a chance to check us out. We looked with favor to have Julie as a part of our family. That May we traveled back to Winona Lake where they were married in the Free Methodist Church. It was a beautiful wedding; we enjoyed everything about it. We also had opportunity to check out where we had once lived and renew friendships at headquarters.

But something was not quite normal on that trip. Mom and Pop Weinel had driven to Indiana for David's wedding. Pop Weinel spoke very little. He spent most of the time during the reception sitting on a chair by the wall. As I talked with him later, he told me he could not remember what roads he had traveled to get to Winona Lake. He managed to drive back to Maryland. Mom did not mention anything unusual about the return trip. Not long after, Mom Weinel went with her friend, Mildred Fulks, to board meetings at Roberts Wesleyan College. Since she would be gone about three days, Pop Weinel drove to Woodbridge to stay with us. When he arrived at our house, he complained that he was tired. He retired to a bedroom to take a nap. At suppertime, I went to wake him. He didn't get up. He was breathing, but it took me at least fifteen minutes to rouse him.

After he finished eating he appeared to regain his normal energy, although I could tell he was just slower than usual. He said he could not remember parts of his drive to Woodbridge. I offered to drive him home several days later but he refused my offer. We called Mom, and she said he was all right.

A couple weeks later I went to my first annual Methodist conference in Virginia with Joe Dunivin. The second day of conference my name flashed up on a large screen in front of the conference room to report to the message desk for information. The person at the desk told me that there was an emergency at home. Pop Weinel had been taken to Suburban Hospital in Bethesda, Maryland.

Joe Dunivin gave me the keys to his car and immediately I left for the hospital. When I arrived I found Lois walking the halls, crying out loud. She seemed to startle the nurses who felt sorry for her. Lois was disturbed to see her father thrashing from side to side in his bed in a semiconscious state. Pop was unable to speak. He was extremely agitated, a truly disturbing sight for anyone who knew his true demeanor. I didn't see how he could survive the night. But later that evening the doctors were able to calm him.

The early diagnosis was a severe blood infection. Several weeks later they learned that he had an aneurysm in the ascending aorta. He was not getting sufficient blood to his brain. He was in Suburban Hospital about a month. During the day he appeared quite normal, but at night he had strange visions and fought to escape. Rather than tie him in bed, Lois and Jack alternated staying with him all night. Lois drank lots of coffee to stay awake. In the morning she left his room in time to get to work. Lois developed heart difficulties with an irregular heartbeat, and we theorized the problem was the massive amounts of caffeine she was using in those days to stay alert.

Pop Weinel was taken to Johns Hopkins Hospital in Baltimore where he was scheduled for open-heart surgery to repair the aneurysm. Before being wheeled into surgery, he called Lois and Jack into his room. He sent Mom Weinel to the nurses' station for something just to get her out of the room.

"I don't know if I'm going to make this or not," he said to his children. "If I don't, I want to meet you in heaven." It was a somber, holy moment.

Pop underwent three separate heart operations. The mesh they used to repair the aneurysm would not hold the blood. Throughout the long day and night he was given 67 units of blood, one for each year of his life, as it turned out. About four o'clock in the morning the doctor came into the waiting room to tell us that Pop was dead.

We were devastated. That drive home was without doubt the most difficult night in my life. I kept thinking about Mom, who cried all the way home from the hospital. God strengthened her during the whole ordeal. She was the oldest of twelve siblings. When all of her brothers and sisters started pouring into the house she showed remarkable strength.

Pop's body was laid out in the Rockville church. Young men from the church kept vigil through the night and three days after his death. A funeral service was conducted by the superintendent and the church pastor. Mom Weinel's family filled one half of one side of the church. They were all good singers. When the congregation sang "All Hail the Power of Jesus Name" to the tune of Diadem, the music was heavenly.

Pop's body was buried at Union Cemetery in Spencerville, Maryland. Once again, the joy of a marriage was followed by the death of a father. Life goes on in an unending rhythm in which the last word with God is not death but life. Jesus said to Martha, "I am the resurrection and the life; whoever believes in me will never die" (John 11:25,26a).

Several carloads of people from St. Paul Church including the pastor, the Reverend Al Honaker, Joe Dunivin and others came to the service and also to the cemetery. Their support was most encouraging and helpful. The large attendance gave evidence that many people revered the Reverend Clarence (Jack) Dawson Weinel. Jack had purchased a retirement home for Mom and Pop Weinel, but after Pop's death, Mom did not stay there. She spent some months with Jack's family or us. Jack sold the house and stored her furniture in a large garage at his place.

45

Woodbridge—Year Two

During my second year in Woodbridge, the Reverend Al Honaker was appointed senior pastor. He was different from Roy Everett in many ways. We seldom sat down to talk over plans for our ministry. Nothing changed in my job description, so we each went about our work rather independent of each other. He took several groups of people to the Holy Land for two-week trips knowing that I was always present to care for the needs of the church.

The second year at seminary was spent in self-study courses, which meant that I only went to the school to get books from the library or to have conferences with my professors. I read every spare moment. Lois helped me immensely by copying material that I marked as I read, pages I would later refer to in completing my future Church in Ministry paper.

Midway through my second year at the Seminary on January 4, 1975, Ronald Craig Stafford Jr. was born in Annapolis, Maryland. We waited five years to welcome our second grandchild. We saw him every week, so we had the joy of watching him grow up. Ronnie developed an early fascination for books, and he was a great singer as a baby and child.

Every summer for about twenty years our family rented a beach house in Rehoboth Beach, Delaware, where we enjoyed a week at the ocean. Ronnie was six months old the first time he went to the beach. He spent long hours under a large umbrella playing in the sand. Because of my sensitive skin, I had to go swimming early in the morning or after five o'clock in the afternoon to avoid getting sunburned. It did not take long for me to burn to the point of developing sun poisoning, a misery one does not soon forget.

Grandchildren at the beach; Darla, Michael, and Amy.

For many years we stayed in the Normandy Apartments on Wilmington Avenue about fifty feet from the boardwalk where Gus' French fries were readily available. Like most Pennsylvania Dutchmen, I enjoyed vinegar on my French fries. What a treat! Those were such wonderful days as we spent the evening strolling the boardwalk, eating junk food, and topping it all off with ice cream.

Months slipped by quickly. I was always challenged by the many opportunities I had as a minister to elderly shut-ins, to hospital patients, and to young people. The sea of faces before me each Sunday was always a challenge, not only when I was preaching, but also when I was worship leader. It seemed at times I was standing with one hand in the hand of the people and the other in the hand of God. I gave a lot of time and consideration to developing meaningful pastoral prayers. Contacting visitors to our church was also a very high priority. Older families I could find home during the day, but contacting working couples meant making calls in the evenings and on Saturdays.

I thought drama would be a powerful avenue to communicate the Gospel. So, I tried my hand at directing a play. I located a script titled "The Room Upstairs." It was an interesting story about a three-generation family living in the same house. I had no difficulty getting a cast of actors. We rehearsed for months and finally finished making or finding all the props for the production. We announced the dates and both performances were given to a packed house in the church's large social hall. It was fun directing a fine cast of characters. As soon as we finished, my actors asked when we were going to do the next production. I was too busy to think about another play. But I had accomplished my goal and I was glad.

I had learned a long time ago, that when visiting elderly people you don't open the conversation with "How are you doing." Invariably the answer was a laundry list of complaints, and they would probably tell you how they were getting on anyway. So, I began my visits by asking, "What have you been doing since I saw you last?"

"Not much," many said. "Just sitting here in this ol' chair."

But occasionally an elderly lady would walk slowly to her bedroom and come back to where I was sitting and show me an Afghan she had just completed; or someone would bring a watercolor painting just completed.

I recall visiting a lady who lived in a small room in a crowded nursing home. She had a dozen or more oil paintings stacked by her chair. She simply had no place to hang them because the walls in her room were already covered with beautiful oil landscape paintings.

Old men escorted me down dark stairs into the cellars of their homes to show me a workshop and then proudly return upstairs to point out all of the hand made custom furniture. Frequently retired military officers told me their war experiences. I would share my story, but only if they asked. I made it a regular practice to always conclude my visits with prayer. Not to have done so would have earned me a sharp rebuke from many of those dear, old Methodists.

I continued my hospital work during that second year. One of the most dramatic scenes was the time the doctors summoned me to the room of a small child who was dying and needed a blood transfusion. However, her parents were Jehovah Witness and refused to allow the transfusion. Doctors asked me if I could try to convince them to allow the transfusion, which would save the life of the child. But my best efforts failed to change their minds. When I offered to pray with the parents, they strongly rejected my offer. "We will offer our own prayers," they insisted.

On another occasion I visited a small child who had a severe case of whooping cough. The child nearly died during long episodes of coughing when she could not catch her breath. About a week later I began coughing, and in a day or two I had developed a full-blown case of whooping cough. When an adult male gets whooping cough, it can be a terrifying and painful experience. It took me more than two weeks to recover. Every time a minister walks into a sickroom where someone has any communicable disease, he runs the risk of contracting the disease.

Not all hospital visits were somber and sad, of course. A young person from our church had to get married at the age of 17. When I visited the new mother, I donned a sterilized gown and mask before I walked into her room. She was holding her baby and she greeted me asking excitedly, "Do you want to hold the baby?" I just about melted as I reached out to her to take the baby and hold him in my arms. Those precious moments became the title for a sermon I delivered at Christmas time that year: "Do you want to hold the baby?"

Months earlier this girl's parents told me their daughter's boyfriend was a Roman Catholic. His parents insisted that they be married in a Roman Catholic Church. When they inquired if their pastor could assist in any way in the wedding, the priest said he would be happy to have a Methodist preacher assist. When they asked if I would assist, they were anxious because they weren't sure how I would respond. When I told them I would be glad to do it, they were very pleased. Not all the members of St. Paul Church would have agreed with that decision. When I was a young pastor such cooperation between the Catholic and Protestant church would have never been allowed. But we have come a little way in interchurch relationships.

Here's another illustration of this. When I was a pastor in Spencerville in the 1950s, some Free Methodist preachers believed the Pope was the Antichrist. A neighbor five houses from the parsonage was struggling to raise two boys by himself; the boys were ages 10 and 12. His wife had died earlier and he had serious heart trouble. He had been a patient at Montgomery General Hospital for a month. Some of our church members looked after his boys by feeding them and washing their clothes.

I visited him several times a week in the hospital. I had just concluded praying with the man and three other men in his room when a young priest about my age stepped through the doorway. When he saw me, he stopped immediately near the foot of the patient's bed. The patient was a rough man about sixty years old who had never been trained in social graces. When he saw his priest, he started telling him about all of the things this man (pointing to me) and his people were doing to help him and his boys. The patient told his priest about my church and the peace of mind he had that his boys were being cared for. He went on and on telling this priest about all the times I had visited him and prayed with him.

"This is the first time I've seen you," he said to the priest.

I was so embarrassed by this I wished I could have fallen through the floor. I did my best to recover, introducing myself to the priest and extending my hand of greeting. He stood as straight as a poker, never looked me in the face, and without moving a muscle, he said nothing. I turned and said goodbye to the patient and walked behind the priest out the doorway. On my next visit I told this man he had been very rough on that young priest.

"He deserved it, and more," he said.

46

Meniere's

Soon after we moved to Woodbridge, Lois began having trouble with her inner ear. She was experiencing hearing loss along with tinnitus. She would become so dizzy she couldn't stand up let alone drive a car. The doctors diagnosed Meniere's disease. She questioned the prognosis when doctors said there was no cure for the condition and there was nothing they could do short of surgery except keep her on medications.

Lois had recently started working as the executive secretary at Pohick Episcopal Church, a historic church on Route 1, South of Alexandria, Virginia. Most of the time, Lois could function without difficulty. But occasionally she would be overwhelmed with such severe dizziness all she could do was lie on the floor and cover her eyes with a dark washcloth as the room spun wildly in her perception. At first Antivert medication helped relieve the vertigo. The horrible thing was there was no warning of these debilitating episodes.

Once Lois was standing at the sink and suddenly crumpled to the floor like she had been shot. Another time she was walking down the cellar stairway. The dizziness caused her to slump on the flight of stairs. She managed to hold on to the railing and not tumble all the way to the bottom.

The most frightening episode happened one night soon before we were preparing to go to bed. Lois entered the bedroom and suddenly slumped to the floor, complaining of severe dizziness. I lifted her onto the bed, thinking she would have some relief if lying down. But there was no relief. I gave her medication. It was usually rather fast-acting, but I could see it was doing no good at all. So moments later I picked her up in my arms and carried her to the car. I drove her to Potomac Hospital where doctors administered an intravenous sedation. She was permitted to return home about six hours later. Months could pass with no problems, and then one day the dizziness would incapacitate her. She called me at regular intervals to let me know she was okay. If she missed a call or was late getting home from work, I would get in the car and backtrack her regular route to see if she had difficulty somewhere along the road. We still follow that procedure to this very day.

During this time, David had enrolled at Louisville Presbyterian Theological Seminary in Louisville, Kentucky. David and I were in seminary at the same time. Lois and I drove to Louisville to visit him at his school. One evening we traveled to the nearby town of Shelbyville, where Colonel Harlan Sanders had started his famous Kentucky Fried Chicken franchise. He still owned the Colonel's Lady Restaurant, and Julie discovered that he sometimes still liked to cook in the kitchen. We happen to arrive on one of the nights Colonel Sanders was there. We met the kind, old gentleman and had our picture taken with him.

That fall we received the happy news from David that Julie was pregnant, something that apparently happens quite regularly to seminary students. Amy Krista Barnett was born June 9, 1977, in Louisville, Kentucky. Amy was a beautiful baby with dark, black hair. Although we did not get to see her right away, Julie sent us many pictures. We looked forward to seeing Amy. When we did finally make her personal acquaintance, we discovered that, unlike most Barnetts, she was a very picky eater. Her favorite meal as I recall was frozen peas. Our visits with David's children were always very special occasions because we never lived close enough to them to see them often.

Years later when I was a pastor at Hopewell, Virginia, I remember David, Darlene, and all the kids had a lot of fun when we spent a day at Virginia Beach. I never saw children take to the water like Amy and Michael. David and Julie could not get them out of the ocean. With his skin as blue as the sky, I asked Michael if he was cold.

"N-n-n-n-no," he answered, his teeth chattering from the obvious chill.

I think that boy must have had a bucket of sand in his britches when he finally was persuaded to come out on the beach. Amy and Michael may not remember that day, but I will never forget it. Darlene and her family were there that day also and Darla kept up with Amy and Michael most of the day. It was good to have all our family together.

My work as a full-time associate minister and a seminary student kept me extremely busy. At times I felt as if I had been a student all my life. I was a serious student as my grades indicated. My last semester was especially hard. At the beginning of the term I met with three professors who would read and evaluate my Church in Ministry paper. They offered some guidance regarding their expectations. After I submitted my paper, I had to endure three hours of oral exams with the three professors asking a wide range of questions. Those who were not prepared for the sessions could not bluff their way through to a diploma. Shortly after my orals, my faculty advisor told me that I did well and qualified to graduate with honors.

Naturally I was pleased as I thought I had brought honor to my father. His long-term council to "use your head" was finally realized ten years after his death. I drove to Pennsylvania to fetch my mother to Woodbridge so she could attend my graduation services. I graduated on May 8, 1978, thirty years after I took my first appointment in Waynesboro, Virginia.

During my final two years at Woodbridge, we had many problems with thieves breaking into the church. One morning we arrived to find that during the preceding night someone had broken in and destroyed all our porcelain drinking fountains. They pulled books off the shelves in the library and scattered them all over the floor. Fortunately they were unable to enter the offices of the secretary or those of the two ministers.

People frequently reported stolen hubcaps when attending evening meetings. At that time I was driving a 1969 Mustang that Jack had located for me as a second car. At lunchtime I went to my car to drive home for lunch, but the car wouldn't start. When I opened the hood, I found that someone had stolen the carburetor and the air cleaner. We finally addressed the problem by posting two men to stand guard all night in the church and after that nobody attempted to break in for the rest of the time I worked at St. Paul's Church.

Following my graduation, my superintendent, Dr. Kern Eutsler, suggested I consider a church in the Rappahannock district further south of Woodbridge. He said that the Carmel-Coles Point charge was in a state of confusion and needed a stable pastor who could put things in order. Since there was little I could do regarding going to Carmel-Coles Point, once again I was a city pastor who was going to a country church.

In the Methodist Church a preacher is guaranteed an appointment, but he must go wherever he is appointed. Reverend Honaker, the senior pastor, was also transferred to another church. The superintendent told me it was wise to change both ministers at the same time. I cannot say I agreed with him, but there was no way to do anything but go and be thankful.

The people at the Woodbridge church expressed their gratitude for my ministry by giving Lois and me a three-week trip to the Holy Lands under the leadership of Bishop C.P. Minnick. Fifteen ministers and their spouses went on this trip in September of 1979.

As many times as I've had to say goodbye to congregations, you would think it would get easier with time. But I always found the ritual painful and emotionally draining. The larger Methodist congregations meant the rituals of leave-taking took longer as different groups honored us with gifts and tributes across several nights of fellowship and joy. It is always a good thing to leave the church when you are still appreciated. A final farewell reception was held in the social hall the last Sunday in Woodbridge for Rev. Honaker, his wife, Arlene, Lois and me. A large group filled the hall. They presented a gift from the church of large silver sets for both ministers. The theme of my brief statement was "I was a stranger and you took me in." No congregation could have done more to make my transition to the United Methodist family more enjoyable or meaningful.

Over the next several years, Lois's ear condition steadily worsened. While we were in the country she had several episodes. We had an excellent country doctor who put us in touch with a specialist in Richmond who we visited several times. At first Dr. Shaia treated Lois with some new medications. But over time, her episodes of dizziness became more frequent.

Lois and I were attending conference that year in Roanoke, Virginia. The second day of the meeting Lois had a terrible episode of dizziness so that she could not get out of bed. A day later she was slightly improved. We drove the three-hour drive home.

I contacted Dr. Shaia, told him of this experience, and he made arrangements to schedule Lois for surgery. We had put it off long enough. It was the only recourse left to us if Lois was to have any chance at a normal life. The plan was to sever the balance nerve in her left ear. Dr. Shaia explained the procedure: he would shave her head, cut a square in her skull like you would plug a watermelon, enter into the inner ear and determine which of three nerves controlled balance, clip it, return the skull bone, and close the wound. It was very serious surgery.

The surgery went well. Lois was placed in a special room where she had a nurse by her side for five days after which she was transferred to another room where she stayed ten days. During this entire stay she was very dizzy. She could not watch television because she was hypersensitive to the flashing light imperceptible to others. She could not walk even to the bathroom without the support of a nurse or me. She could not turn around and when she walked in the halls, she couldn't determine how far she was away from the wall. She had no depth of field in her vision. She could not lean over to put on her shoes.

When she was discharged from the hospital, it was like torture to look out the side window of the car and see the world whizzing by. It would be months before she could ride in a car, a full year before she felt comfortable enough to drive.

In the hospital, Lois received a beautiful bouquet of flowers from David and Julie. Lois had them placed on a high shelf at the foot of her bed. I watered them faithfully until I discovered they were artificial flowers. We still have the bouquet at the doorway of our apartment.

47

Culture Clash

The Carmel and Coles Point churches were served by one minister. It was the first time I had ever served what is called "a two-point charge." Coles Point Church was an old country church begun in 1891. The congregation was small and the church building was located close to the Potomac River, so there was a larger percentage of "come heres" in this church than at Carmel. A "come here" was a retiree from Richmond or the Washington, DC area who had "come here." Come heres were frequently lawyers, geologists, retired professors, and others who encountered a huge culture shock coming to live and worship in this community of watermen and farmers.

The two churches were probably five miles apart geographically, but quite a bit farther apart culturally. I considered the Carmel congregation somewhat more "high church," but not necessarily in an urbane way. Our neighbor to the right of our house was a member at Carmel Church. He was a member of the state legislature in Richmond. He owned a lot of land farmed by sharecroppers. The neighbor to the left was a pig farmer whose pigs sometimes wandered into our yard, where they enjoyed acorns fallen from the large oak trees around our house. The politician was a member of Carmel Church; the pig farmer was not. Both families were friendly to Lois and me, but I don't think they had much to do with each other.

At Coles Point, six members owned oyster houses. The largest was owned by a young man named Ronnie Bevans. He had a large family of girls and a pretty wife. They were devout members of Carmel Church. Ronnie was a hard-working millionaire by the time he was 30 years old. His fleet of fishing boats tended seine nets that were strung far out into the Potomac River where they caught tons of fish. The so-called "junk fish" were frozen in three-foot squares and sent by truck or airplane to the Gulf States where it was used as food for shrimp. The large piles of oyster shells he dredged from the river bottom were used to make driveways or lanes to farmhouses set back off country roads. The fish were sold to restaurants and hotels in Richmond, Northern Virginia, and Washington, DC.

Coles Point Church at Christmas

When people in Northern Virginia would ask me what I meant when I told them that my churches were in the country, my simple answer was that it was 20 miles to the nearest McDonalds. However, we had many small grocery stores. I counted ten stores that were owned by members of my churches. It seemed to me that at just about every country crossroads there was a small grocery store where I suspect that, next to milk and bread, fish bait was a very important item. A man in the Carmel Church used to say to me that he was in the "mercantile business," but his place of business looked like all the other stores to me.

Both congregations welcomed us warmly. I had never served people who were friendlier. The two church groups seldom got together for any combined meetings. Together the membership of the two churches was 700. The worship service at Coles Point was scheduled from 9:30 to 10:30 a.m.; Carmel Church went from 11:00 to 12:00 noon. The Sunday school hour was the reverse time. The schedule made it impossible for me to serve in both Sunday schools.

The first Sunday we arrived at Coles Point we were greeted by a group of members. One lady was 100 years old. When I introduced myself to Mrs. Godman, she looked at Lois and then to me and she said, "She must be your second wife."

"She's my one and only wife," I said laughing.

"You know," she chattered happily, "when you're a hundred years old you can say anything and get away with it."

Mrs. Godman was a remarkable lady who lived alone and cared for a garden in her back yard. Almost every time I visited her, she would saunter into her garden and return with an armload of vegetables for me to take home. I had a garden five times larger than hers, but there was no way I could deny this dear lady the joy of sharing her treasure with me.

There were two drawbacks of having two churches. One was that the administrative work doubled. I now needed two annual reports, two charge conferences, two nominating committees, two finance committee meetings, and a host of other organizational meetings. Those activities are held in the fall, therefore soon as I returned from the Holy Land trip I was kept very busy. The district superintendent conducted what is called a charge conference at which all the reports of activities, gains or losses of membership, and financial reports are made. We also shared our goals for the coming year and projected where the churches might be in five years. The Methodist Church is second only to the government in paperwork.

The other drawback to having two country churches was I was going to be putting more miles on my car. I was driving an Oldsmobile Cutlass sedan getting 17 miles to a gallon of gas. My hospital calls were to Richmond, 70 miles away, Kilmarnock, 40 miles distant, and Tappahannock, which was 20 miles away. I decided to buy a small Datsun sedan to save on the cost of gasoline. The Datsun delivered 38 to 40 miles per gallon. There was only one problem: the Carmel church's most prominent member owned a large Chevrolet dealership in the nearby town of Kinsale. Some members teased me about buying a Japanese car, but Melvin Moss never said a word about it.

Those people were so generous. A member at Coles Point who owned a garage in Richmond installed an air conditioner in my Datsun. The following spring he gave me a rototiller to work in my large garden. When they learned that Lois and I were scheduled to leave on that three-week trip to the Holy Lands made available by my previous congregation, the churches got together and purchased an expensive 35mm Minolta camera for us along with a projection screen.

The chairman of the administrative board at Coles Point was Sonny Allen, a prosperous oysterman in that community. The waterman's job was long and difficult one. Crab pots were strewn throughout the coves of the river. They were baited and harvested every day. I could easily spot the watermen in my congregations. From the eyes down, their faces were deeply tanned by the sun, but their foreheads would be snow white, protected by the caps they always wore on the water. These watermen kept this preacher well supplied with oysters, crabs, and fish. I had more fresh fish than I could eat. Almost everybody who lived along the river had a dock with crab pots that kept the family supplied with the delicacy throughout the long season. Wives of watermen generally picked the crabs and prepared them for sale.

Adell Lampman and Libby Jones loved to fish. I often told these two older ladies in the Coles Point congregation that I thought they would rather fish than eat. It was not unusual to receive a phone call from one or the other three or four times a week in the summertime.

"Preacher, high tide will be at six o'clock this evening. If you're not busy, come out and we will go fishing."

When the incoming high tide was in the evening, I would ride with them in their boats just off shore. In an hour we could catch enough Norfolk spot fish, the tastiest fish in the river, to fill half of a five-gallon bucket. We caught sea trout weighing as much as two pounds. We used tackle that allowed us to catch two fish at a time. When Adell didn't hook a fish that took her bait, she always said, "He done took me to the cleaners."

I went fishing with Libby Jones more frequently. The ladies were always the captain of their fishing boats. Lois would go with us some times, but she never took a rod or experienced the joy of hooking a large fish and the struggle to get it into the boat. There were men who also enjoyed fishing, but none of them were better at the game than Adell and Libby.

I enjoyed preaching in these churches because the people were eager to hear Bible-based sermons. Many who attended were not life-long Methodists and seemed more eager and open to receiving the Gospel. By the time I left that charge there were nearly as many people attending the Coles Point Church as Carmel. I was probably closer emotionally to the people at Coles Point than I was at Carmel. But Carmel members were also very dear to me.

A lobbyist for the American Dairy Association attended the Carmel Church every Sunday. He thought I was a good preacher and more than once he quietly said to me at the door, "Why are you wasting your time with this bunch of farmers and watermen?" I think that was how he experienced the culture shock. He voiced feelings that other "come heres" shared with me from time to time. Somehow the culture shock did not shock me as hard as it shocked him. I loved those people, and they knew it.

The superintendent had sent me to Carmel and Coles Point to bring stability and order to that charge after a previous pastor had created turmoil in the congregations. I fulfilled that purpose the only way I knew how. I saw myself as a modern Barnabas. In the New Testament church, Barnabas had the gift of being able to bring people of different views and traditions together. After I retired I became a woodcarver of ducks and birds, which requires a lot of patience. My teachers told me I learned quickly and did a good job working on these creatures because I had a lot of patience to do fine work. Patience can work miracles among people of good will.

One of the wisest men I ever met was a waterman who never entered the fifth grade. His wife died; they had no children. He had been very devoted to her. Now his sorrow was as deep as his devotion. I visited him regularly in his small humble home in Coles Point. Week after week I found him sitting alone.

"Come in, preacher," he always greeted me. "Glad to see you."

"What have you been doing this week?" I asked, taking a seat.

"Nothing much, been thinking a lot," he said.

"Tell me about it, if you want to," I said, my voice trailing off silently.

"You know," he spoke after a slight pause, "when my wife died, I thought I couldn't live without her. I cried some. Well, I cried a lot at night, but here it is four months later and I'm doing all right. I don't think I'll ever get over it, but I am getting used to it."

I never heard grief recovery stated any better than that to this day.

About a year later Tom was hospitalized in the Tappahannock Hospital. I had visited him several times the week earlier, but on this particular day, as I approached his room I heard someone speaking to him. I paused outside in the hall out of sight. It didn't take long to realize that the person talking was another preacher who was trying very hard to get the old man saved before he died. After five minutes or more of evangelistic hard sell, he gave a long prayer. As he was preparing to leave I stepped into the room.

"Excuse me," I said.

"That's all right, brother," the other minister said. "I'm finished."

We shook hands and he left. I moved to Tom's bedside and said, "He was really telling you fellows all about it, wasn't he?"

Tom's answer was a classic. "You know, preacher, I believe it did him a lot of good."

Two years later Tom was hospitalized again, this time his situation was critical. He was taken to St. Mary's Hospital in Richmond. I visited him twice the first week. It was obvious that he was dying and he knew it. I took his hand and asked him if he was prepared to meet God should He call him soon.

"I have right smart faith, Preacher," Tom answered.

He died a week later and I conducted his funeral on April 17, 1981. The text for my remarks came from Philippians Chapter 1, verse six, and my topic was "The Place of Completion."

"Tom Jenkins was my friend," I began, "a rugged individualist whose kind is fast becoming extinct in our times. He lived a simple life loving the outdoors and especially the Potomac River. He was a unique person endowed with the wisdom one does not get in school."

48

Holy Lands

Lois and I joined fourteen other ministerial couples for a Holy Land tour under the leadership of Bishop C.P. Minnick. We flew to Kennedy Airport in New York where we boarded a 747 aircraft to Amsterdam. During our afternoon layover we did some sightseeing in the Dutch city before boarding a Jordanian 747 that flew us across the Alps and Europe to land in Amman, Jordan. The airport was crowded with a strange mixture of Westerners and hundreds of Arabs, who had come with all of their possessions on their backs from the desert. They were a frightening mass of humanity. They focused on us like we were aliens from another planet. They appeared to look at us with scorn and we looked at them with fear.

The Palestinians and Israelis had been fighting and killing each other since 1946, when Britain created the Jewish state of Israel. Following the 1967 Six Day War, Israel occupied the West Bank and Gaza and took control of the Temple Mount and all of Jerusalem (it had previously been a divided city). Arab animosity spilled out of the Middle East. In 1970, the terrorist group, Popular Front for the Liberation of Palestine, hijacked and blew up two American jets and a Swiss airliner to punish the United States for its support of Israel. In 1972, another Palestinian terror organization killed 11 Israeli athletes at the Munich Olympics. Almost a year to the day before we arrived in that part of the world, Anwar Sadat signed the Camp David Peace Accord with Menachem Begin of Israel, further inflaming the homicidal mania of the terrorists.

We knew about these tensions, but we were assured by our tour guides that tourists were generally safe since most of the income of both Jews and Arabs in Israel came from sightseers.

It took a long time to check our baggage and passports, but finally we boarded a bus and left the airport.

As we traveled through Amman in the early evening, our guide told us to close the shades on the bus so local residents could not see we were Western tourists. Security precautions were quite tight.

The bus took us to the Ambassador Hotel in Amman, a modern hotel with all of the amenities one could hope for. We ended the long day with a tasty meal. All of the waiters were men. Women were expected to stay at home. I don't recall seeing a female waitress at any time we were in Jordan, Israel, Egypt, or Greece.

The next morning I was awakened by what sounded like an old man crying for help. I wondered whether someone was being mugged. It was early but the sun was up when I stepped out onto the veranda of our second-floor room. I looked around, but saw no one on the street below or on the hotel lawn. However, across the way was a tall pointed spire fitted with a loudspeaker. Then I realized what I had heard was the first call to prayer when Muslims are to stop whatever they are doing, bow toward Mecca, and pray.

After breakfast our group boarded a bus. We left Amman to cross the Jordan River at the Allenby Bridge. At the Israeli-Jordan border female Israeli soldiers carefully searched our luggage. Allenby Bridge is the main entry point into Israel for Palestinians. One soldier ripped out the lining in our suitcases and rummaged through our clothing. She tore out a mirror built into the top of our overnight suitcase. Taking my camera out of its case, she told me to take a picture.

"You want me to take your picture," I asked good-naturedly.

"Don't be funny," she scowled. "Shoot the table."

These young soldiers were all business. She was making sure the camera was not a cover for some weapon. This inspection took hours, but finally we were allowed to proceed to Jericho, the ancient city as well as the modern town. We saw the excavations of the ancient walls and there is evidence that at some point they did fall down.

Near Jericho we crossed the Jordan River once again at the site where tradition says Jesus was baptized by John the Baptist. I was surprised to see the river was not "the mighty Jordan" as described in the familiar song, "I Walked Today Where Jesus Walked." Well, I was walking where Jesus walked but I didn't see the mighty Jordan roll, but a trickling stream not 25 feet wide.

In the range of rugged hills just west of Jericho, we explored the site identified as the Mount of Temptation. Of course, no one knows whether any of the places in modern Israel are the exact locales of events recorded in the Bible. But many traditions go back to very early times. If this particular mountain wasn't the site of Jesus' temptation, it certainly had to be some place nearby and very much like this desolate hill.

From the desert high country we could see the Jordan River valley, like a narrow green ribbon of vegetation. On either edge of that green belt lies a formidable desert where virtually nothing grows. I quickly understood why they say in that part of the world that water is as precious as oil.

At the southern tip of the Sea of Galilee was a suitable place to wade into the river. The Sea of Galilee is beautiful fresh water lake with a wide variety of fish. One food fish taken from the Sea of Galilee is called St. Peter's Fish. We ate lunch in a restaurant called Peter's Fish House, where they served up the small but tasty fish. The restaurant was located in the modern town of Tiberius, on the western shore of Galilee. Following lunch many in our group waded into the crystal clear water and walked on the rocky floor of the Sea of Galilee. The warm water was refreshing to poor achy feet.

At Tiberius we boarded a boat for a one-hour cruise across the Sea of Galilee to the site of the Biblical city of Capernaum. It was an inspirational journey. I could easily picture all the stories in the Scriptures that focus on that beautiful body of water. I could almost hear Jesus calling the sons of Zebedee to come follow him, and as we neared Capernaum, to hear Simon Peter cry out "Lord, save me."

We took a bus trip to the Golan Heights, a strategic piece of land where Israel borders Syria, captured and occupied by the Israelis after the Six Day War. We saw many Israeli military garrisons posted throughout the area. Our bus traveled to the border, where a guard greeted us and told us we could go no farther. He was a soldier from the United Nations. He pointed out their garrison about a mile away.

We returned to the Ginton Hotel in Tiberius, which became our base for day trips to Nazareth, Cana, and other sites in northern Israel.

The source of the Jordan River is a large spring at the base of Mount Herman. I remember stooping over and drinking from that spring. The water was clear as crystal and ice cold. We went as far north as to the southern border of Lebanon. From the town of Metulla we saw and heard Israeli jets bomb PLO positions in southern Lebanon. When we returned to the Ginton Hotel that evening, we found a large group of people gathered around the television in the lobby listening intently to the news report of a terrorist bomb that had gone off in a sidewalk café in Jerusalem. One person had been killed and 58 injured in the pedestrian mall. The terrorists said the bombing was in retaliation for the attacks on Metulla

The following day we traveled to Mount Tabor, believed to be the site of the Transfiguration of Jesus. From the wind-swept height of Mount Tabor, we could see the Jezreel Valley and the plains of Armageddon.

At the base of the Mount Tabor was an Arab who rented his camel to tourists. He tried to persuade us to ride the camel to the summit. Lois and I approached the camel but stopped suddenly when the strong odor from that critter reached us.

"Whew, he stinks," Lois said, squinting her eyes and holding her nose. I think she was referring to the camel, but it might also have been said of the Arab. There was no road up Mount Tabor until the 1930s when a gravel road was constructed so that material to build a church could be delivered to the site. Having declined the camel, we were packed into old taxicabs with daredevil drivers who relish the opportunity to throw us from side to side in the cab as he turned one hairpin curve after another. The driver seemed thrilled to shift into second-gear and with the engine roaring drive around those hairpin curves. It was so hair raising an adventure I almost wished we had taken the camel. About eight or ten minutes later we reached the summit, greatly relieved until we thought about the return trip.

The view from Mount Tabor was interesting; to the east one could see the Sea of Galilee and the hills of Moab; to the west was Mount Carmel were Joshua defeated 400 prophets of Baal.

We entered the beautiful Church of the Transfiguration and sat in the rear of the sanctuary. Two priests were conducting a service of mass. After the congregation was dismissed, we walked toward the altar where Bishop Minnick introduced us as a group of Methodist ministers from Virginia in the United States. When he said Virginia, one of the Franciscan priest's eyes lit up and he told us he was from a small town in Virginia. You would have thought he had found some long-lost relative as he introduced himself to each of us. When I introduced myself and Lois, he said, "You don't sound like a Virginian." I told him he was correct. I was a Pennsylvania Dutchman.

When the Bishop suggested it was time for us to leave, the priest from Virginia asked us to sing some hymns before we left. Early in the tour I had been designated the group's song leader. So, the Bishop nodded to me and I started to sing "All Hail the Power of Jesus Name" to the tune of Diadem. When we sang the third verse, "Sinners whose love can ne'er forget the wormwood and the gall," I saw tears rolling off the cheeks of this frail priest.

We joyously sang the triumphant fourth verse, filling the Church of the Transfiguration with these words: "O that with yonder sacred throng we at his feet may fall, we'll join the everlasting song and crown him, crown him, crown him, Lord of all."

By this time most of us were crying tears of joy along with our new friend.

"Would you please sing another song," the priest from Virginia asked.

"We will sing a Methodist hymn," I said.

I began singing the familiar lines, "O for a thousand tongues to sing my great Redeemer's praise." Our group never sounded better as the acoustics in that large stone church were excellent.

The ride down from Mount Tabor was more thrilling than any I ever had in a theme park. Rounding the hairpin curves one after another with stones and dust exploding beneath the wheels of those old cabs was enough to make you close your eyes and pray for mercy.

On our way to Jerusalem, I noticed as we drove further south in Israel the larger buildings were rimmed with soldiers on the rooftops.

We stayed in Jerusalem for five days. The following morning we began a five-day visit in Jerusalem. We visited so many historical sites in the holy city, but I will mention only a few. We visited the site called Gordon's Calvary not far from the hill of the skull and the site of the tomb where Jesus was reported to have been buried. It was a moving experience to enter that tomb. On a nearby hillside I conducted a communion service with our group.

We marveled at the Wailing Wall, the holiest shrine of the Jewish world, where I watched with fascination the bar mitzvah of a Jewish boy. From there we entered the Temple Mount, a 35-acre site currently occupied by two Muslim mosques, the Dome of the Rock and Al Aqsa Mosque. The Dome of the Rock sits today where the Jewish Temple once stood.

We were made to remove our shoes before entering the mosque. Inside we saw the large white rock that is the top of the ancient site of Mount Moriah, where Abraham prepared to sacrifice his son, Isaac, and which was the foundation of the altar of burn offerings in the Old Testament Temple.

The Al Aqsa Mosque is a large carpeted open floor that holds 5,000 worshipers. While we looked around inside the mosque, our guide tied all our shoestrings together as a joke.

We walked through the old city of Jerusalem along the Via de la Rosa (the sorrowful way) to the Church of the Holy Sepulcher and then out to the Garden of Gethsemane at the foot of the Mount of Olives. Olive trees from the time of Jesus still grow and bear olives there. Next to the garden is the Church of All Nations, the site where Jesus prayed and sweat drops of blood before he was arrested.

Our days were so full. We would return to the Ambassador Hotel in the late afternoon foot weary and hungry. I made a habit of checking at the hotel front desk to check for messages. Darlene was expecting their second child any day. We had left a complete itinerary with her and Ron so they could call us when the baby arrived. We were anxious to get a call.

The following day we went to the Church of the Nativity in Bethlehem. Israeli soldiers guarded virtually all of the historic sites in Jerusalem and in Bethlehem. I walked through Hezekiah's 1,777-foot tunnel through solid rock which ran from Gihon spring outside the wall to the pool of Siloam in the old city of Jerusalem. Those ancient tunnel diggers had started from either end and when they met in the middle the elevation was only about a half-inch off. Along with 10 or 12 other fellows I was given a small candle as we entered from outside the city wall. The tunnel was from five to seven feet tall and nearly two feet wide although some places I had to turn sideways to be able to pass by. We walked in water that was two to three feet deep. The water that flowed through that tunnel in antiquity saved the city of Jerusalem when it was under siege from the Babylonians in Old Testament times.

We took a day trip to Qumran on the shores of the Dead Sea. In 20 miles we dropped 4,000 feet. Jerusalem is 2,700 feet above sea level; Qumran is 1,300 feet below sea level. The Dead Sea Scrolls were found in caves near this Essene community. Although some members of our group went swimming in the Dead Sea, Lois and I chose not to do that. Anyone who had shaved that morning and gone into the salty water was miserable.

A black man from our group nearly drowned as he couldn't get himself upright in that salty water. If another preacher had not been close by to help him, he may well have died. He swallowed a lot of the brackish water. When we returned to Jerusalem, he was taken to a hospital and the following day he and his wife flew back to United States for further examinations.

As we drove south along the Dead Sea, we saw large blocks of salt, the size of an ironing board floating on the surface of the Dead Sea. We reached the fortress of Masada were Jewish zealots made their last stand against the Romans in 73 A.D. Rather than surrender to the Romans, 960 defenders committed suicide. All Israeli recruits are taken to Masada as part of their orientation and induction into the armed forces.

After exploring the mountaintop excavations, we returned to Jerusalem for dinner and bed. At 3:00 a.m. the phone in our room awakened us. The man at the desk said, "You have a call from the United States. I'll connect you."

It was Ron calling to tell me that we had another granddaughter and mother and daughter were doing fine.

"Thank God," I said. Darla Jean Stafford was born on September 25, 1979. She was a little redhead, and we looked forward to seeing her when we got home.

When Darlene and Darla went home from the hospital, Mom Weinel was there to help attend them. When we told our group that Darla was born, they congratulated us and shared our joy.

The author at the Temple of Apollo in Corinth, Greece

The following morning we packed our bags and once again drove to the Allenby Bridge, went through customs quickly, and boarded a Jordanian bus with a new guide. We returned to the Ambassador Hotel in Amman, Jordan. Amman is the biblical city of Philadelphia. Then we drove a few miles west to Mount Nebo.

I cannot describe the deep feelings that flooded my soul as I stood where Moses stood. He had been permitted to see the Promised Land, but God told him he could not enter it. I thought about how I had been traversing all over that land that Moses was not permitted to enter. I don't know what he saw when he stood there that day. I hope he saw more than I could through the hazy heat.

We proceeded south on a high plateau to Petra hundred fifty miles away. The bus stopped several times while caravans of camels crossed the highway. We passed one gas station and a restaurant, if you could call it that. Butchered sheep hung from the rafters as we entered the building. Fortunately, we had boxed lunches.

As we approached Petra we passed a large well called Moses' Well which provided water to the ancient city of Petra. A short time ago in geological time a river had cut a gorge through sandstone. We entered the ancient city on horseback because the road was far too narrow for any vehicle. Presently, the gorge widened to reveal an immense treasury building, a temple, and other great buildings etched out of vertical sandstone walls along the giant cliffs. There were as many as 2,600 caves originally occupied by the early descendents of Esau and still inhabited by the Bedouins. We walked on stone roads built by the Romans thousands of years ago. What a wonderful experience!

When the sun got high in the sky and became unbearable, we loaded into our bus for three and a half hour ride back to Amman.

The following morning we boarded a Royal Jordanian 747 aircraft where we were outnumbered three to one by Arab Bedouins going to Cairo, Egypt. We visited the Pyramids of Giza and the great Sphinx. We stayed on the tenth floor of the Shepherd Hotel, located on the banks of the Nile River. We trekked around all the famous sites in and around Cairo.

The following day we flew up the Nile River to Luxor and the Valley of the Kings where many Pharaohs are buried. We spent about three hours in that ancient city and saw temples built to honor ancient Egyptian gods.

We spotted a restaurant and a rest area where most of the ladies needed to go to the restroom. When Lois entered the ladies bathroom, a man followed her. He carried a bucket in one hand and some toilet tissue in the other. Lois pushed the door on him saying "No, no, no."

When she came out from the toilet, she walked past the man.

"Cheap, cheap, cheap," he said.

Lois was frightened by the man, and when she told me what happened I laughed every time I thought about it the rest of the day.

That evening we boarded the dirtiest train I have ever seen in my life. The ride was to take us to Cairo. When we boarded the train the temperature was 110 degrees. We were told that it had not rained in Luxor for five years.

Twelve hours later we finally reached the city of Cairo and later that day we boarded another aircraft and flew to Athens, Greece. When the plane landed and we entered into our hotel we thought we had landed in heaven. Our home for three days in Athens was the Golden Age Hotel, a modern clean hotel where we feasted on seven course meals. We visited the famous historical sites in and around Athens and Corinth. Much of the Apostle Paul's writings came to life in Athens.

After three wonderful days of sightseeing we boarded a plane for our return flight. Our plane arrived too late to make a connecting flight to Washington, so we were put up in a large motel near Kennedy Airport and the next morning we caught a plane to Washington, D.C. The trip was sometimes frightening but always interesting.

The knowledge gained in those three weeks made me a better pastor. The Bible became a living book in the Holy Lands. What a wonderful gift from the people in St. Paul Church.

When we got back home, we drove to Annapolis, anxious to meet our newest grandchild. What a wonderful joy to see her, take her up in my arms, and hold her. She was so very precious. Darlene informed us that Darla had difficulty eating. The uvula did not grow together in the back of her mouth. She had to be fed very carefully or the food would get into her nostrils. Darlene was the only one who learned the technique for feeding her.

When we got back home to Virginia, we were totally exhausted. After a good night's rest I called around to see what, if anything, had transpired while we had been traveling those three weeks. I was relieved to learn that everything was OK with our church members. No one had died or was critically ill in any of the hospitals. I arranged to show the pictures and lecture about our trip. Our people were eager to hear about our travels.

49

Sharing Abundance

In many ways, the time I spent at Carmel and Coles Point was one of the most idyllic times of my life. Everything I enjoyed most in life was there in abundance: wonderful people, great fishing, gardening, and the opportunity to minister in meaningful ways.

Planting with grandson, Ronnie

My second year there I had the largest garden of my life. My neighbor told me that his farmer would plow and disk a field and fertilize it. He told me to mark off how large a garden plot I wanted. I chose a plot that was 70 by 100 yards. That's a large garden. Early in the season I planted a few things that could take the cool weather if necessary. Later I planted beets, carrots, cabbage, corn, and tomatoes. I planted cantaloupes, broccoli, and so many other vegetables. Everything flourished. My neighbor told me he didn't think I knew what I was doing when I had marked off such a large patch. He used to laugh and tell his wife there was no way this new preacher would be able to care for such a large garden. But I kept the garden perfectly; there wasn't a weed to be found anywhere.

About the middle of July he saw me working in the garden and pulled his truck into our driveway. I walked over to his truck and greeted him.

"Preacher, I owe you an apology," he said. "I've been making fun of you all spring for putting in such a huge garden."

He got out of his truck and shook my hand. "'Deed, if you don't have the best looking garden up and down this road. You're the best. I was wrong; you're the best."

"Thank you, brother," I said.

He didn't know that I had an excellent teacher, my Dad.

When Darla was a year old, she was taken to Children's Hospital in Baltimore for surgery to correct her uvula. In the recovery room, she evoked all the pity in this grandfather's heart. Blood was oozing out of her mouth, which was stuffed with cotton wads tied with string that hung from her mouth also coated with blood. This string would be used to eventually extract the wads and also to keep her from swallowing them. But the sight was more than Darlene could handle at the time. So, I walked with Darla around that whole area. I didn't sit down for the longest time because Darla seemed more at ease if we were walking. My shirt was covered with blood where she cradled her face on my shoulder. That was one difficult day. Darlene stayed with her in the hospital for five days. Thankfully, the surgery to close the opening in her mouth was successful and she had no difficulty whatsoever in recovering. Today no one would ever know that she ever had a problem.

Two of the most difficult events I faced in the country were a couple of suicide deaths. A man from Coles Point suffered for months with severe cancer. He had gone through surgery in Richmond had been in remission for almost a year. But his cancer returned and after several months his doctors recommended that he undergo a second operation. He was 65 years old. Two days before he was to enter the hospital he went into his back yard and shot himself. I can only imagine why he chose to take his life. He had been through it all once before—the long months of intense suffering and the huge expenses that had drained his meager savings. His wife had to drive 70 miles one way every day to visit him in Richmond. She had been worn to a frazzle in the first go-around. I suspect the thought of repeating that awful scenario with no guarantee of a positive outcome became an unbearable burden, so he chose what he thought was his best option. His death shocked the town of Coles Point. I rushed out to comfort his wife as soon as I heard what had happened. I tried to offer whatever assistance I could at that crushing time, but there's really nothing anyone can say. Suicide funerals are difficult not only for the family but also for the minister.

The next story was even more tragic. A young white man from one of my member families fell in love with a young black lady whom he wanted to marry. Social change happens more slowly in the country than in the large cities or on television. Racial lines were still drawn pretty sharply in Westmoreland County in the northern neck of Virginia. When his parents learned he was dating this girl who lived about 20 miles away, their anger was all consuming. They threatened to take the boy's pickup truck and they forbade him to ever see her again. But he was 20 years old, and the powerful forces of society, culture, and family were in conflict with the power of love and something had to give way. I cannot imagine the struggle that young man faced every waking moment of the day. Finally he drove to her house and, after spending an evening with the girl he loved, rather than go home, he shot himself in his truck parked in her yard. The pressure of conflict was more than he could bear.

The young man never came to church nor ever sought my counsel. I don't know what I would have said if he had come to me. I would hope that I would trust the Holy Spirit at the moment to guide me, but I honestly don't know what I could have said to the boy. I felt tongue-tied as I went to his parents' home to express my sympathy and offer my assistance. I stayed a long time to hear them vent their anger and express their grief. I cried with them. I did not visit the black girl or her parents. I wondered how her parents felt about her relationship with the white boy. Racial prejudice worked two ways in the country. I had ambivalent feelings about going to the black community, but I had a lot of sympathy for the girl. Several days later I conducted the funeral. I could not find any notes of my sermon for that service. It may be that I never prepared a written outline. I remember that I cited the 23rd Psalm as an affirmation of faith, which I usually use at most of my services. My message was "He Restores My Soul." I know whatever I said must have come from a broken heart that was being restored by the grace of God, and I wanted to share that power of grace with others whose hearts were broken, especially those parents and family members. As if to punctuate the tragedy, there was not a black person at the funeral.

I planted a large garden the following spring with the idea that I would share the produce of the harvest. I canned and froze many vegetables for the winter.

When I had more than I could use, I took tomatoes, squash, and cantaloupe to the Coles Point Church. I would set the produce in the church vestibule and city folks picked up whatever they desired. I often took the produce to elderly people who had no gardens. This is what I enjoyed most about gardening—the community it created when the earth produced so much one had to share the abundance.

An elderly geologist who owned a large tract of land on the Machodoc River came to the parsonage one day on some business. As he was preparing to leave, I asked him to wait a minute while I went into the garden and cut a large head of cabbage. I handed it to him. He looked somewhat bewildered and said, "I never had a preacher give me anything."

He was used to giving things to the preacher. His wife was a gifted artist. We have one of her original oil paintings in our living room, a picture of Robert E. Lee's birthplace, Stratford Hall Plantation.

On the day before my 56th birthday Michael David Barnett was born on May 8, 1980, my fifth grandchild who hopefully will pass on the Barnett name for another generation. Michael got a good start in life and just recently stopped growing. All of us have to look up to him and soon we will call him Doctor Barnett.

I loved living in the country, but Lois only tolerated it. In some ways, we experienced our own little culture clash. I liked the peace and quiet of the country; she missed the convenience and contacts of the city. The people were magnanimous and receptive to my leadership and especially to my preaching. Come to think of it, I have liked every place I have ever lived. I had learned to be content where ever I lived.

After three years a superintendent friend who had been one of our Holy Lands group asked me if I would leave the country and take an appointment to Wesley United Methodist Church in Hopewell, Virginia. No matter how many times we had packed our belongings and prepared to leave, it never became easy for me to say goodbye. The elderly people seemed the most disappointed to learn that we were leaving for the city of Hopewell 25 miles south of Richmond. But my mission was accomplished in the country.

50

Hopewell

We were greeted by members of the parsonage committee when we moved to Hopewell the end of June, 1981. That church was highly organized; they prided themselves on doing their work in an organized and efficient way. Wesley Church was the second Methodist congregation in Hopewell. It was beautifully situated in the western end of the city. The parsonage was a fine four-bedroom, two-story house. It sat on a corner lot about two blocks from the church. Surrounded by medium-sized lawns, the house featured a carport, a double car garage, but it had no garden plot.

My predecessor had done a good job preparing the congregation for an extensive building program that had just begun. Footings for a new sanctuary and office complex were laid. Week after week, I enjoyed watching the beautiful colonial church take shape until at last the steeple was placed on the roof. The congregation and I celebrated every part of our new church construction. Finishing out the interior was not as exciting, but every bit of the work was done to perfection.

We laid the cornerstone in the spring of 1982 and on May 9, 1982, on my 58th birthday, Bishop Robert Blackburn led our service of consecration. It was so exciting to be back in the city and to watch this church building rise from the soil. I wasn't growing vegetables this year; I was cultivating and growing a church. It was thrilling.

Wesley Church had an excellent music program. We had two excellent choir directors and an organist who was also my secretary for two years. The choir served up a steady diet of classical music. I tried to bring balance to the music by singing contemporary solos. Sometimes I could persuade the choir to sing something contemporary and evangelical by requesting music that complemented the theme of my sermon. The directors were graduates of Westminster school of music and it showed. Every year the choir presented Christmas and Easter cantatas, but the director absolutely refused to sing with taped music.

The routine of sermon preparation, preaching, teaching short-term studies for adults, hospital and shut-in visitation, and committee meetings kept me busy day and night. I did not go fishing once in the three years I was pastor at Wesley Church.

Before she had her ear surgery, Lois promised Darlene she would baby sit Ronnie and Darla when Darlene had to teach for a semester in order to graduate with a teaching certificate. The drive from Hopewell to Annapolis took three hours. Lois left Hopewell Sunday afternoon and returned Friday evening. She made this trip several times when she began to have dizzy spells while attending the children. It was becoming too dangerous for Lois to drive. A member of the congregation who was stationed at Fort Meade but came home to Hopewell on weekends volunteered to take her to and from Annapolis. Lois was determined to make good on the promise she had made to Darlene if it was the last thing she ever did. When she was no longer able to care for the children, we contacted Mom Weinel, who finished babysitting the children until Darlene completed her teaching assignment. Later, Lois' mother came to our house that summer to help care for Lois after her surgery. Otherwise, I would not have been able to do my work at the church. Lois needed a lot of care for months.

John Weaver was a man about my age who lived on the outskirts of Hopewell. He looked exactly like my Grandfather Baer, which may have been why I had such a special affinity to him. He also had a large garden. He loved gardening as much as I did. He had some extra land so he urged me to start my garden on his plot and plant as much as I wished. My garden was about half the size I had in the country. It provided plenty of vegetables that summer and fall. Mr. and Mrs. Weaver became our closest friends in Wesley Church. When John Weaver died several years after I was moved to northern Virginia, I attended his funeral and eulogized my dear friend.

Our church showed steady growth in attendance both in Sunday school and worship throughout my tenure at Wesley Church. One very special occasion was the celebration of the church's 30th birthday. About half of the 84 charter members were still living and attended the anniversary party. We paid tribute to them in that birthday celebration.

I thought we had a lot of deaths for a young congregation. I wondered why until I realized there were numerous chemical and plastic manufacturing plants located along the Appomattox River, which formed the northeast border of the city of Hopewell. Dupont was manufacturing the latest synthetic carpets at that time. Many believed that emissions from those chemical plants had an adverse effect upon the health of many people in Hopewell.

I could relate dozens of deaths from cancer the three years I was pastor, but I will share only two stories. I believe my training as a medic in the Army enabled me to deal with serious illness and death with less anxiety than some pastors. Henry and his wife, Elizabeth, always sat in the same place for worship, the back seat on the left side of the sanctuary. They had been members of the church for a long time. They had no children. Henry was my age at the time when he started to cough a lot and have difficulty eating food. Early in the diagnosis, doctors were uncertain of the cause of his coughing, but a CAT scan showed a growth in his esophagus. A biopsy revealed that he had an inoperable cancer. Every day Henry's pain increased, and he coughed incessantly. It wasn't long before he couldn't eat anything, so a stomach tube was inserted to sustain him. Elizabeth could hardly bear to visit him in the hospital and see him in such pain and agony. I will never forget hearing Henry beg for water. I spent a lot of time endeavoring to comfort and to prepare Elizabeth for the eventuality of Henry's death. I arranged for some ladies in the congregation to visit her in the evening.

I visited him in the hospital just about every day. As his situation worsened, Henry started asking me to pray to God to let him die. I did ask God to lead him patiently through the closing days of his life. I promised Henry that I would look after Elizabeth and see that she was cared for. I asked God to enfold Henry in his care and hasten the day when he would be set free from his suffering and pain. When Henry asked for water I placed a straw in his mouth, he took several sips of water and soon the water would seep out beside the stomach tube. Moments later he begged for water with the same result. Mercifully, God answered our prayer when he died after unbelievable pain and agony. I conducted his funeral service, where many people came to honor and celebrate the life of a quiet man who met death not as an enemy but as a friend.

Francis was on the sick list left by my predecessor and it noted that I should see her soon. So, soon after I arrived at Wesley Church, I visited Francis and her husband, Archie, who had recently retired from his job. They appeared to be a very compatible couple. Francis had been diagnosed with cancer several months before. She was just getting over the shock and was beginning to adjust to her new condition. They had just returned from a three-week vacation when I stopped by their house. They had a nice trip, but Francis said the best part of the trip was coming home.

The following months she was in and out of the hospital. Doctors performed various surgical treatments as well as chemotherapy, all of which made her very ill. Archie was by her side day and night. How they loved each other. But her health deteriorated steadily until she was in the hospital more than she was at home. Her cancer had spread to several other organs in her body. Her friends tried to encourage her by telling her to keep fighting. Archie was always by her side, but I doubt he ever gave her false hope of recovering.

After six months or more of misery, weakness, and pain, I visited her at John Randolph Hospital in the evening. Her strength was gone. She looked at me and said, "I'm tired of fighting, Pastor. I'm just too tired."

I told her I thought she had fought long enough. "Why don't you relax and commit yourself to God right now as I pray."

She reached out her hand to take mine, as did her husband. When I finished praying with her, her grip released, she opened her eyes, and said, "Thank you, Pastor."

I sensed that she was greatly relieved that I gave her permission to stop fighting. She remained conscious with Archie holding her hand constantly surrounded by his love. Several days later she died peacefully with the knowledge that God would meet her when she got home. The best part of life for the Christian is arriving home safely.

When I conducted her funeral at Wesley Church, her many friends packed the church to celebrate her life. I have before me my notes from that service on November 10, 1982. I knew her for only five months, but I had visited Francis and Archie dozens of times so I had any number of themes I could have used in my sermon. I always base my sermons on a biblical text and always personalize my remarks as much as is appropriate. The text I chose for her service was from Ecclesiastes Chapter 7, verses one through eight with a focus on verse one and verse eight which reads, "A good name is better than fine perfume, and the day of death better than the day of birth…the end of the matter is better than its beginning and patience is better than pride." I think I could have spoken from these texts relating it to her life for several hours, but I spoke 20 or 25 minutes. I closed my sermon with these words: "Planning a trip can be exciting. The trip can be fun, but isn't the greatest joy arriving home safely? If Francis could speak to us now, she would respond to that statement with her familiar words, "I know it, I know it."

I do not recall any real conflict with anyone during my years at Wesley Church. That is not to say that everyone agreed with everything I said in my sermons, my teaching, or committee meetings. Some of my holiness sermons were not received too well by some of my members. I recall one sermon I titled "Conversion a la Mode" in which I spoke about the importance of sanctification by faith; I tried to make the point that sanctification is to conversion what ice cream is to apple pie. I don't know whether the illustration was confusing or if the congregation wasn't spiritually minded enough to get the point of my sermon.

I enjoyed teaching confirmation classes. One year I handed each student an old Sunday bulletin and proceeded to explain the purpose of each part of the order of worship. Everything was fine until I made the mistake of asking what part of the service each child liked the best.

One boy said, "The benediction because I get to go home and eat."

The class broke down in great laughter. So, I gave the benediction and told the class, "I'll see you next week. Class dismissed."

51

St. James Church

Darlene and her family came to see us about twice a month. I was always glad to see them round the corner and pull into the driveway. "They're here!" we would say when we saw them pull into the driveway. Ron always had a briefcase full of papers to grade. Ronnie and Darla brought books and toys to keep them occupied when we were not playing board games or card games. Darlene might bring the laundry for the week. They lived in an apartment and were often too busy during the week to visit the laundromat. Darla enjoyed going a short block from the parsonage where a freight train passed each evening about 8:30.

The last big event for us at Hopewell was the celebration of our 40th wedding anniversary. The church got together each year around Valentine's Day for a Sweetheart's Dinner. Darlene and my secretary, Judy Williamson, planned a number of surprises that evening for Lois and me. Darlene contacted our family members and friends in Pennsylvania and Maryland who showed up. But the biggest surprise was when David and Julie appeared. They had flown in from Indiana without anyone telling us. We were surprised beyond words. The church presented us with a large microwave oven. Darlene and Judy pulled off the event without a hitch. That was an unforgettable evening.

About that same time, I told my superintendent that we were hoping to be appointed to a church in Northern Virginia where we would be closer to Lois's mother, who lived in Maryland and to my mother, who was in a nursing home in Pennsylvania. In addition being a diabetic, Mom Weinel had developed osteoporosis, but she refused to slow down. She still loved to go shopping as she had done her all life. Lois and I were concerned that on one of her adventures she might fall or that her health might suddenly deteriorate and she would need us to be close.

David plays at 40th Wedding Anniversary; granddaughter Darla listens, too

Final arrangements were completed by the end of May, and at the annual conference in June I was appointed to St. James Church in Alexandria, Virginia.

Many people in Wesley Church were sorry to learn that we would soon leave. The three years in Hopewell had been so rewarding and fulfilling. Our new church building was beautiful. The acoustics were excellent for both preaching and singing. The people were kind and generous. In a history of Wesley United Methodist Church written after I was Pastor, my legacy was described as follows:

> *Reverend Clarence Barnett was appointed to Wesley at the annual conference in June 1981. Clarence came at a crucial time for Wesley. The construction of the sanctuary had just begun. He assumed this task with courage and aplomb and saw it to its glorious finish. He and Lois made a significant contribution to the music program, Lois sang in the chancel choir and Clarence was a soloist. Because of Clarence's genuine concern for his people and his warm and personal prayers, it was easy for him to become one of us. His love of the arts enriched his ministry at Wesley.*

St. James Church was located near three large retirement homes with nursing facilities. The Hermitage was a United Methodist affiliated facility with a one hundred bed nursing home. The Washington House was founded by United Methodists but had no official affiliation with the United Methodist Church. A larger facility was Goodwin House, which was affiliated with the Episcopal Church. The membership at St. James was about two-thirds elderly people from the three retirement homes. The remaining third lived in single family dwellings or in high-rise condominiums and apartments just off I-95 in the sprawling southern suburbs of Washington, DC.

Many members of St. James were retired and active military personnel. Others were professional people who could afford to live in one of the large retirement homes. The congregation had a number of retired preachers, superintendents, college and seminary professors, and professional men and women. They were the most distinguished group of people I had ever served as a pastor. It was a real challenge to me every time I entered the pulpit. They attended services faithfully. All were seasoned Christians who were used to "calling the shots," but now struggled to find meaning in the closing years of their lives. They were as supportive of my leadership and preaching as any congregation I ever served. What wonderful people! As I write this story I realize that I am now the age of those folks and today I look to the church for the ministry I endeavored to provide.

Pastors who served St. James usually requested a transfer after a year or two because they could not handle the unique challenges of serving sick and dying people on a continual basis. It was not unusual to have two funerals a week. One week I presided at three burials. My superintendent and Bishop believed I had the temperament and the gifts that fit the needs of St. James Church. I would stay at St. James until my retirement at age 65.

The church listed some 350 members on the rolls, with an average attendance of 120 in good weather. In addition to preaching, I taught an adult Sunday school Bible class. Air Force General Wilma Vaught was the chairperson of the Board of Administration at St. James Church and she taught a Bible class at the Hermitage. General Vaught was the chairperson of the committee responsible for the memorial to the women who served in Vietnam near the Vietnam Memorial.

The Pentagon was not far from our church. I was privileged to attend several promotion ceremonies in the Pentagon for officers who attended our church. I conducted numerous funeral services for veterans at Arlington National Cemetery where the chapel service could not last one minute longer than the scheduled half hour. Following the caisson from the chapel to the gravesite was always a stirring, patriotic walk for me. This was holy ground. Watching the soldiers remove the flag from the casket, fold it precisely according to protocol, and then present the flag to a spouse or a family member was a moving, somber moment. The words of thanks from the sergeant in charge of the detail often moved me to tears.

The church parsonage was a two-story, four-bedroom house with a sun porch. It was conveniently located just three blocks from the church in a pleasant community with lots of trees. A ten-foot high wooden fence was a quick escape route for the squirrels that stole green apples from my apple tree. They were always running to and fro with some purloined delicacy. When I saw one of the varmints running away with nearly ripe tomatoes from my garden, that was more than I could take. I borrowed a trap from a neighbor and in the course of two weeks I caught 35 squirrels. I took the critters to a nice park two miles away. I don't believe they ever came back. I tried to plant a garden, but I didn't get enough sun through the treetop canopy to do very well. But I did get some worthwhile exercise in the process.

Having an older congregation meant I did not have a busy mid-week schedule. I was home most evenings unless I was called away for an emergency. Lois got a job working at Northern Virginia Doctors Hospital in Arlington, Virginia, not far away. She worked in the business office part time while she was still recovering from ear surgery. I drove her to work for nearly a year. As she felt stronger, she returned to full time employment and was put in charge of the cashier department.

I volunteered to be a Chaplain every Friday at National Orthopedic Hospital near the Pentagon. People came from all over the country for knee and hip replacements. I became a pastor to those patients who were far away from home. I received many assignments to visit patients who were angry about being discharged too soon. At that time, Medicare outlined how long a patient was allowed to stay in the hospital after any given procedure. To save money, recovery time was typically cut short by a day or two and the patients did not like it. Of course, the hospital had to comply since Medicare would not cover the cost for the additional time spent in the hospital. Patients asked me to intercede.

"Can't you do something, Chaplain?" they would ask. But there was nothing I could do.

I was appointed to serve on the hospital's ethics committee along with several doctors, an administration officer, and the nursing supervisor. Each month the committee met over dinner. We reviewed complaints and actions taken by hospital staff. Many complaints involved living wills and what determined extraordinary life support procedures. Family members complained when certain measures were taken or if extraordinary measures were not taken. We discovered that many of these problems arose because doctors' orders were not written clearly, and often the nurse who was on duty at the time was left with the life and death responsibilities. I thought it was wrong to lay this burden on the nurses. Many crises resulted when surviving family members could not agree on what procedure should be followed, which left the staff in the hospital in a hopeless position. It was interesting work and I felt honored to serve on the committee.

I became personally involved in one such case when an elderly lady from my church was being kept on life support at National Orthopedic Hospital. She had no living relatives in this country, no one to speak on her behalf. She had drawn up a living will, which clearly stated that no extraordinary measures were to be taken in the hospital to prolong her life. I visited her several times a week for two months and saw no change in her condition. I became convinced that the hospital was collecting money from Medicare for her care, but that she was in fact receiving little if any medical attention. I was the only person who could speak for her and I thought the time had come to do something about it.

I confronted her personal physician with my concern. I asked why no action was being taken in her case. At first he was defensive, but after I reminded him about the living will, he agreed that there was no reason to continue and he ordered the life support to be discontinued. She died, of course, very quickly, and I conducted her funeral several days later. Only two or three staff members from the Hermitage attended and no one went to the cemetery except and the funeral director and myself. Two workers from the cemetery were drafted to join the funeral director and me as pallbearers. I felt very sad as we carried the casket from the Hearse to the grave, but I believed that I had done the right thing. There's no way to know how long she might have been left on life-support if I had not interceded. My decision to act on her behalf was supported by the ethics committee members when it was discussed at a later meeting.

This didn't happen once or twice, but many times I counseled with family members who wanted to know and do what was right for a terminally ill family member or loved one. I think this is an important aspect of modern ministry. I don't remember that I ever took a class in medical ethics during my seminary days. I hope young pastors are being prepared to help their congregations with this difficult dilemma.

Area ministers conducted worship services in the three retirement homes several times each quarter. We became very well acquainted with the residents. I knew virtually all the residents in the Hermitage. There was a full-time chaplain there and we shared many funeral services together. I spoke one evening at a service where as many as 150 residents and family members were present. When the chaplain introduced me, before I had an opportunity to speak a lady in the second row said, "Somebody told me you're long-winded."

I smiled then said, "Ma'am I'm not long-winded; I just seem to be long-winded."

The congregation laughed and I proceeded to read a Scripture lesson and preach a sermon. I sang at nearly all of the services; sometimes Lois and I sang duets.

Two residents from Washington House asked me to marry them. Both the man and the woman were 83 years old. When I met with them the first question I asked was what do your children think about this? They were surprised at the question because they hadn't really asked what their kids thought. After learning their children gave them their blessing, they had a lovely wedding in the social hall at Washington House. One of the man's sons came up to me at the reception.

"I heard it said there is no fool like an old fool," he said. What could I say! The couple was still living two years later when I retired from St. James Church.

52

But They Write Nice Letters

One of the most challenging events of my entire ministry was dealing with scam artists who were stealing from a resident of the Hermitage who was also a member of St. James Church. One day while visiting her she said, "I don't think I'll ever get caught up with all my work."

"What work?" I asked. All she had to do was get up each morning, dress and go to the dining hall three times a day.

"This work," she said, producing a stack of letters about two inches thick from beside her chair. "I simply don't know how I can find time to answer all these letters."

She handed the bundle of letters to me. I was astounded to learn that she was sending a check for no less than $25 to every charity who wrote to her. I had heard of some, but most were causes I had never heard of. She told me that she had been giving between $25,000 and $35,000 a month to these so-called charities. I noticed that many return addresses were only post office box numbers and not street addresses. I called this to her attention, saying it was a sign that many of these may not be legitimate charities.

She looked at me with a genuinely puzzled expression and said, "How could they write such nice letters if they weren't being honest?"

I inquired if she had spoken to the administrator or any staff member about all this mail. She told me she had not. Scam artists had found a gold mine in the gullibility of this woman, and they were working hard to get everything they could from her. I asked if she would allow me to check into four of the charities that showed addresses in Washington. I was especially interested in one charity called "Feed My Hungry Children in Africa." I wrote letters requesting information on the organizations, using the enclosed self-addressed donation envelopes to mail the letters. A couple weeks went by and I received no replies.

I contacted the Better Business Bureau in Washington, who informed me that they had received some complaints on file about Feed My Hungry Children in

Africa, but they had never been able to reach anyone to confirm the organization's purpose. The BBB advised me that, until they could verify the identity of these so-called charities, I should have nothing to do with them. When I told to my church member what I had discovered, all she could say was, "How could they write such nice letters?"

When I learned that a local bank was the executor of her estate, I was surprised that some bank officer had not contacted this lady regarding the huge outflow of money from her account. I even wondered if someone at the bank could somehow be involved in the scam. I contacted the bank and requested they send a representative to meet with me and their customer at the lady's apartment the following day.

One of the bank's vice presidents showed up for the meeting. I explained the situation and showed the officer stacks of canceled checks from the previous three months. The lady from the bank was flabbergasted. She could offer no explanation for the oversight on their part and assured me the bank would be more attentive in the future and advised the gullible woman in such matters. I tried to explain to this trusting soul that there was no good reason for her to respond to all the requests she received from charities, especially those of which she had never heard. I alerted the Hermitage administrator to the problem and asked him to warn all the residents to beware that they were prize targets for these mail order scam artists.

Imagine my surprise one Sunday morning when I looked over my congregation and spotted two familiar faces I had not seen in many years. John and Harriet Walton were dear friends who joined the Spencerville church following their graduation from college in the 1950s. John was a project manager for an aerospace contractor. They lived in Alexandria, not far from the Pentagon. John and Harriet were outstanding singers and soon they joined Lois and me singing mixed quartet numbers in church as well as for social gatherings. We spent many hours reviewing events that had transpired in their lives and in ours since we had seen them in the early 1960s.

Elderly people get a little mixed up sometimes. It was not uncommon for someone to walk into the church and sit down waiting for worship to begin and be oblivious to the fact it was Friday morning or Tuesday or some other day. I took the opportunity to talk with them and tell them how much I appreciated their faithfulness. One Sunday I spoke to a lady as she left worship service.

"I missed you in church last week," I told her.

"I was here last week," she said, looking puzzled. "But I'm not here today."

I cannot tell you how often I ministered to elderly people in hospitals who never had anyone visit them, not a family member, not one friend. Except for the nurses who looked after them, I was the only person who expressed any care for the fact that they were in the hospital. When I inquired if they had relatives in the area, patients frequently told me they had nieces or nephews, but they never showed up at the hospital. If one of those solitary patients died, the funeral parlor swarmed like bees with relatives who made sure they signed the visitors' book. That may sound terribly cruel but it's the absolute truth.

The AIDS virus was front-page news during the 1980s. Since I spent a lot of time in hospitals, I visited quite a few AIDS patients. Jane worked with Lois in the business office at the hospital. Jane had a son in his mid-20s who was very ill in the Alexandria Hospital. Jane asked Lois if I would consider visiting him, never saying he had AIDS. As his condition worsened, his mother was afraid he would die without seeing a minister. It is interesting to me that even people who would not describe themselves as "religious" will instinctively turn to the church for the blessing of a marriage or for comfort when death touches their lives.

I don't know what she expected. Ministers cannot work magic. But when Lois told me about the young man, I suspected he was dying of AIDS. Jane never talked with me directly, but I told Lois to tell her that I would visit her sick boy.

I saw him later that day. He was severely emaciated with hollow cheeks, not unlike the ghastly people rescued from POW and concentration camps following World War II.

I introduced myself to him. He welcomed me with his eyes for he was so weak he could not raise his hand. He spoke in a labored whisper. He told me that he and his family never went to church, never had anyone to call on for help as he made his way down the road to the grave. Like many other young homosexual men, he told me he had learned the hard way that the lifestyle was not all it was cracked up to be. I learned that his favorite uncle, Jane's brother, was also a homosexual. It seems hardly necessary to tell you more of this young man's sad story. I told him it was never too late to call upon the Lord and I assured him that God was a merciful God. He gave no indication that he understood what I was saying. I'm not sure the word "God" had any meaning to him. Nevertheless, following our brief conversation, I prayed with him, asking God to meet him in some way that he could understand and to which he could respond.

Two days later the young man died and I was asked to conduct the funeral. I met Jane and members of her family at the funeral home the following evening. Not many people were at the funeral home when Lois and I went to meet them. The casket was to remain closed. Usually I can gain some insight into a person's life as I talk with the family, but I couldn't get a clue from his mother or other relatives what I might say about him in the service. This family didn't have a clue about what it meant to be a Christian, but they wanted a Christian funeral. I did my best the following day when I read words of comfort and hope from the Scriptures. I spoke of the young man kindly without recrimination (something not often heard in those days from Bible-believing preachers, many of whom were convinced AIDS was a curse from God). I hoped that something I might say would help family members realize that God wanted to comfort them in their sorrow and grief. Jane never talked about her son in the days and weeks that followed. She was an extremely private person and proud. She confided in no one, and she kept whatever heartache she carried completely to herself.

53

Retirement

Except for our time in Winona Lake, Lois and I had lived in parsonages through-out my professional ministry career. Unfortunately, the church does not provide housing for its retirees. We had saved some money over the years and had considered buying a small house or entering a retirement home. But Darlene came up with a plan that seemed to be our best option at that time. She and Ron wanted to purchase a home where Lois and I might have our own "apartment." In exchange for helping with the down payment, we could live in the house rent-free for as long as we wanted.

The tri-level house Darlene and Ron bought was located on a large lot in a wooded subdivision of Annapolis called Rolling Knolls. There was a large front yard and woods on the back third of the property. We would have the bottom floor for a living room and kitchen and sleep in one of the four bedrooms upstairs.

After Ron and Darlene moved in, we worked through the spring to remodel the unfinished part of the basement into our kitchen. We hung cabinets, laid the flooring, and put in new windows. The elevation of the house was such that the bottom floor was not completely underground. Our windows were at eye level.

The best thing about new living arrangement was that we had the joy of being part of Ronnie and Darla's growing up years. We felt very close to both of them because they had visited us so much as infants. Now we were together and there is nothing more important than that. We attended many of their school activities and followed Darla to softball, basketball, and field hockey games throughout the county. I enjoyed working with Darla to develop her athletic skills. When Coach Brady asked Ronnie to videotape all of the high school basketball games, we saw to it that Ronnie got to all the games at home and away.

Our annual trips to Rehoboth Beach were always the highlight of fun every year. Early bicycle rides on the boardwalk, hours on the beach under a big umbrella, riding ocean waves, playing games at the arcade, hanging on during the amusement park rides, and playing miniature golf filled our day. We carbed out on Gus's French fries. Days ended with evening walks on the boardwalk shopping in the stores, watching night volleyball games on the beach, and ice cream to top it all off. We might sit on the porch of our apartment with the aroma of pizza filling the air. Finally we tumbled into bed, knowing that the next day we would repeat the fun all over again.

With some reluctance Darlene permitted me to dig up a 12' by 35' patch for a garden in the sunny portion of the backyard. I was as happy as a clam. The vegetables I harvested from that garden were amazing. I canned dozens of quarts of green beans and tomatoes, which we ate all winter long. I had the most delicious large tomatoes for several years. Darla was my best worker, or maybe I should say she was my only worker. She wanted to sell the tomatoes. At first we set up a stand in front of the house, but traffic was pretty limited as we lived at the very back of the subdivision. But she sold tomatoes to virtually everybody who drove by. Later we secured permission to set up a table in the front of Leydorf's home on the main road into the community where she sold a bushel of tomatoes in a couple of hours. When she counted all the money, I asked her for my share.

"No, Poppy," she said. "I sold them."

As I got older I found that I would get lightheaded if I bent over, so it became a struggle to pick beans. Darla was there to help me much of the time. I sat on a stool to pick the beans, zucchini squash, acorn and yellow crook squash, lima beans, potatoes, kale and spinach in the fall. I gave vegetables to the neighbors who also relished the sweet basil I planted every year.

When we moved to Annapolis, I had expected that many men in the church or in our community would be fishermen. I had hoped I would receive many invitations to fish in the Chesapeake Bay, one of the world's finest places for seafood. Some of my friends promised me they would take me fishing, but Ritchie Park, who lived on the South River not far from the mouth of the bay, is the only person who took me fishing the first six years we lived in Annapolis.

Lois and I joined Trinity United Methodist Church in Annapolis. We sang in the sanctuary choir; Lois sang soprano and I sang bass. Occasionally I was asked to sing a solo. As it turned out, my retirement lasted for all of two months, July and August of 1989.

The previous December, the pastor at Trinity, Eldon Watts, began having fainting episodes. He was hospitalized and ultimately learned that he had blocked carotid arteries to the brain. The doctors determined that the placement of the blockage was such that they could not operate to remove it. I was asked to fill the pulpit for the six weeks the pastor was hospitalized. When Reverend Watts was told that he had to go on disability leave, he and his wife moved into an assisted-living facility in Westminster, Maryland. The District Superintendent in the Baltimore Conference, the Reverend Byron Brought, appointed me to be the interim pastor until a new one could be appointed at the June, 1990 annual conference.

I was glad to accept the appointment at Trinity Church. Once again I had all of the responsibilities of the pastor. I could sing solos every Sunday if I chose to do so.

Five months later, the new pastor arrived. The Reverend Donald Matney was a much younger man. He asked me to stay on the staff as the minister of visitation. It wasn't long before I was back in the bass section of the choir.

Matney's theological views and my own were miles apart, but I endeavored to support him in every way possible as this was essential for the good of the church. During the first two years of his pastorate, he allowed members to request my services for weddings and baptisms, but later he began not to honor all the requests. It became clear to me that he resented the fact that in times of crises people often sought my counsel rather than his. When members requested that I be put on a regular preaching schedule, he refused to permit it, which was fine with me. After all, I was supposed to be retired.

We maintained cordial relationships until one day he called me into his office. I could tell he was really upset, so I was prepared for anything.

"We have a problem," he said.

"What do you mean?" I asked.

"These people think they have two pastors. They only have one, and I'm that pastor."

"I understand that perfectly well," I replied. "So we don't have a problem. You have a problem."

He glared at me.

"I never performed a wedding or a baptism until members first secured your permission," I continued.

He acknowledged the truth of what I had said. Whenever someone requested a service from me, I told them to check with the pastor. If Reverend Matney agreed to it, I would do it. I didn't particularly like that arrangement, but that's the way it was.

I worked with him about four years. But it became clear that I couldn't maintain my integrity and work with the man, so I resigned my position and started attending another Methodist church in Annapolis. Here's how I felt my integrity was compromised.

Visitors came to worship. My job was to visit them. The newcomers would tell me how much they liked the singing in church and how friendly the people were, but they couldn't understand the minister's sermon. So they might ask me, "What was the pastor trying to say?" I couldn't tell them because I hadn't understood the sermon either. So, this was my dilemma. How could I be a loyal staff member and tell visitors that the pastor's sermons were usually very good when in four years I never heard him preach an intelligible sermon? I couldn't defend him and be honest with myself, so I resigned.

About a year after we moved to Annapolis, I was asked to preach at Ginger Cove Retirement Center, an elegant, new community for relatively affluent retirees. I preached at least once and sometimes two Sundays each month. I enjoyed my ministry there for more than four years.

All during this time, Mom Weinel was in a nursing home in Annapolis. She had Alzheimer's disease. Lois visited her almost every day because she needed a lot of care. Lois and I began to think of our own long-term needs. We had to climb two sets of stairs at Darlene's place, and we were concerned my arthritis could make that impossible in the years ahead. We learned of a retirement community on Maryland's eastern shore that was managed by the Wesleyan Church (a sister denomination to Free Methodists). Their retirement community consisted of regular housing, assisted living, and a nursing home. As part of their community, we would have exactly the level of care we might need for the rest of our lives. As we talked with them about buying into a duplex, we were encouraged to bring Mom Weinel to their facility. They promised they would take very good care of her. We decided we would move to that retirement community in Denton, Maryland. We had a duplex home built in June, 1995 and planned to move Mom Weinel into the nursing home as soon as we got settled.

That summer Mom became very ill. Our granddaughter, Jill, was to be married the first weekend in August in Winona Lake, Indiana. I had been asked to assist David in the ceremony. Lois was beside herself, wanting to attend the wedding, but feeling that Mom's situation was grave. Jack urged Lois to attend the wedding while he and Jean agreed to spend the evening and night with Mom. Mom Weinel died August fourth around 11:30 p.m. The next day, Jill and Adam Schutz were married.

What a day that was: a day of great joy and unspeakable sadness all at once. We said nothing to the family members about Mom' death until after the wedding.

By the time we returned from Jill and Adam's wedding, Jack had made funeral arrangements for Mom's service. Her body was taken to Donaldson Funeral

Home in Laurel, Maryland. All her family members were notified and funeral arrangements were finalized by Jack and Lois.

Her funeral service was held in the Spencerville Free Methodist Church with Reverend Timothy Rush as the preacher. Timothy had been in the youth group at the Rockville church when Pop Weinel entered the ministry and served that congregation. No one had more respect for Mom and Pop Weinel than Tim Rush. Lois' uncle, Gerald Diddle, led the singing at the funeral service. The service was both inspirational and comforting.

Mildred Ruth Weinel was laid to rest beside her husband in the Union Cemetery in Spencerville, Maryland, on August 8, 1995. The Spencerville Church prepared a large meal for all persons who attended the service. A shared meal is a good way to conclude a difficult day.

When it was all over and we had time to think about such things, we realized that the primary reason for our move to Denton was now a moot point. How ironic that so many decisions we made during those years were always with a view of caring for Lois' mother, who had devoted so much of her time to us. I'm not sure we would have ever moved away from Darlene and our friends in Annapolis if we had known Mom Weinel would not need the nursing home facilities of that retirement community on Maryland's eastern shore.

54

Western Shore People

Denton is 45 miles east of Annapolis, across the Chesapeake Bay Bridge and 50 years back in time. The county seat for Caroline County, Denton is a typical American small town with the county courthouse, the bank, two gas stations, a grocery and drug store, the post office, a smattering of small wood frame churches, and a large Methodist church. In the summer, farmers bring fresh vegetables to town on Tuesdays and Fridays, selling them at open-air stands along the road. This was really my kind of town, but Lois felt isolated and trapped there. There was no place to go, and like some "come heres" in Carmel and Coles Point churches, we felt like outsiders even after living there nearly five years. If one was not a member of the Wesleyan Church in our retirement community, in some respects they were regarded as second-class citizens.

We attended the large Methodist church in town where we sang in the choir. At night we went to the Wesleyan Church. As a United Methodist, I was looked on with some theological suspicions. It reminded me of how Free Methodists thought about the Methodist Church back in the 1950s. Many of my colleagues in the Maryland-Virginia Conference thought I had backslidden into all kinds of sin and deprivation when I transferred to the United Methodist Church in 1973. So, I wasn't surprised when some of my Wesleyan neighbors did not embrace us wholeheartedly.

When you retire, it's important to have access to good medical care. There was no hospital in Denton. The nearest hospital was in Easton, about 16 miles from Denton.

Our duplex home on the retirement campus was a lovely but modest two-bedroom brick-front home with a great front porch that Lois and I enjoyed very much. About a hundred yards in front of our home was a man-made lake about the size of a baseball field that was stocked with fish. It was a favorite wintering place for Canadian geese. We would watch them circle the lake and glide to a feet-first watery landing.

I had beautiful flowerbeds all around our house. A half block from our house I planted a vegetable garden plot about 20 feet by 35 feet in full sun. As I had done so many times before, I canned the abundance of tomatoes and green beans that garden produced and we enjoyed the harvest throughout the winter.

The pastor from the Wesleyan church became one of our best friends in Denton. He visited us regularly and took a lot of interest in us. I think he looked to me as a spiritual mentor. I gave him a number of my best books, which I believed would be helpful to a relatively young pastor. He was a good preacher and a good man.

The author and his mother at Zerbe Sisters Nursing Home

After my Dad's death in 1968, my mother did a lot of traveling with senior groups from the town of Ephrata where she had moved into an upstairs apartment that could only be reached by climbing a long set of stairs. She was in exceptional health. Dad did not like to travel, so Mom made up for lost time. She traveled to Europe, the Caribbean, Hawaii, and many places throughout the United States. While on a cruise in Jamaica, she suffered a mild heart attack.

When she arrived home, her doctor advised her to curtail her travel because of her weakened heart. At first she showed no signs of heart problems, but she began to accept the reality of her condition when climbing the stairs to her apartment became an ordeal. Then came fainting spells and other health concerns. She entered Zerbe Sisters Nursing Home near Churchtown in Lancaster County, Pennsylvania.

This new facility, built on a lovely wooded Pennsylvania hilltop, was staffed with conscientious workers. No longer able to travel, Mom turned her attention to working on afghans and other handiwork which she enjoyed very much. She moved into Zerbe Sisters when I was pastor at Carmel-Coles Point in Virginia. I visited my mother every month or two in the summertime. We often took Ronnie and Darla with us because Mom loved seeing them. It was a five-hour drive from Virginia. Those early visits were fun times when my Mother and I did a lot of reminiscing about days past. She had a good memory and her mind was clear.

My brothers, sisters, and I always made it a point to see her on her birthday, May 24, each year. How she enjoyed those family reunions on her birthday. After she reached 90, her health deteriorated more. She fell and broke her hip. Doctors did not believe she was strong enough to endure the stress of surgery, so the last years of her life she lived with a broken hip, confined to bed and a wheelchair.

After I retired and moved to Annapolis, I was able to see her more often. Not only did I have more time, but it was only a two and a half hour drive to her place. I prayed often with my mother, who was always encouraged by the visits of her children. During the last two years of her life, every time I said goodbye, I thought it may well be the last time I could talk with her. Rather than contributing to morbidity, that thought made each visit a very special occasion.

She died peacefully on November 22, 1991, five and a half months before her 93rd birthday. The cause of her death was kidney failure. All my brothers and sisters felt deep sorrow as we gathered at the funeral home. She looked beautiful in the casket, better than we had ever seen her. We had such mixed feelings, sadness for ourselves, but relief and joy for her as she was now free from her constant pain and confinement to bed and wheelchair. She had been ready for a long time to meet the Lord Jesus. Her funeral service was held in Ephrata, and her body was laid to rest in Hain's Church Cemetery beside my Dad.

My brother, Earl, was the executor of her estate. He made arrangements for the entire family to have dinner at a large restaurant in West Reading following the burial service. We got re-acquainted with family members we had not seen in many years. We all commented that it is regrettable that the only time we have opportunity to see our extended family is at funerals.

Following my mother's death, Lois and I followed her example and we did more traveling. My sister, Emily, and her husband, Bob, had time shares, so we made many trips together, mostly to Florida. I owned a large Mercury Grand Marquis so I did all the driving.

Never go to Florida in hurricane season. One year we planned to stay in Florida for one week and then travel north to Myrtle Beach for the following week. The second day we were in Florida we were ordered to evacuate because a hurricane was bearing down the coast. We packed the car and headed north for Myrtle Beach only to learn on the day we arrived that the South Carolina city was also to be evacuated. So, we just decided to just keep driving north until we arrived back home. A few weeks later we took a trip to the Pocono Mountains in Pennsylvania. No hurricanes were forecast.

I would vote that our best trip was the one we took on our 50th wedding anniversary. In April, 1994, Emily, Bob, Lois and I went to Hawaii for three weeks. We were not with a group so we were free to go wherever and whenever we wished. Hawaii is truly a paradise. We went to a luau and the roasted pig was delicious, but I enjoyed the music and the singing even more than the food.

One Sunday during a congregational hymn, I began to feel light-headed. I sat down and slumped over unconscious in the front-row pew. When I regained consciousness, I could move my arms and legs. I was pretty sure that I had not suffered a stroke. I stood up and Lois and I exited along the side aisle with very few people knowing I had passed out. Lois drove me to the hospital in Easton, 16 miles away, where I was diagnosed with a ventricle fibrillation. After four days of tests, I seemed to be fine. I was prescribed medications that kept me going with no ill effects from the event.

But that experience frightened Lois. She began to worry about how she would cope in Denton if I should suddenly die. I knew she wasn't happy there and so we made plans to return to Annapolis where we would be closer to our doctors and our family.

Old people love to bore others with stories about their illnesses and surgeries. I will not go into details about my 30-year struggle with BPH and three TURs. (Look it up if you're curious.) Suffice it to say we had our share of surgeries so that now, when we go to a doctor who wants to know our medical history, Lois has a list she maintains for herself and one for me. We give them the list and let them make a copy for their records. Through it all, God's grace has sustained us and we have supported and cared for each other for more than 62 years.

During our five years in Denton I had no regular preaching schedule, although I did preach several times in both Methodist and Wesleyan churches. I also gave devotional messages in the assisted-living units and in the nursing home in our retirement community.

We located an apartment in Arnold, an adjoining town to Annapolis. We told our friends that we discovered we were definitely more Western Shore people than Eastern Shore people. I was without a garden, but I took up the hobby of carving and painting wooden ducks and birds. I attended two classes in two senior centers weekly for about 15 years. I seldom missed a class, which lasted from nine o'clock in the morning until three o'clock in the afternoon. I only stopped carving about a year and a half ago because tremors in my hands made it difficult for me to do the fine detailed painting. I hope soon I'll be able to resume carving, for I truly do enjoy it.

We went back to Trinity Church, where a new pastor had been appointed while we were away. People were able to understand his sermons. A friend in one of my carving classes who lived on the Magothy River was an avid fisherman and he provided us with a weekly supply of blue crabs. It does not get much better than that in Maryland.

Our second floor apartment in Arnold was spacious and overlooked an Arnold Palmer-designed golf course. But it became Lois' Waterloo. Not long after we moved there, Lois could not get out of bed one morning. When she tried to move severe back pain nearly incapacitated her. I called 911 and the medics took her to the hospital. After a couple of days of tests, doctors discovered that she had a pinched sciatic nerve. She was given prednisone and other medications, which had the effect of lowering her resistance to infections. She was in and out of the hospital five times in the following months for infections resulting with high fevers. One episode raised her pulse rate to 160 beats per minute, which caused her heart to go out of rhythm, and left her with a permanent atrial fibrillation.

Lois had seven electric shock procedures to try to get her heart back in rhythm. One procedure was successful, keeping her heart in rhythm about a year. But even then, she had difficulty climbing steps. So, although we had been in Arnold less than two years, it became necessary to find a place to live that did not have steps.

In 2001 we moved into Claiborne House in Annapolis where we had a two-bedroom apartment on the fifth floor. Lois had an operation to relieve the pressure on her sciatic nerve called a laminectomy. Even after that surgery, however, she had trouble negotiating stairs. She had to use a walker.

Soon after we moved to the Claiborne House, Lois learned that she needed a second operation for she had a ruptured disc. The second surgery to improve this condition was far more serious than the laminectomy. In 2002, she had steel rods and clamps inserted in her spine.

About the same time, living conditions in Claiborne House began to deteriorate rapidly. The county needed a place to house patients from state hospitals that were judged able to live on their own with no oversight. Claiborne House was soon overrun with some pretty strange characters. Folks who might otherwise be hanging out under bridges or on the streets were now hanging out in our lobby. The authorities had miscalculated because some of these people began causing a lot of trouble. We were embarrassed to have visitors come to see us, and they would be stopped by these persons begging for money or harassing them on the elevator. One fellow who lived on a floor above us cursed at me one day for stopping the elevator at the fifth floor where I lived when he wanted to get out at the first floor. Beyond embarrassing, it was sometimes frightening to be accosted by our new neighbors.

Darlene insisted that we should not have to live in these conditions. Lois was recovering from her serious back surgery walking with the aid of a walker when the three of us came to see the apartments in the Gardens of Annapolis. The place was first class if not somewhat more expensive than we were used to. Lois claims that Darlene and I told the agent we would take the apartment while she was still walking down the long hall from the elevator. Darlene did whisper to me, "Dad, take it. This is really nice." So, I told the agent we would take the one-bedroom apartment. We made plans to move as soon as we could make arrangements with the moving company. Darla's husband, Tim, helped us move in during a bad snowstorm in February, 2003.

Soon after we returned to Annapolis, I was invited to become the chaplain at Ginger Cove Retirement Center. They said they needed someone for twenty hours a week, but I knew how that twenty hours would easily stretch into twenty-five or thirty hours, not counting staff meetings. I informed the manager that I enjoyed preaching, but at 76 years of age, I wasn't looking for a demanding job. I agreed to preach two Sundays a month, but I was not anxious about the chaplain's duties.

I enjoyed the ministry there and they paid well, which helped a lot on our fixed income. Every Sunday I preached, Lois and I were invited to enjoy dinner in their elegant dining room. I continued my ministry at Ginger Cove until I reached my 80th birthday on May 9, 2004. I have returned three or four times since then to substitute for the present chaplain. Occasionally, former church members moved into Ginger Cove and invited us to dinner. Invariably one of the residents will say, "Why don't you come and sing for us?"

Someone once asked Jean's father, Melvin Woodward, what he would do if he knew he only had one day to live. He said he would plant a tree. On my 80th birthday, I planted a maple tree in the front yard of the house Darlene and Ron eventually sold to Tim and Darla. I placed a marker beside the tree. It's two years now since I planted it in the spring, and you should see how beautiful it has become. I only hope to live to see that tree at least 30 feet tall.

55

Reflections

Throughout the course of writing this autobiography and searching the depths of my memory, I have said to myself I'm glad I retired from the professional ministry when I did. In truth, I have never fully retired as I still preach on occasion and teach a Bible study class every Thursday evening to this day.

Clarence and Lois, 60th Anniversary

As a young pastor, I thought the church was the moral conscience of society. Now it appears that society ignores the church, which in my opinion is far worse than if the world hated the church. In recent years, church denominational leaders have either completely rejected or at the very least have ignored the orthodox tenets of the faith. So, is it any wonder that they are now ignored as having no moral standing before the world and society? We used to strive to get the world into the church where people would come to know the saving grace of the Gospel. Now it seems to me church leaders are striving to get the church into the world so that we become antinomians; that is, each individual doing what he or she thinks is right in his or her own eyes. Moral standards have vanished and "thus saith the Lord" falls on deaf ears. Is it any wonder that people have no sense of direction or purpose in life? I can only echo the words of the prophet Isaiah's complaint about the absence of faith when he writes, "all we like sheep had gone astray, we have turned everyone to his own way" (Isaiah 50:36a).

In times past, we celebrated conversions along with church and Sunday school growth at our annual conferences. Evangelism strategies were planned, and programs were developed for implementation in the local churches. We celebrated new churches being added to the conference role. During the 1970s, "Catch the Spirit" was the last great effort. But not long after that preachers in the Virginia Conference began debating whether pastors should be allowed to purchase their own homes rather than live in church parsonages. The whole idea of the itinerant ministry on which Methodism was founded came under attack. John Wesley must have turned over in his grave.

One of Wesley's watchwords, "sanctification," was seldom heard from the pulpit in the conference sessions. When the Bishop examined candidates for membership in the annual conference, questions formulated by Wesley himself for every Methodist preacher were asked and had to be affirmatively answered to become a full member of the annual conference. Those questions were:

"Have you faith in Christ?" The answer "yes" was heard clearly across the floor of the conference.

"Are you going on to perfection?" One had to strain to hear the whispered response. Bishop Goodson would then look at the candidates and remark, "Well, if you're not going on to perfection, just where are you going?" This caught many candidates looking like deer in the headlights.

"Do you expect to be made perfect in love in this life?" A low groan of "Ohhh" from the conference made it impossible to hear the candidates' response.

"Are you earnestly striving after it?"

Apparently, these questions have long since been forgotten by church leaders. It gives me no pleasure to share these deep disappointments, but it is why I say I'm glad I retired when I did in 1989.

Today someone might well ask in all seriousness, "What did you talk about before the question of human sexuality became the predominant topic for discussion in annual conference sessions?" In the past 25 years no other topic has been discussed more. There have been endless questions, study groups and resolutions relating to homosexual and lesbian lifestyles and whether homosexuals should be ordained to the ministry. The fact that all of these questions have been definitively answered in the Discipline for decades is ignored as gay rights activists fight their battles of attrition year after year, laying siege to the fortress of the faith, protected by a mote of religious experience that is a mile wide and an inch deep. I wonder how long delegates to the General Conference will prevail over the never-ending demand of those members who wish to rewrite the Church Discipline. I have been ashamed to read about Bishops, Superintendents, and Pastors who apparently have forgotten their vows for admittance and ordination into the Annual Conference.

Not long ago, conference ministers voted to dismiss a fellow minister from his church because he refused to receive a homosexual person into church membership. The Pastor appealed his dismissal to the General Counsel of the United Methodist Church (the denomination's Supreme Court), who sustained the appeal and ordered the Bishop to give the Pastor an appointment. Our Church Discipline clearly states that the pastor has the authority to determine who is received into the membership of the local church. I never had to deal with that issue in my 50 years, but I admire the pastor who stood his ground in the face of opposition from the politically correct. My health prevents me from attending conference now, so I'm not engaged in the struggle. But you can be sure if I had been at that conference, I would have stood with the victor in this battle. I'm a peacemaker at heart, so I'm glad I retired in 1989 before the battle lines were drawn so sharply.

I believe if we resist change when God confronts us with the need to change we become progressively more false. Whenever planning the church calendar for a quarter or for the year, I found one of the hardest tasks was getting committee members beyond the question, "What did we do last year?" Last year's programs, regardless of their success, may not be adequate to the challenges of the future. Twice-a-year revival services is a case in point.

Many years ago, revival services were often times of spiritual renewal. Many people professed faith in Christ during these meetings. Attendance was good in the 1950s. There were some people who professed to be saved at every revival. By the 1970s, women were working and people didn't have time or energy to go to church every night for ten days. Attendance dwindled, so revivalists started having weekend revivals, but that conflicted with Friday night high school sports activities.

Americans seem busier than ever. Time at church for most professed Christians has been compressed into one hour on Sunday morning. In fact, only one third of church members are in church on any given Sunday. No matter how the church tries to accommodate modern schedules, people find it hard to make time for God. But the change that's needed is a change in our priorities. Here's what I've learned after more than 50 years as an observer of these things: people find time to do what they want to do. Therefore, the challenge facing pastors today is no different than it always was: getting people into a relationship with God so that serving and pleasing a personal God becomes the highest priority in life. This change will require more than praise bands and informal services where you can come to worship in your jeans or shorts. Solid Bible-based sermons delivered under the inspiration of the Holy Spirit will move sincere believers to reach their potential in Christ. People who attend worship services should be challenged to be all that they can be. For many years "Be All You Can Be" was the slogan of the U.S. Army, but I think it should be the goal of every believer. Good preaching will do more to build the Church of Christ than all the gimmicks that have been employed in the past three decades.

My impression is that too many pastors today view their work as a profession rather than a calling. The pastors in our conference groaned at Wesley's conference membership questions; how different from the Apostle Paul's sense of calling that prompted him to write, "Woe is me if I preach not the gospel" (I Corinthians 9:16). When I was a young pastor, a lawyer in my congregation said to me, "You're the first pastor we've had in this church in my lifetime that gives me the impression you could make a living doing something besides being a preacher."

I answered Mr. Brown in all honesty, "I'm doing what I believe God wants me to do."

"You do it well, Pastor," he replied.

I saw Leroy Brown recently at the 100th birthday celebration for Beulah Moore who had been the Sunday School Superintendent at that church. After I paid tribute to Mrs. Moore in a short talk, Leroy came to me and said, "You still do a good job, Pastor."

Most of my colleagues fifty years ago believed they were called by God to preach. Whenever ministers got together, we talked about the impact our churches were having on the spiritual life of our community and in the lives of individual members. We encouraged each other with conversations about the people who were being saved and the growth we saw in our worship and Sunday school.

By the time I retired in 1989, when ministers met, the questions I heard discussed with animation and interest were "How's your golf game?", "Where are you going on vacation this year?", and "Can we get together this week for a couple of games?" Not until the chairman called the ministers to order and we proceeded with the announced agenda, did the church become the topic of discussion. There's nothing wrong with playing golf. I just wondered many times if these pastors cared more about perfecting their golf game than perfecting their walk with Christ. I didn't play golf, but many of my ministerial colleagues accepted me anyhow.

I'm persuaded that if a young man came to the typical modern pastor with the testimony that God was calling him to preach, he would probably be referred to a psychiatrist as suffering from hallucinations or delusions of grandeur.

Since I retired in 1989, I have attended many United Methodist Churches. Very few sermons I've heard preached from their pulpits anticipate any response from the congregation. I had the impression that if someone came forward for prayer, the pastor would not know what to do. In fact, on several occasions I've seen a pastor ignore the person who came to pray at the altar during the singing of a closing hymn. I'm convinced there is a hunger for sermons that call people to repentance and commitment to Christ. When I preach at Ginger Cove or at the Gardens of Annapolis, frequently someone tells me at the close of the service, "You preach like the preachers did when I was young."

After reading the last few pages you may get the idea that I'm an old grouch who was around long ago when somebody came up with the idea of sin. To the contrary, I am a happy, thankful man endowed with a good sense of humor. I may not laugh as loud as my sister, Gertie, but we share the same capacity to enjoy something funny. I remember how my mother would laugh until she cried. I have done that more than once myself.

In spite of the actions of some church leaders today, I'm convinced that there are still thousands of Methodist preachers and millions of members who intend to steadfastly stand by the historic statements of our faith. I shall always be grateful to the Virginia Conference of the United Methodist Church. I was a stranger from a sister Methodist denomination and they took me in and provided me the opportunity to fulfill and expand my call to the ministry. I am every inch of me a Methodist. I revere John and Charles Wesley. Like John, I, too, have had a "heartwarming" experience and I have thrilled all my life to sing the hymns of Charles Wesley. I am still amazed by the power of God's grace and so thankful to

God for calling me into service in the church. God has blessed my preaching by using it to bring many persons to a saving faith in Jesus Christ.

From the world's standpoint, I never had much throughout my life, and yet I had everything. I had honorable, loving parents who never gave me a single reason to be anything but proud of them. I attended good schools and had outstanding teachers. I suffered no injuries in World War II in answer to many prayers. I married a good Christian wife whose family treated me as a son. Lois gave me two outstanding, talented children, David and Darlene. Their spouses, Julie and Ron, love me and call me Dad. Our children have blessed us with five gifted and handsome grandchildren. David's daughter, Jill and her tall husband, Adam, gave me two strong, intelligent great grandsons, Trevor and Tyson Schutz. David and Julie gave me Amy and her husband Marc Corbett (married on June 5, 1999), and Michael and his wife, Cheryl (married October 8, 2005). Darlene and Ron have given me two gifted grandchildren. Ron Jr. and his wife, Tracie (married April 18, 1998). Darla and her husband, Tim McDonald, were married on August 15, 1998 and gave me three great grandchildren: Luke, whose red hair is identical to mine as a child; Eva Ruth, named after my mother and Lois' mother; and Jonah Clarence, named after me. For these great grandchildren and more still to come, God willing, I have penned my story as a testimony to the faithfulness of God and to the enduring power of love.

Writing my story has been a therapeutic process. When I began I was into the second year of a difficult physical struggle with a disease that none of my doctors had ever heard of or knew how to treat. Called Grover's Disease, its cause is unknown, but it manifests in a very painful and extremely itchy rash on my back and arms that has taxed my endurance many times.

At 3:00 a.m. one morning, I was nearly frantic with pain. Lois called 911 and I was taken to the hospital. When the emergency room physician looked at my back, he stepped back and said, "What is that?"

I asked if he could just give me a sedative to knock me out because my skin felt like it was on fire. Since that time, three different dermatologists have prescribed pills, creams, ointments, and ultraviolet treatments with little or no effect. Writing my story has taken my mind off the itching and pain for hours at a time. The Apostle Paul said, "Lest he should be exalted above measure he was given a thorn in the flesh, a messenger of Satan to torment him" (II Corinthians 12:7). No one knows what Paul's "thorn" may have been, but I have no doubt the affliction I carry in my own flesh; it's called Grover's Disease. I must continually battle the debilitating pain and the psychological discouragement, as did Paul who wrote in another place, "We have this treasure of Christ in jars of clay (someone has said in cracked pots) to show that this all surpassing power is from God and not from us" (II Corinthians 4:7-9).

As I complete this book, I have recently celebrated my 82nd birthday. I never expected to live this long. Perhaps I was overly pessimistic since my Mother lived 92½ years. After reflecting on my life, I conclude that I have become like my Mother in so many ways. Her sense of humor, her compassion, her sense of adventure, and her love of working with her hands to create objects of beauty—this is her legacy to me.

My Dad would get very agitated if he came home from work and found Mom sitting in a chair, knitting or perhaps just resting.

"Get up," he would tell her, "get moving. You sit too much and you'll get so stiff you won't be able to walk."

After Dad died and Mom could no longer travel, she continued working with her hands, always seated in a chair. I asked her once what she thought now of Dad's advice.

She put her head back and laughed until she almost cried. "I've outlived him by 20 years," she observed.

I have sometimes wondered if all the activities of ministry over the past half century have really accomplished anything. It is a task, a calling, without many markers to measure progress. The same need that motivated my Mother to create her crafts worked itself out in the enjoyment I derived from carving ducks and birds. Each day I could look at the carving and clearly see the difference I had made for that day. Three or four months later I could hold in my hand a wooden bird so life-like I wished I could breathe life into it and watch it fly away.

But this retrospective look at my life has helped me to see that my life's work did make a positive difference. I was there to comfort a young mother when death snatched her infant. I was there time and time again when a couple in love pledged themselves to each other in marriage. I was there when the police officer knocked on the door to inform a young mother and her three children that her husband had been killed in an automobile accident. I was there when young and old convicted of their sin needed guidance in their search for forgiveness. I was there to open Scriptures to people wanting to grow in grace. I was there whenever there was an emergency and my people needed me. Ministry isn't about being clever or being liked or even being a good churchman. Ministry is being there in times of human need as a living reminder that God is near and that God deeply cares.

My father taught me that if something was worth doing, it was worth doing right. Perhaps that is why my spirit so resonates with John Wesley's emphasis that Christians strive for Christ's perfection in all we do. Whether I was doing the work of a minister or planting a garden, I was perpetually driven by a desire to do my best. I am so thankful for the words of praise from parishioners who have told me that my sermons have moved them to love and serve God. Bessie Dunn, a 92-year-old member at St. James Church, often said as she shook my hand after worship, "You make me feel real good." Or, to hear a farmer from Virginia's Northern Neck say, "'deed, if you don't have the best garden up and down this road."

I was content wherever I lived and God empowered me to love the people in the churches to which I was appointed. My love for the work of the ministry and my love of gardening share a lot of things in common. A church and a garden require constant attention and hard work. A man once stopped at Mr. Woodward's roadside vegetable stand located in front of his peach orchard.

"This is surely a beautiful orchard the Lord has given you," he said.

Mr. Woodward looked at him and replied with a smile, "You shoulda' seen it before I started working on it."

Church growth is the Lord's doing in which a faithful pastor and people are privileged to share. I saw a church building under construction with a large sign that read, "This church is being built by the hand of the Lord." A smaller sign nearby read, "Plumbing and heating by Johnson and Sons."

Whatever success I have enjoyed as a minister in the Free Methodist and the United Methodist Church has been God's blessing on my work. I was often given credit, but God gets the glory.

Great gardens require that good seeds be planted in late spring to reap the harvest in the early fall. In ministry, the seed is the Word of God that is planted in people who have been befriended and loved sincerely by the people of God. Cultivating those friendships by giving personal attention to candidates for conversion provides nourishment for church growth. People are won to Christ by what they see of Him in us. Although that may seem to be an unfair arrangement, that is the way it is. The Scripture promises, "He who goes out weeping, carrying seeds to sow will return with songs of joy, carrying the harvest with him" (Psalms 126:6).

One of the great joys I experience as a gardener is to share what I grow with others. I delight to watch the eyes of someone who has only known store-bought vegetables bite into a slice of a luscious, vine-ripened tomato so big it covers an entire piece of bread. As a pastor I have stood before hundreds of people who have known only frustration and sin and ask, "Do you believe in Jesus Christ as your personal savior?" When they answered "Yes," I knew I had played a part in introducing them to Jesus Christ. There is no greater joy!

In the fall the gardener reaps the fruit of his labor. No more weeding or pest control. When the plants dry up and the stalks of corn have yielded their bounty, the gardener breaks and cuts up the residue and tills it back into the soil for next year's planting. My hope is that all the necessary labor to create this book will serve succeeding generations of my family and anyone else to know where I came from, who I am, what I have done with my life, and the joy I've been privileged to share with those who call me Dad, Poppy, Grandpa, and Pastor.

978-0-595-41189-4
0-595-41189-4

www.ingramcontent.com/pod-product-compliance
Lightning Source LLC
Chambersburg PA
CBHW030259290526
45785CB00001B/152